TRANSNATIONAL LAW IN A CHANGING SOCIETY

Transnational Law in a Changing Society

ESSAYS IN HONOR OF *Philip C. Jessup*

Edited by WOLFGANG FRIEDMANN, LOUIS HENKIN *and* OLIVER LISSITZYN

COLUMBIA UNIVERSITY PRESS

NEW YORK AND LONDON   1972

Preface

THE EDITORS are teachers of international law at Columbia University. Our institutional and professional ties to Philip Jessup, who taught international law at Columbia University for many years, are reinforced by intellectual admiration and personal affection. The present volume is a modest expression of our respect and affection for a man whose influence as scholar, teacher, diplomat, and judge has been profound and worldwide.

We sought to reflect in this volume the universality of Philip Jessup's influence, and therefore invited contributions from a number of eminent international jurists from various countries —linked to Philip Jessup by professional and personal associations. Many other distinguished jurists would have wished to contribute to this volume, but practical considerations limited its size; we also wished to maintain some geographic balance. This has in particular restricted the number of American contributors. A few jurists who had accepted our invitation found themselves compelled to withdraw. We, of course, wished to contribute to the volume that we have organized.

It seemed fitting to introduce this volume with a word about "Philip Jessup, Diplomatist," reflecting on his other major contributions to his country and to peace and order. This tribute was written by Dean Acheson several months before his death. Another contributor, Francis Deák, a lifelong friend and collaborator of Philip Jessup, died as this book went to press.

We have sought to give a measure of unity to this volume by making "Transnational Law in a Changing Society" the central theme. Perhaps Philip Jessup's most important scholarly contribution has been to widen the ambit and goals of international law, bridging the gap between private and public international law, and breaking down boundaries which had confined international law essentially to the regulation of relations between states. We believe that this volume gives some indication of the broadening structure of international law, of which Philip Jessup has been a principal architect.

The editors wish to acknowledge their indebtedness to the School of International Affairs of Columbia University (Dean Andrew W. Cordier) and to the International Legal Research Program of the Columbia University Law School for the financial support given toward the publication of this volume.

WOLFGANG FRIEDMANN
LOUIS HENKIN
OLIVER LISSITZYN

Contents

I

INTRODUCTION

DEAN ACHESON

Philip C. Jessup, Diplomatist

DIPLOMATIST, RATHER than diplomat, is the right word here. The latter took on a denigrating cast when we were young. Then a new Jacksonian democracy—this time all Bachelors of Arts—beat against the barriers that set off the supposed elite inhabitants of embassies and foreign offices. Garbed, so legend has it, in "striped pants," these were said to occupy themselves "cookie-pushing" at tea parties. However, the rabble recognized here and there a man like Philip Jessup's hero, Elihu Root, who seemed to come of sterner stuff and to be worthy of respect. For these a syllable was added to their titles to indicate elevation to a peerage.

In the twenty happy years of my morning walks with Felix Frankfurter, among the many subjects of our talk was the best preparation, apart from apprenticeship, for work in diplomacy. Frankfurter would contend that this was training for and at the bar. To tease him, I would deny it, citing Sir John Simon as a horrible example and ascribing Frankfurter's views to a prejudice akin to the shoemaker's conviction that there was "nothing like leather." He would advocate next, I supposed, "world peace through world law." The truth was, of course, that for the most part he was right. The law and the Church

THE LATE DEAN ACHESON was formerly United States Secretary of State.

offered the oldest intellectual professional training, and both leaned heavily on philosophy. Many centuries would pass before the profession of arms would have much intellectual content and still more before medicine would emerge from the barber shop. One could deride the law—"law sharpens the mind by narrowing it"; however, while logic sharpens the cutting edge, philosophy broadens the understanding and a grasp of relevancy confines issues and makes analysis possible.

Furthermore, much of modern (that is, nineteenth and twentieth century) diplomacy derives from the two great cardinals, one of the beginning, the other of the end of the sixteenth century—Wolsey of England and Richelieu of France. The purpose, organization, method, and, to some extent, the ideology of modern diplomacy were first adopted by one or the other of these cleric-statesmen who guided their sovereigns' foreign policy. Both tended to forget, as do their modern counterparts today, a wise principle laid down a century before by a French diplomatist, Philippe de Comines: "Two great princes who wish to establish good personal relations should never meet each other face to face, but ought to communicate through good and wise ambassadors." The Seigneur d'Argenton saw no good in meetings at the summit.

The purpose of the two sixteenth-century cardinals was not only to reach agreements between princes, but to reach lasting agreements. Particularly perplexing was the problem of lasting agreements to keep the peace in Europe while European armies were off on a crusade in the Middle East. Pope Leo X was preaching the latter and worrying about the former in 1517. Cardinal Wolsey was not interested in the crusade but very interested in some arrangement to keep the exuberant energies of Francis I under control before they came in conflict with Emperor Charles V. The problem was a practical one; the solution he found is a now-familiar one—a multilateral treaty binding all the powers of Europe to perpetual peace and providing that, should any signatory suffer aggression, the others on appeal would demand that the aggressor withdraw and, upon refusal, would make war upon him by land and sea until the peace was restored and recompense made.

The Treaty of London was signed by England and France in 1518 and soon after by the Pope, the Emperor, Spain, and over twenty lesser states and principalities. Curiously enough, this treaty of splendid innovation is now wholly forgotten, though the great meeting held to celebrate it at the Field of the Cloth of Gold still glitters through the years. One reason, perhaps, is that within three years of its signature Francis had violated the treaty by attacking the Emperor, who promptly invoked it. Wolsey procrastinated in devious maneuvers, whereupon the victim of aggression defeated the aggressor at the Battle of Pavia in 1525, destroyed the French army, and made Francis his prisoner. Europe disintegrated into general war and the Turks entered southeastern Europe.

A hundred years later Grotius proposed an institution that would compose quarrels by the judgment of those not involved. The problem of the "means . . . to constrain the parties to agree" to the judgment remained unsolved.

Cardinal Richelieu's contributions to diplomacy were solid. He was a realist. Not that Wolsey was not, but in disguising his project to control Francis through a grandiose device, he lost sight of the fact that initiative by England was essential to putting it into action. Richelieu went to work upon the means, instruments, and methods of maintaining his intelligence, communication, and confidence, which he believed essential to reaching agreement and agreed action. The permanent foreign office, diplomatic missions, regular reports, and available files all received his meticulous attention. The tricks, deceptions, and kaleidoscopic combinations so prominent in earlier Italian practice were dropped. Above all, Richelieu believed that diplomacy was a serious, continuous operation, not spasmodic attention to crises, and should be aimed at creating respect and confidence. The interests it served should be the long-term interests of the state, not ephemeral, sentimental, or ideological concerns, as is too often the case today. Nothing should be undertaken until well thought-out. Then it should be undeviatingly adhered to and, if eventually incorporated in a treaty, should be precisely formulated and rigorously observed. To accomplish this, Richelieu succeeded in having the direction of foreign policy unified under one ministry, his own, though both he and especially his successors suffered from the personal and secret intervention of the monarch, a difficulty not unknown today. Finally, he well understood the importance of broad backing for his policies and, in achieving it, became a skillful and persistent propagandist.

Philip Jessup came to the practice of diplomacy with qualities of body and mind admirably adapted to it. His physique was imposing, so much so that after his appointment as ambassador at large his secretary, Miss Vernice Anderson, would refer to him as the large ambassador. His wit, gay and ready, and his irrepressible humor would survive the longest and dullest meetings with their endless translations. These qualities alone would have made him a cherished companion in an occupation that is by no means all fun; however, another quality, a courage that brought them to the fore in times of adversity as well as during mere dullness, made him an indispensable reserve of strength. A trouble was a trouble and taken as such. It was no occasion to pull a long face and push the panic button. His ingenuity was sufficient to meet the most novel demands.

A few days after I had returned to the Department of State as its chief, need arose to put Mr. Jessup's abilities to a most important and secret test. The Soviet blockade of Berlin had dragged on for many months. In January 1949 Stalin, answering questions of a newspaper correspondent on ending the blockade, had not mentioned the chief reason for imposing it, the Allied application to West Berlin of the new West German currency. Was this significant? Was it a possible sign that Stalin was prepared for serious talk of ending an operation that had turned out so unprofitably for him? A highly secret and casual approach to the Russians was needed. The route through Jessup to the Soviet Ambassador to the United Nations, Jacob Malik, by way of a chance meeting in the United Nations building seemed the most innocent. Jessup arranged this. He asked as a matter of personal curiosity whether Stalin's omission of any reference to monetary matters was significant. Malik did not know. If he learned anything, he would remember Jessup's interest.

A month later he reported that the omission was not accidental. While monetary matters were important, they could be discussed at a meeting of the Council of Foreign Ministers. Was such a meeting contemplated, asked Jessup, after lifting the blockade? Malik would have to inquire. This inquiry revealed that, if a definite date for the meeting could be set, the blockade could be lifted before the meeting took place. However, Malik asked, in such event would the United States postpone preparations for a West German government until after the meeting? Jessup replied, as he had been instructed to do, that, since the preparations could not be completed for some time, the meeting could be held, if the Russians really wanted one, in the meantime. Beyond this, he refused to move, making no commitment of any sort.

These negotiations resulted in the raising of the blockade and the countermeasures imposed by the Western Allies. Six weeks of talk by the foreign ministers in Paris accomplished nothing beyond what Jessup and Malik had outlined. The Russians were clearly unwilling to go a step further, and Jessup had skillfully avoided any suggestion of further commitment on our side that might have confused the subsequent discussion. Nor was there any breach of secrecy on the American part that might have undermined the desire of Moscow to go forward with a limited agreement. At no time did more than five people on our side know that talks were under way. This in itself was a triumph of the diplomatic art in America.

In the next four years Philip Jessup remained my constant companion and colleague in the diplomatic field. One can only give a few examples of his contributions. In 1949 he passed from the role of secret diplomatic agent to that of editor-in-chief of what was popularly called the China White Paper, a massive work prepared in the Department of State with the President's agreement and officially entitled *United States Relations with China with Special Reference to the Period 1944–1949*. In spite of the storm of abuse directed at this document by the ideological and partisan political foes of the policy it reported, it has stood up admirably for thirty years as the definitive factual history of the period. This is due to Jessup's editing and supervision.

As I have said before, the conclusion of the report "was unpalatable to believers in American omnipotence, to whom every goal unattained is explicable only by incompetence or treason":

The unfortunate but inescapable fact is that the ominous result of the civil war in China was beyond the control of the government of the United States. Nothing that this country did or could have done within the reasonable limits of its capabilities could have changed that result; nothing that was left undone by this country has contributed to it. It was the product of internal Chinese forces, forces which this country tried to influence but could not. A decision was arrived at within China, if only a decision by default.

And now it is abundantly clear that we must face the situation as it exists in fact. We will not help the Chinese or ourselves by basing our policy on wishful thinking.

Cardinal Richelieu would have seen in the White Paper a development of what he called *"mes petits écrits,"* though this *écrit* could not have been called *petit*. It was and remains a work of the highest quality, compiled under great pressure. Unhappily, its orderly and thorough presentation of facts did not impress contemporary emotion.

The four years 1949–1953 brought great activity in multilateral diplomacy through the two newest centers for its practice, the United Nations and the North Atlantic Treaty Organization. Philip Jessup was active in both. At that time the United Nations had considerably less than half the member nations that compose it today. The prevailing view of its powers and function was far more modest then than the views of the present majority. Secretary General Dag Hammarskjöld stated them in his annual report of September 4, 1957:

The events of the past year have, I believe, cast a clearer light upon the role of the United Nations in these times. The Charter, read as a whole, does not endow the United Nations with any of the attributes of a super-state or of a body active outside the framework of decisions of member governments. The United Nations is, rather, an instrument for negotiation among, and to some extent, for, governments. It is also an instrument added to the time-honored means of diplomacy for concerting action by governments in support of the goals of the Charter. This is the role the organization has played, sometimes successfully, sometimes with disappointing setbacks, throughout its life.

This was the conception of the United Nations that was held in the State Department at that time—as an aid to diplomacy, not as a world government. Philip Jessup's gifts were well suited to work in this setting.

In 1950 Soviet intransigence and incitement to force in both western Europe and eastern Asia brought urgent need for further institutional support in both the United Nations and the North Atlantic Treaty to effectuate concerted action by governments in support of the goals of both agreements. Jessup played an important role not only in negotiating an answer to this need in both these groups, but also in devising what the answers should be.

Among the North Atlantic Treaty states the answer was to add to the treaty commitments of mutual help, in case of attack, civilian and military executive bodies, strategic plans, and forces-in-being with their command structures. As Averell

Harriman put it, it was to put the "O" for organization into NATO. This was begun at the May 1950 NAT Council meeting in London and continued at the Brussels meeting in December of the same year, when the Supreme Command was established under General Eisenhower and forces were allocated to it.

While this was under way, need arose on the other side of the world to organize and mount a common defense to meet armed aggression against the Republic of Korea. This was successfully done under the aegis of the United Nations and the leadership of the United States. The need was too urgent to brook delay. The United Nations Security Council declared the attack a breach of the peace and called on all members to repel it with armed force. This action happily escaped a Soviet veto, as the Soviet Union was at the time boycotting meetings of the Security Council because of the exclusion of a Chinese Communist representative. Soon afterward, the Security Council asked the United States Government, which was supplying the bulk of the armed forces, to appoint the U.N. commander. The President appointed General Douglas MacArthur.

Thus, within the year, two organizations of states asked the United States to assume the leadership—indeed, the command —of two common efforts to meet aggressive, armed attacks instigated, supplied, and directed from the same source on opposite sides of the world. This clearly indicates something important in their attitude toward the United States. Of course, it indicated respect for the power of this country, but these same states also had respect for the power of the Soviet Union. So it represented more than respect for power. I suggest that it represented what Cardinal Richelieu believed to be one of the primary purposes, if not the primary purpose, of diplomacy— confidence, belief in the integrity of the purposes and conduct of this nation, trust. Philip Jessup had contributed mightily to creating this trust. I wish that one could believe that trust in the United States was so widely shared today.

Not all diplomatic exchanges are on so high a level of purpose as those described. As 1951 succeeded 1950, the Western Allies were drawn into another diplomatic exercise of far more dubious purpose. It required, however, just as much skill as the previous endeavors and, in avoiding the Soviet trap, achieved an almost equal success. Philip Jessup was our protagonist in this encounter also. His performance entitles him to the highest professional rating.

Our attempt to open to Germany in 1950 essential participation in the defense of Europe had created great strains within the NAT alliance and the NATO system, especially within France. That indispensable ally was of two minds as to whether Germany should be embraced as a new-found friend or suspected and disarmed as a twice-proven enemy. This fiery issue, the most publicized secret in Europe, was quickly seized upon by Moscow as the means of dividing and nullifying the Western alliance. The first half of 1951 Stalin devoted to demanding, repeatedly and stridently, a four-power conference "on the German question." He was right in his appraisal of the divisive qualities of this demand. Paris insisted that only after French opinion had been satisfied that no stone had been left unturned to reach agreement with the Russians on the neutralization of Germany and European security would it face the infinitely more distasteful question of German rearmament. Furthermore, the French fervently hoped that success in achieving such an agreement would make unnecessary ever facing that painful alternative. Adenauer saw disaster in any toying with the idea of second-class status for Germany. The British government, representing a bitterly resentful and anti-German people, had no stomach whatever for the discussion. And the President, General Marshall, and I saw in the conference on the German question only a clever and almost certainly spoiling operation.

The Russians had correctly appraised the disruptive dilemmas that a conference on the German question would present to the Western Allies and which the Soviet diplomats could exploit. It soon became plain that the first Soviet theater of operations would be in negotiating an agenda for such a meeting. Here Russian tendentious resources were endless. They could refuse to discuss matters not specifically included on the agenda, argue endlessly on the interpretation of agenda items, refuse to pass an item until agreement had been reached on it, refuse to return to an item once it had been passed over, and so on. For a month Ambassadors Jessup, Bonnet of France, and Franks of the United Kingdom wrestled with this problem and then produced a bright idea. Why not precede the ministerial conference on the German question by a four-power meeting of deputies to try to settle the agenda for their principals? This had many advantages: they might not succeed and the major conference, with so many dangers and so few hopes, might never occur. In any event, as an arena for propaganda the technical one promised to hold advantages for the Western Allies in showing the same Russian unwillingness to change the status quo in Germany as had been evident in May 1949.

The deputies' conference met at the Palais Rose in Paris on March 5, 1951 and dragged on wearily and repetitiously until mid-June. Philip Jessup and Charles Bohlen, brilliantly representing the United States, were fortunate in their opponent, pedestrian Andrei Gromyko, Deputy Minister of the Foreign Affairs of the Soviet Union, and less so in their collaborators, Alexandre Parodi, Secretary General of the French Foreign Office, and Ernest Davies, Undersecretary of Foreign Affairs in London. Gromyko was lumbering; Parodi and Davies, timid and slow. The Americans had a handicap in maintaining the initiative in peppering Gromyko with variations on the themes of their proposals and denouncing the immovability of his. They had trouble, too, in keeping a firm Allied line and not being led into futile discussion of Soviet proposals designed to alarm the Germans.

Nevertheless, they did so for eight weeks, at the end of

which they produced a maneuver, called "the triple play," in which they offered Gromyko a choice of three agendas. Each contained five items, all of which both sides, at one time or another and in some form or other, had appeared to favor. Gromyko turned them all down. They then proposed a foreign ministers' meeting without any agenda at all. Gromyko rejected this, too. After another period of arguing that nothing proposed would pass Gromyko's veto, they adjourned the Palais Rose meeting.

In this encounter American diplomatic skill succeeded, with the approval and support of all three democracies, in parrying a strong Soviet move to confuse and weaken the alliance. This was no mean success. It was by no means the end of Jessup's diplomatic achievements, which went on for another eighteen months. This account, however, illustrates the work of a rare and gifted diplomat, set against goals and standards provided by the two masters and authors of today's diplomatic method. It shows him at work constructively in the effort they both prescribed of improving good relations between states and establishing lasting agreements, and in the practical task which can often be of such importance that St. Paul is not denigrated for describing it as the "shield of faith, wherewith ye shall be able to quench all the fiery darts of the wicked." Well, if not "all," at least a good many. We must not claim too much for diplomacy.

II

THE CHANGING FRAMEWORK
OF INTERNATIONAL LAW

CHARLES DE VISSCHER

Stages in the Codification of International Law THE HAGUE 1930—GENEVA 1958—VIENNA 1969

THE WISH to give greater precision and strength to international law through written formulation antedates the League of Nations, which deliberately embarked on the work of codification. As early as 1920 [1] an international organization was established which gave a decisive impulse to this project, an impulse which survived the first disappointments. Errors were committed, but they taught precious lessons.

In 1924 the Assembly of the League of Nations decided to embark upon this enterprise, "gradually and progressively," by concentrating on subject matters sufficiently ripe for codification, so that such codification would be both "possible and desirable." This approach was perfectly justified; it was the in-

CHARLES DE VISSCHER is a sometime President of the International Court of Justice and Honorary President of the Institut de Droit International.

[1] A significant manifestation of this plan is found in a resolution passed on the initiative of Root and Descamps by the Consultative Committee of Jurists entrusted with the task of drafting a statute for a permanent Court of International Justice. The Committee was well aware of the close link between international jurisdiction and the state of the law which an international court would have to apply.

sufficiency of the means put at its disposal which impaired its results. Let it be said at once that, in this first attempt, such experiences were inevitable.

Between 1924 and 1927 a committee of experts, under the presidency of the eminent Swedish jurist Hammarskjöld, proceeded to select the suitable subjects as well as to prepare questionnaires and preliminary projects to be submitted to the various governments. Already at this stage the weaknesses of this method became apparent. In the absence of a central organism which could give direction to the enterprise, the experts had to pursue their project in a haphazard fashion and did not succeed in establishing the necessary contacts with the governments. In fact, the object of the entire enterprise remained somewhat nebulous. At the end of one of the sessions Henri Fromageot observed: "We do not know what we want, but we want it very much." This caustic remark characterized well the state of mind prevailing at that time.

The need to formulate the objectives to be attained more precisely and to substitute for academic studies the precise formulation of goals in a program or plan of action directed to practical ends was not sufficiently appreciated in 1927, when the Assembly of the League of Nations fixed 1930 as the date for the first codification conference.[2] If this conference nevertheless was able to attain a measure of success, this was due to the excellent work done by a distinguished preparatory committee.[3] This committee succeeded in organizing the often very unsatisfactory replies given by the various governments and to provide the foundation for an ordered discussion. The task was all the more difficult since the Assembly resolution of 1927 asked for the formulation not only of the *lex lata* but also

[2] Despite the fact that the Committee of Experts had notified the Council of the League of the insufficiency of governmental responses in its 1927 report. For further details about the efforts of the League in this area, see 41 *Am. J. Int'l L.* 66–93 (1947 Supp.).

[3] The president of the committee was M. Basdevant, and its other members were Sir Cecil Hurst, Castro Ruiz, and François Pilotti.

of a *lex ferenda* adapted to the new conditions of international life. This distinction—on the meaning of which agreement has never been reached—became in practice a source of unnecessary complications.

The remarkable effort of the preparatory committee, which had a more realistic appreciation of the problems, could not, however, make up for the insufficiency of concrete governmental objectives and of a clear intention to achieve practical reforms. It was wrong to press forward at a time when it would have been more important to scrutinize and patiently measure the degree of self-interest which alone can prompt governments to act.

Unfortunately, the very use of the term "codification" has constantly contributed to enmeshing the whole enterprise in formal distinctions which were bound to lead to an impasse. Delegates without precise instructions have often spent more time with the technical aspects of a well-arranged code for lawyers than with the more or less novel content which governments have had an interest in introducing. This latter task is always far more important than the relatively simple one of converting certain rules into logically arranged texts. In order to attain this more important objective it would be necessary to obtain agreement among responsible statesmen as well as among expert jurists.

If one adds to these basic considerations the fact that the delegates who met in the Peace Palace at The Hague in 1930 had not had any preliminary contacts and, for the most part, did not even know each other, it is easy to understand how poorly the ground was prepared for a fruitful collective endeavor. Perhaps the task of coordinating, and of communicating to the invited governments the opinions of the other governments, could have been undertaken by the secretariat of a well-organized League of Nations; but at that time the League was too weak to embark on it.

The replies received by the preparatory committee brought

out profound divergencies, due to the tendency of the governments to keep to their traditional viewpoints. This state of
mind was naturally reflected by the delegates at The Hague;
they were generally more intent on affirming their particular
views than on embarking on enterprises the responsibilities
and risks of which they understood.

Experience has shown that the work of codification requires
a structure; this did not exist in 1930. We, the jurists, felt ourselves in a kind of vacuum. A sincere but vague general desire
to improve the law cannot substitute for this sense of isolation.

Three subject matters had been singled out as having
reached a sufficient degree of maturity: nationality, territorial
waters, and state responsibility. In the matter of nationality,
some modest results were achieved that tended to reduce
somewhat the number of cases of statelessness and double nationality. This was also the only subject where the competent
commission had before it sufficiently precise legislative reform
proposals. The other two commissions found themselves
charged with the thankless task of finding agreement on matters
on which the various governments had profoundly divergent
attitudes, and which were politically highly sensitive. The
most that can be said is that the second commission prepared
the way toward the acceptance of that somewhat hybrid and
confused concept nowadays known as "contiguous zone." As
for the third commission (state responsibilities), it failed completely after agitated sessions. From the beginning, it was impossible to reconcile the proposed theoretical approaches—
which were, by the way, perfectly well known to all
concerned before the conference convened.

With the passage of years, one is less disposed than in 1930
to speak of a "catastrophe" of international law. After all, in
1972 we are still far from reaching international agreement on
the major problem of the law of the seas, i.e., the width of territorial waters. And as regards international state responsibil-

ity, which has been on the agenda of the International Law Commission for some years, we are still far from even preliminary drafts.

The chief result—and it was far from negligible—of The Hague Conference of 1930 was to bring out the inadequacies of the method of approach chosen, and to put into the realm of reality the hopes for patient codification of international law. It proved impossible to revive the enterprise in the League of Nations in the following years, since the failure of the first conference had left too deep a mark. It was not, however, too early to outline the deficiencies of the approach chosen. The Drafting Committee of the 1930 Conference addressed itself to this task at the end of the session and succeeded in getting inserted into the final protocol a declaration which, notably, emphasized the necessity of preparing codification studies long enough in advance so that discussions could be pursued with the necessary degree of authority. It recommended selection of subject matter from the perspective "of reasons which make it appear possible and desirable to arrive at international understandings on the chosen subject matters." In turn, on October 3, 1930, the Assembly of the League of Nations adopted a resolution recommending that codification procedures in the future should concentrate on subjects of "immediate and practical importance."

Fortunately, the disappointment caused by the failure of the Codification Conference of 1930 did not prevent the United Nations from resuming the task Article 13 of the U.N. Charter entrusts to the General Assembly the task of commissioning studies and of making recommendations "for the purpose of . . . encouraging the progressive development of international law and its codification."

In the light of past experience, it now became necessary to put the whole enterprise on a firmer foundation. The guiding thought was the creation of a permanent organization. This oc-

curred in 1947 with the establishment of a special body, the
International Law Commission, which was to have close ties
with the General Assembly of the United Nations.

In the course of the following years, the composition of the
international community and the direction which it gave to
the flow of ideas were determined by a worldwide evolution,
which gave a powerful impulse and better defined directions
to the work of codification. Decolonization, which brought a
large number of new states into the realm of international relations, made it necessary to widen certain objectives of codification. It was now out of the question to concentrate on the
formal task of substituting written rules for customary norms.
It was essential to give to the new states a feeling of confidence in a law in the development of which they had not previously taken any part, and to accept reformulation of principles, with the participation of the newcomers, in certain fields.

From that moment the political perspectives of the whole
enterprise were more openly articulated. This made it necessary for the organs of codification to take cognizance, at all
stages of their work, of governmental attitudes and, consequently, to institute a procedure of systematic consultation. In
this respect, there is no doubt that continuous contact with the
General Assembly of the United Nations, and in particular
with the Sixth Commission, constitutes a great improvement in
efficiency over the tentative procedures of the League of Nations.

One of the most important guarantees of effective work is
the composition of the International Law Commission, which
today, in accordance with its statute, insures representation to
the great forms of civilization and the principal legal systems
of the world. As Roberto Ago has observed, this means that "in
reality the Commission is almost a small-scale model of a general conference, for it contains the basic tendencies, concepts,
and interests which would be represented in a conference

within its own structure." 4 Such an Organism would not be much inclined toward imprudent improvisations; *festina lente* appears to be its wise maxim of conduct.

The work of the jurists is now part of a political plan and structure which has proved to be effective. It is backed by the United Nations Organization, which supervises its progress. A simple resolution of the General Assembly decides on the convocation of a general codification conference; there is a constant exchange of views between the International Law Commission and the Sixth Committee of the General Assembly which insures contact with the governments concerned; finally, the legal services of the United Nations provide the machinery for the codification conferences and have developed conference procedures which benefit from established practice.

In all this one senses a firmer direction, sustained by adequate technical apparatus, conscious of the dimensions of the enterprise and capable of responding to its needs.

It is important to note that, within the International Law Commission itself, the methods of operation have gradually developed in a sense favorable to really concerted codification. On the one hand, the function of its drafting committee has been enlarged by the practice which has gradually developed of referring to it now only questions of a purely technical drafting character, but equally, and after discussion in plenary session, points where the drafting touches on questions of substance. On the other hand, the Commission has more and more abandoned the rather annoying practice of prematurely emphasizing points of disagreement by voting. It has sought more and more—in accordance with the spirit of an organization whose members are not tied by rigid instructions—to obtain a consensus by patient exchanges of views designed to clarify and persuade.

4 "The Codification of International Law and the Problems of Its Execution," *Mélanges Guggenheim* 104 (1968).

GENEVA 1958:
THE INTERNATIONAL LAW OF THE SEA

In order to promote interest in and help the movement toward
codification, it was necessary to launch a codification conference with a theme of great compass that presented both a political and a legal aspect. The Conference on the Law of the
Sea, which was convened in Geneva in 1958, fulfilled this
need. By the breadth of the subject with which it dealt, by the
collaboration among lawyers, statesmen, and technical experts
which it achieved, it marks the starting point for a new dyna-
mism which has not yet diminished.

An old controversy the futility of which had been demonstrated by experience had, fortunately, already abated at that
time: the sterile distinction between "progressive development" of the law and "codification." The first was supposed to
be reserved for subjects not yet regulated or insufficiently regulated by the law, the second for those where the law was
generally accepted and nothing more was needed except re-
finement or formal precision. The International Law Commission, despite the terms of its Statute, did not take long to rid
itself of this distinction. The question was important not so
much with respect to the proper words and formulas to use
as because of the tendency of the participants to adopt a more
or less broad conception of the work to be done in response to
new needs.

In this spirit, the Conference of 1958 introduced into the
traditional law concepts and notions which went beyond the
simple restatement of the existing law. By way of example, one
may mention certain provisions which have been directly inspired by recent decisions of the International Court of Justice: the adoption of the baseline method to measure the width
of territorial waters in regions where the coastline has deep in-
dentations or is dotted with isles along the coast or in its

immediate proximity. This method of measurement, however, is confined to cases where the baselines do not appreciably depart from the general direction of the coast. In a related matter, where the discussion is still open, the conference sought to give precision to a generally accepted notion of the bay by adopting again a criterion spelled out by the court: that of the more or less intimate relation between certain expanses of the sea and the terrestrial formations which surround it.

More boldly innovative were the solutions adopted by the Conference on the Continental Shelf. But here, as was to be expected, the opposing interests had not yet had time to settle on a precise definition; controversies have been reopened on the exact nature of the rights of the coastal state, on the utilization of a double criterion for the limits of the shelf (exploitability and maximum depth), on problems of delimitation between adjoining coastal states, and notably of the lateral delimitation of a single shelf adjacent to the territories of two adjoining states—which was the object of the decision of the International Court of Justice in the *North Sea Continental Shelf Cases*.[5]

The major problem of the international law of the sea, that of the width of the territorial waters, has not yet been solved. A second conference on the law of the sea, convened in 1960, fared no better. Taking into account the votes cast in the course of these conferences, it is nevertheless possible to believe that an international agreement, probably on a maximum width of twelve miles, is in process of formation. Although it is true that in this field, which in many ways is political, the opposed theses for the time being have contributed to a hardening of conflicting positions, it is equally permissible to believe that the confrontation that occurred in conferences largely representative of the members of the international community

5 [1969] *ICJ Reports* 1.

can in the long run modify the extreme views and lead them
toward middle positions from which a large measure of agreement can be attained.

In the meantime, the Conference of 1958 has consolidated a
concept which had already been developed at the Hague Conference of 1930: the institution of a contiguous zone. On this
point its work was less felicitous: Article 24 of the Convention,
the only one dealing with this matter, leaves great uncertainties. One can only discern in this ill-advised concept a provi-
sional compromise which probably will not arrest for long the
general move toward enlargement of the limits of full sovereignty. Provisionally, as Paul Reuter has observed,[6] "The contiguous zone appears to be an instrument of nogotiation and
understanding; everything that is conceded with respect to a
contiguous zone has the aim of containing an extension of territorial waters."

One of the merits of the work on codification is that it
brings out at short intervals the need to regulate interconnected subjects, some of which envisage the improvement and
completion of existing legal regimes, although in certain respects they go beyond present needs, whereas others tackle
really new problems. In the domain of the law of the sea one
might allot to the first category the 1958 Geneva Convention
on Fishing and the Conservation of the Living Resources of the
High Seas,[7] which very quickly led to the conclusion of the
European Fisheries Convention (London, March 9, 1964).[8] To
the second category one might allot the work which, on the
occasion of the Conference of 1958, concerned the bed and
subsoil of the sea; it has stimulated recent attempts to formulate principles that can lead to international cooperation in the
exploration and exploitation of the seabed and to place the resources of the seabed at the disposal of all mankind.

---

[6] *Droit international public* 206 (3d. ed. 1968).
[7] 17 U.S.T. 138, T.I.A.S. 5960, 559 U.N.T.S. 285.
[8] [1966] Gr. Brit. T. S. No. 35 (Cmnd. 3011).

Since the 1958 Geneva Conference, the study of these programs has increasingly demonstrated the basic unity of the entire maritime domain, and the impossibility of delimiting and organizing maritime territories without a comprehensive view of all the elements involved. In adopting the principle of a new conference on the law of the sea to be held in 1973, the General Assembly of the United Nations (in December 1970) had in mind, notably, on the one hand establishing an international regime for the exploration and exploitation of the seabed and the oceans beyond the limits of national jurisdiction, and on the other hand, dealing in a fundamental manner with the questions actually in suspense concerning the high seas and its limits, the revision of the provisions concerning the continental shelf, the territorial sea—including its extent and the question of international straits—the contiguous zone, fisheries, biological resources of the high seas, and the prevention of pollution. This vast program has the merit of including from now on in a comprehensive perspective matters which it is no longer possible to deal with by means of fragmented regulation. One can see how the codification enterprise, provided it is sustained by homogeneous direction, contributes to enlarging the horizons of international regulation.

VIENNA 1969:
THE LAW OF INTERNATIONAL TREATIES

In many respects, the codification of the law of treaties is of particular importance and urgency. The accession to international relations of a large number of new states made it necessary to obtain their agreement on a precise formulation of the principles and rules which govern this chief instrument of interstate relations. The multiplication of multilateral treaties caused by this accession made it necessary, on the other hand, to formulate positions with regard to a number of specifically legal problems and to reexamine traditional solutions.

The Vienna Conference of 1969, which after long preparation was convened under the auspices and with the blessing of
the United Nations, successfully discharged this double task. Its
work, which did not require the same degree of cooperation
among technicians, politicians, and lawyers as did the Law of
the Sea, has not to the present provoked serious challenges. Its
preparation, in accordance with proven methods, was adequate. Contact with political circles through the intermediary
of the United Nations brought out government positions which
were sometimes hardly mentioned in the literature of international law.

Certain problems could not, however, fail to embarrass the
Conference. This was true of the question of coercion in the
conclusion of treaties, which, in turn, was connected with the
use of force in international relations. The Conference could
not contest the validity of peace treaties imposed by the victor
on the vanquished without endangering the stability of a political order. On the other hand, it was even less able to give its
endorsement to all agreements obtained by coercion. It therefore confined itself to pronouncing summarily the nullity of
treaties obtained through threats or the use of force. This simple reference to Article 2(4) of the Charter is hardly satisfactory; in certain respects it is too narrow. On the other hand, its
indiscriminate application could compromise the stability of
the entire system of international law.

More felicitous are the Vienna texts that deal with the important question of the interpretation of treaties. The solutions
there given are in accordance with recent judicial and arbitral
applications. The Conference, which, no doubt, did not entertain the illusion that it had exhausted the matter, had the satisfaction of seeing a draft proposed by the International Law
Commission accepted unanimously. This is an important result, especially if one bears in mind that a large number of
new states have acceded to the Convention.

The delicate legal problems raised by reservations in multilateral treaties have long been approached from the point of view of the logic of contracts, according to which a reservation formulated after the conclusion of the agreement is valid only if it is accepted by all the other parties to the contract. This approach is valid for treaties of an essentially reciprocal character; it is challengeable for multilateral conventions where the parties pursue ends superior to their particular interests. On this point the advisory opinion of the International Court of Justice "Concerning Reservations to the Convention for the Prevention and Punishment of the Crime of Genocide" [9] had paved the way. According to the Vienna Convention, acceptance by all the parties is required when "it appears from the limited number of negotiating states and the object and purpose of a treaty that the application of the treaty in its entirety between all parties is an essential condition of the consent of each one to be bound by the treaty. . . ." Where this is not the case, the Convention admits that a certain objection to a reservation made by another contracting state does not prevent the treaty from coming into force between the state that formulated the objection and the state that has made the reservation, unless a contrary intention has been clearly expressed by the state that has formulated the objection.

The most remarkable innovation of the Vienna Convention of 1969 is that which introduces into positive international law the concept of *jus cogens* (Articles 53, 64, and 66, Sect. a). This challenges the positivist position according to which states are free to give any content they choose to their conventions. Was it not necessary, in our age, to admit exceptions to this principle and to recognize that states are bound by certain imperative norms from which they cannot derogate, even *inter se?*

Opposition to *jus cogens* is logical for the defenders of positivist doctrines, for whom the content of a treaty can be challenged only through the procedures that governed its for-

---

[9] [1951] *ICJ Reports* 15.

mation. The delegate of the Federal Republic of Germany, Mr.
Gropper, has rightly observed that the concept of *jus cogens*
"necessitates a reexamination of the positivist doctrine."

Nevertheless, the Conference of Vienna accepted the doctrine of *jus cogens* by a very large majority. This is an important fact: it signifies a retreat from positivist formulas, the incorporation into international law of certain moral and social
postulates. And this is a cause for satisfaction.

But does this mean that the formulation of Article 53 of the
Convention, with respect to the concept of *jus cogens* has
given it sufficient normative force to insure its incorporation
into positive international law? On this point some doubt must
be expressed. The Convention is far from having given a precise sense to that somewhat vague and ill-defined entity of international law which it describes as "the international community of states as a whole." An attempt has been made to
mitigate this grave lack of precision by a procedure which permits "any one of the parties to a dispute concerning the application or the interpretation of Article 53 or 64 . . . by a written application, [to] submit it to the International Court of
Justice for a decision . . ." (Article 66(a)).

The moral and theoretical importance of this problem probably goes beyond the range of its practical application. The
need for showing that a norm qualified as one that cannot be
derogated from not only must have quasi-universal application, but also must be applied as imperative, will no doubt
make recourse to *jus cogens* rather exceptional.

The rapid succession of codification attempts under the auspices of the United Nations has given new actuality to a question whose doctrinal importance, it must be admitted, is
greater than its practical significance. The question is under
what conditions a convention of this type can by itself, i.e.,
outside any specific element of its text and structure, give rise
to a new customary norm which can be raised against states

that are not parties to the convention. The importance of this question is somewhat diminished by the fact that the International Law Commission did, quickly and expressly, abandon the sterile separation between "codification" and "progressive development," and also by the fact that the mandates assigned to the codification conferences abstain from any indication concerning the relation of the codification in question to customary law. The codification treaties do not say anything on the declaratory or constitutive character of their provisions; the only exception is the preamble to the Geneva Convention on the High Seas,[10] which affirms the generally declaratory character of its provisions, no doubt because of the almost universal adherence to these provisions.

The new rules formulated by the codification treaties are not automatically imposed on states that have not participated in them. They can be invoked against the latter only to the extent to which they have been confirmed by the practice of an important group of states. Such confirmation remains distinct and outside the treaty itself.

The solid reasoning developed in the decision of the International Court of Justice in the *North Sea Continental Shelf Cases* should, it seems to us, dissipate all doubts on this subject. The Court admits the possibility of a "norm-creating provision which has constituted the foundation of, or has generated a rule which, only conventional or contractual in its origin, has since passed into the general corpus of international law, and is now accepted as such by the *opinio juris*, so as to have become binding even for countries which have never, and do not, become parties to the Convention." But the Court also adds that "this result is not lightly to be regarded as having been attained."

Having formulated this caveat, the decision carefully outlines the traditional positions from which the formation of cus-

---

[10] 13 U.S.T. 2312, T.I.A.S. 5200, 450 U.N.T.S. 82.

tom can be deduced. It states first that the structure of Article 6 of the Convention on the Continental Shelf does not testify in favor of its normative character. This first observation rests "inside the Convention"; it is the only one which, in our opinion, supports the reasoning developed by Professor A. D'Amato in an interesting article published in the American Journal of International Law.[11]

But the decision does not confine itself to this internal, contractual aspect of the elements necessary for the formation of custom. It develops simultaneously other factors which are, as it were, situated outside the treaty. The decision cites above all the very large and representative participation in the Convention, including the states particularly interested in this subject. Passing from there to the question of the time factor, it underlines that "an indispensible requirement would be that within the period in question, short though it might be, state practice, including that of states whose interests are specially affected, should have been both extensive and virtually uniform in the sense of the provision invoked; and, moreover, should have occurred in such a way as to show a general recognition that the rule of law or legal obligation is involved." (Section 74.)

This shows convincingly that the Geneva Convention was not, either by virtue of its origin or by its premises, declaratory of an obligatory principle of customary international law which would impose the principle of equidistance, nor has it, by virtue of its subsequent effects, led to the formation of such a rule, since state practice has not been adequate in this respect.

In a remarkable study published prior to the Court's decision,[12] Professor R. R. Baxter of Harvard University had al-

---

[11] "Manifest Intent and the Generation by Treaty of Customary Rules of International Law," 64 *Am. J. Int'l L.* 892 (1970).

[12] "Multilateral Treaties as Evidence of Customary International Law," 41 *Brit. Y. B. Int'l L.* 275 (1965–1966).

ready observed that a codification treaty which purports to be declaratory of customary law at its adoption can be used in support of such an argument only where it has received the approval of a substantial number of states.

To conclude this point, we may say that however well prepared and drafted a codification treaty may be, it can aspire to being declaratory of customary law only where the intentions expressed in the treaty are confirmed by adequate international practice.

There is one aspect which is particularly critical for the future of general codification treaties. This is the problem of ratifications. Too many states which have signed codification projects or have adhered to them are very tardy in ratifying them, sometimes at the risk of endangering the state of the law or of making it more uncertain than before codification.

Quite apart from the political reasons which may persuade states to modify their positions, such delays can usually be explained either by the tendency of governments to observe each other's behavior and to enter into a commitment only when others have done so, or simply by the ponderousness of the ratification mechanisms prescribed by internal constitutions. This problem had already engaged the attention of the League of Nations, and various matters had been envisaged to counter this tendency toward inertia. Among such countermeasures recently mentioned has been the adoption, by the General Assembly, of a more or less solemn recommendation inviting the member states to ratify the conventions which they have failed to ratify. Such a procedure can be effective mainly where the conventions in question have no great political importance, such as those which deal with human rights or have humanitarian objectives. Nevertheless, the best assurance of ratification within a reasonable time is the continuing interest of the governments in a convention in which they have participated.

T. OLAWALE ELIAS

Modern Sources of International Law

THE AIM of this study is to demonstrate, if indeed any demonstration were needed, that there is a real sense in which it is possible to say that modern international law now exists. Just as Europe historically has had its old and its medieval periods and now has its modern period, so international law may be said to have had its old and its medieval periods and to be now in its modern period. The classical age of international law may be said to date from the days of the Greek city-states until the time immediately preceding Hugo Grotius (circa 1651); the medieval era can be conveniently described as falling between Grotius and the demise of the League of Nations; and modern international law, although presaged in some ways by certain significant landmarks, like the Hague Conventions of 1907, the Treaty of Versailles of 1919, and the Briand-Kellogg Pact of 1928, may nevertheless be taken as dating from the end of the Second World War, particularly with the emergence of the United Nations Organization.

The first and earliest period was characterized by often rudi-

T. OLAWALE ELIAS is Attorney General of the Federation and Commissioner of Justice, Republic of Nigeria; Dean of the Faculty of Law, University of Lagos; and an Associate of the Institut de Droit International.

mentary arrangements for regulating the almost ceaseless Old-World struggles between empires, kingdoms, and city-states. The medieval period witnessed the breakup of Western Christendom under the Holy Roman Empire as a result of the Treaty of Westphalia (1648) and the consequent rise of nation states based upon the cult of political sovereignty adumbrated by Jean-Bodin and others. This produced the new traditional dichotomy between the monist and the dualist schools in international law, the one holding that municipal law and international law are two distinct entities, each valid in its own sphere, and the other maintaining that there is only one international legal order based upon the primacy of international law over municipal law wherever there is an interaction between the two. Allied to this view has been the rule that international law exists to regulate the relations between sovereign states alone. It will be shown presently that neither the monist-dualist controversy nor the theory of states as the only subjects of international law is still tenable in contemporary juristic thought and practice. A strong feature of modern international law is its three-dimensional character—its encompassing of the whole range of relations between states and states, between states and individuals (including institutions), and between two or more international institutions. Modern international law is new not only in respect of the new ground it has broken and continues to break, but also in its treatment of and orientation toward established subjects and concepts. For several decades, the strict state versus state relationship has been giving way to one in which, increasingly, states are confronted by individuals and organizations, as in the sphere of humanitarian law (notably, the European Commission and the Court of Human Rights) and in the area of international economic and financial law (notably, the Convention on the Settlement of Investment Disputes between States and Nationals of Contracting States). The establishment of the specialized agencies of the United Nations and the proliferation of inter-

governmental organizations within the last twenty-five years
have led to a growing network of intercourse among these new
subjects of international law which has had to be regulated by
agreements; for these international institutions have, we have
been told by the International Court of Justice,[1] their own individual legal personalities.

Apart from the temporal factor in our evaluation of modern
international law, there is the question of expansion of the
frontiers of customary international law since the beginning of
the modern period. Whereas up to 1945 the public international law that was studied in universities and academies was
limited mainly to the general principles of customary law and
practice governing interstate relations, there has since taken
place an explosion that almost leaves one breathless in attempting to enumerate its offshoots. In addition to the study of
the general principles of international law, an international
economic law and a law of international institutions have developed rapidly since the end of the Second World War. Other
fields of specialization have since followed: diplomatic law,
treaty law, international constitutional law, humanitarian law,
international space law and air law, the international law of
communications and, now, environmental law. And this list is
by no means exhaustive. So dynamic is modern international
law that there is no sign of an ebbing of the tide.

This great expansion in the frontiers of public international
law may be traced in three main factors: (1) the increase in the
number of independent, sovereign states and their accession to
membership in the United Nations within the last two decades; (2) the resulting growth in cooperative economic and
social activities which the very proliferation of sovereignties
fosters within an increasingly interdependent world, such as
the League of Nations system never envisaged, but which
forms the point of departure for the United Nations' "brave

[1] See Reparation For Injuries Suffered in the Service of the United Nations, [1949] *ICJ Reports* 174.

new world"; [2] and (3) the phenomenal advances made in the fields of science and technology, opening up vistas of man's inescapable involvement with nature and his environment. We shall elaborate upon all these later. It is sufficient to note here that in no single municipal legal system has there been such profusion or such abundance of legal rules and practices as we have witnessed in modern international law in the last quarter of a century.

Under Article 38 of the Statute of the International Court of Justice the following sources of international law are listed:

(a) international conventions, whether general or particular, establishing rules expressly recognized by the contesting states;

(b) international custom, as evidence of a general practice accepted as law;

(c) the general principles of law recognized by civilized nations;

(d) judicial decisions and the teachings of the most highly qualified publicists of the various nations, as subsidiary means for the determination of rules of law.

As these so-called sources also denote the scope of the material content of public international law, an attempt will be made to analyze their nature and character in order to indicate how they add up to the modern international law which we treat in the present study.

THE INTERNATIONAL LAW COMMISSION

Unquestionably, the most significant development in contemporary international law has taken place in the field of international legislation in the traditional sense of the term. The genesis of the idea is to be found in Article 13(1)(a) of the United Nations Charter, which provides that the General Assembly "shall initiate studies and make recommendations for the purpose of . . . encouraging the progressive development of inter-

[2] See Article 13(1b), chs. IX and X of the U.N. Charter.

national law and its codification." Pursuant to this, the General Assembly adopted Resolution 174(II) on November 21, 1947, by which it established the International Law Commission and also approved its Statute,[3] according to Article 1 of which the Commission is "to have for its object the promotion of the progressive development of international law and its codification." It is further required to "concern itself primarily with public international law, but is not precluded from entering the field of private international law." Article 15 of the Statute draws a distinction between "progressive development," which means "the preparation of draft conventions on subjects which have not yet been regulated by international law or in regard to which the law has not been sufficiently developed in the practice of States," and "codification," which means "the more precise formulation and systematization of rules of international law in fields where there already has been extensive State practice, precedent and doctrine." In its twenty-one years of work, the Commission has submitted fifteen final reports on as many topics but has not found it easy in practice to make the distinction between progressive development and codification when drafting the several articles for a convention. This point was put graphically by the Commission when it decided in 1962 to change from drafting a code to drafting a convention on the Law of Treaties:

First, an expository code, however well formulated, cannot in the nature of things be so effective as a convention for consolidating

[3] The precursor of the ILC was the 17-member standing Committee of Experts for the Progressive Codification of International Law, composed to represent "the main forms of civilization and the principal legal systems of the world." This committee made recommendations which laid the foundation for the Codification Conference which was held at The Hague from March 13 to April 12, 1930, which failed, however, to adopt any conventions on the first two of the three topics before it—territorial water, state responsibility, and nationality. See *League of Nations Official Journal, Special Supplement*, No. 21, at 10. What the ILC owes to these ideas can be seen in the existing provisions of the Statute of the ILC. [Cf. also de Visscher, *supra* p. 17.—Eds.]

the law; and the consolidation of the law of treaties is of particular importance at the present time when so many new States have recently become members of the international community. Secondly, the codification of the law of treaties through a multilateral convention would give all the new States the opportunity to participate directly in the formulation of the law if they so wished; and their participation in the work of codification appears to the Commission to be extremely desirable in order that the law of treaties may be placed upon the widest and most secure foundations.[4]

Probably the most significant developments in public international law have been due to the work of the International Law Commission.[5] Even if we put aside its reports on such topics as *The Draft Declaration on the Rights and Duties of States, Formulation of the Nuremberg Principles, Question of Defining Aggression,* and *Ways and Means for Making the Evidence of Customary International Law More Readily Available,* we must take note of its notable achievements in the Law of the Sea (1958), made up of the four conventions on the High Seas, on the Continental Shelf, on the Territorial Sea and the Contiguous Zone, and on Fishing and Conservation of the Living Resources of the High Seas;[6] in the Vienna Conventions on Diplomatic Relations, (1961) and Consular Relations (1963);[7] in the Vienna Convention on the Law of Treaties

[4] 2 *Y. B. Int'l L. Comm'n* 160, Doc. A / CN.4 / Ser. A / 1959 / Add. 1.

[5] The Commission's work has been enriched by its cooperative relationships with the Inter-American Council of Jurists and its standing organ, the Inter-American Juridical Committee, with the Asian-African Legal Consultative Committee and, since 1965, with the European Commission on Legal Co-operation. The periodic interchange of observers and documents between the Commission and each of these bodies has been of mutual benefit to both sides. This rapprochement is based on Article 26(4) of the Statute of the ILC, which provides for "the advisability of consultation by the Commission with intergovernmental organizations whose task is the codification of international law, such as those of the Pan-American Union."

[6] Respectively, 13 U.S.T. 2312, T.I.A.S. 5200, 450 U.N.T.S. 82; 15 U.S.T. 471, T.I.A.S. 5578, 499 U.N.T.S. 311; 15 U.S.T. 1606, T.I.A.S. 5639, 516 U.N.T.S. 205; 17 U.S.T. 138, T.I.A.S. 5969, 559 U.N.T.S. 285.

[7] Respectively, 500 U.N.T.S.; 21 U.S.T. 77, T.I.A.S. 6820, 596 U.N.T.S. 261.

(1969); [8] and in the Convention on Special Missions (1969).[9]
Although their coverage is still not complete,[10] the Law of the
Sea conventions nevertheless represent a notable advance
upon the uncertainties of the past in this area. The conventions on the Law of the Sea contain many elements of progressive development; for example, the new definition of piracy su-
persedes the one which served as the *ratio decidendi* of the
English decision in *Re Piracy Jure Gentium*,[11] the rule in respect of state jurisdiction over crimes committed on board foreign vessels in territorial waters in the *Lotus* case [12] has been
overthrown, and the customary rules relating to the right of
"hot pursuit" have been extended. As the recent *North Sea
Continental Shelf Cases* [13] show, the new rule laid down in the
Convention on the Continental Shelf is sufficiently equitable
to warrant its affirmation. The diplomatic, the consular, and
the special mission conventions, together with the Convention
on Relations between States and International Organizations
now nearing completion by the International Law Commission, will constitute a new diplomatic law superseding customary rules and practices on the subject. The Vienna Convention on the Law of Treaties, "The Treaty on Treaties," as
it has been called,[14] although it has yet to receive the requisite
number of ratifications, is already the accepted authority on
the subject, despite the elements of progressive development
which it contains, such as its reformulation of the principles

[8] Not yet in force. *Done* at Vienna, May 23, 1969, U.N.Doc. A / CONF.
39 / 27. For the text, see also 63 *Am. J. Int'l L.* 875 (1969) and 8 *Int'l Legal
Materials* 679 (1969).

[9] Not yet in force. *Opened for signature* December 16, 1969. See Annex to
G.A. Res. 2530 (XXIV), 24 U.N. GAOR Supp. 30, U.N. Doc. A / 7630 (Dec. 8,
1969).

[10] As witness the December 1970 Resolution 2750 C (XXV) of the General
Assembly calling for a plenipotentiary conference on the Law of the Sea in
1973.

[11] A.C. 586 (1934).   [12] [1927] PCIJ, series A. No. 10, p. 10.

[13] [1970] *ICJ Reports.*

[14] See Kearney and Dalton, "The Treaty on Treaties," 64 *Am. J. Int'l L.*
495 (July 1970).

underlying *pacta sunt servanda* and *clausula rebus sic stantibus*, rules for the interpretation of treaties, and the grounds of invalidity, termination, and suspension of treaties —particularly the *jus cogens* rule, which is defined as a peremptory norm of general international law from which states will not be permitted to derogate in their future dealings with one another. Indeed, the International Law Commission itself has called the convention the "modern law" on the subject.[15] By outlawing fraud, coercion, and the use or threat of force from the sphere of interstate relations, this convention is laying down a revolutionary standard of international morality which, under the overall aegis of *jus cogens*, represents the high-water mark of international legislation in the history of international law. Whether or not it eventually enters into force, international law cannot be the same again.

Among the topics now under active study by the International Law Commission are also the question of succession of states and governments, which is of considerable contemporary relevance to the new states and to others, and the question of state responsibility, a subject of great complexity and delicacy. It must be conceded that, when these and the other subjects now under study, such as relations between states and international organizations and international waterways and watercourses, are completed, international law will have been rewritten and restated to such an extent that it will have ceased to be a European-orientated law and will have become a modern world law.

OTHER LAW-MAKING BODIES

Although the International Law Commission is the most important law-making body established for the *general* purpose

[15] Int'l L. Comm'n, Report on the Work of its Eighteenth Session, 21 U.N. GAOR, Supp. 9, U.N. Doc. A / 6309 / Rev. 1 (1966), Article 49, para. 7 of commentary. [Cf. also de Visscher, *supra* p. 27.—Eds.]

of studying and submitting draft articles to the United Nations on almost any subject whatsoever, there are other bodies established by the General Assembly, such as the United Nations Commission on International Trade Law (UNCITRAL) and the United Nations Conference on Trade and Development (UNCTAD), which are also filling up gaps in the customary law regulating international trade, economic relations, and problems of economic development, especially between the capital-exporting and capital-importing countries. There is, in view of the dynamic activities of such bodies, a developing new *lex mercatoria,* this time developed and adopted by *all* and not only by some of the states that are to be subject to its sway. In addition to these permanent bodies are temporary ones like the Committee on Principles of International Law Concerning Friendly Relations and Co-operation among States, which, after nearly five years of study and prolonged conferences, drew up the Draft Declaration on Principles of International Law Concerning Friendly Relations and Co-operation among States,[16] adopted by the General Assembly in December 1970 as one of the principal instruments in commemoration of the Twenty-Fifth Anniversary of the United Nations Organization.[17] The seven principles of the United Nations Charter, the progressive development and codification of which have been attempted in the instrument, are: (1) the principle that states shall refrain in their international relations from the threat or use of force against the territorial integrity or political independence of any state or in any other manner inconsistent with the purposes of the United Nations; (2) the principle that states shall settle their international disputes by peaceful means in such a manner that international peace, security, and justice are not endangered; (3) the duty of states not to intervene in matters within the domestic jurisdiction of

[16] 25 U.N. GAOR Supp. 18, U.N. Doc. A / 8018; A / AC. 125 / 12 (1970).

[17] The instrument itself is U.N. Doc. A / RES / 2625(XXV) of November 4, 1970.

any state, in accordance with the Charter; (4) the duty of states to cooperate with one another in accordance with the Charter; (5) the principle of equal rights and self-determination of peoples; (6) the principle of the sovereign equality of states; and (7) the principle that states shall fulfill in good faith the obligations assumed by them in accordance with the Charter. Now, these principles as elaborated in this important declaration constitute, in the words of a preambular paragraph, "a significant contribution to contemporary international law." Insofar as they constitute "basic principles of international law," the General Assembly "appeals to all States [that is, not only member states] to be guided by these principles in their international conduct and to develop their mutual relations on the basis of the strict observance of these principles." Although the Declaration is not an amendment of the Charter and is without prejudice to the latter's provisions, it marks a development in the underlying ideas that inspired the Charter in San Francisco in 1945.

Outside the United Nations system, there are also a number of independent bodies participating in the task of refashioning and developing international law, of which the most important are the *Institut de Droit International* (1873), the International Law Association (1873), and the Harvard Research in International Law (1927), all of which have rendered invaluable services by providing draft codes and articles on the basis of which many an international convention has been reconsidered and improved before its adoption.

The foregoing does not take into account the invaluable legislative work going on in the various United Nations specialized agencies, particularly the International Labour Organisation, which for over fifty years has enriched public international law with numerous conventions on labor law, social welfare legislation, and general humanitarian law. The significant thing about the ILO's contribution in this area of international law is that the legislation it promotes often results in modification of relevant municipal enactments, thus showing in a conspicuous manner transnational law in action today. Other specialized agencies—for example, UNESCO, the Universal Postal Union, the International Telecommunications Union, the International Civil Aviation Organization, and the World Health Organization—continue to widen the scope and insure the effectiveness of modern international law, not only through conventions but also by means of decisions, resolutions, and practices within the several organizations.[18]

THE ROLE OF DIPLOMATIC CONFERENCES
IN INTERNATIONAL LAW-MAKING

The one great worldwide diplomatic conference under the League of Nations was the Codification Conference of 1930, to which we have already referred. Aside from the San Francisco Conference of 1945 which inaugurated the United Nations Charter, all the important conferences of a law-making character have taken place since 1949, almost all under United Nations auspices. The first notable conference was that held in Geneva on August 12, 1949, which adopted the four conventions relating to the protection of war victims.[19] Almost all the subsequent conferences have been held to study and conclude conventions on the basis of draft articles prepared and submitted to the General Assembly by the International Law Commission. We have already mentioned the four Geneva Conventions on the Law of the Sea of 1958, the Vienna Diplomatic and the Consular Relations Conventions of 1961 and 1963, and the Vienna Convention on the Law of Treaties of 1969.

Whereas the normal pattern has been for ILC and other draft instruments to be submitted by the General Assembly to

[18] For a recent account of the process, see E. Yemin's *Legislative Powers in the United Nations and Specialized Agencies* (1969).

[19] See 75 U.N.T.S. These four conventions owed their origin to the Geneva Red Cross Conventions of August 22, 1864.

plenipotentiary conferences for consideration and adoption, such texts are sometimes dealt with by the General Assembly itself without reference to a conference separately convened for this purpose. Thus, on December 8, 1969, the General Assembly adopted the Convention on Special Missions and the Optional Protocol Concerning the Compulsory Settlement of Disputes, based on the ILC draft articles. The U.N. Conference on Transit Trade of Land-Locked Countries held in New York in 1965 adopted the Convention on Transit Trade of Land-Locked States, the draft having been prepared by the UNCTAD.[20] Similarly, a number of declarations,[21] such as the Universal Declaration of Human Rights (1948) and the Declaration on Principles of International Law Concerning Friendly Relations and Cooperation among States (1970), have been adopted by the General Assembly on the basis of texts prepared either by another subordinate organ or by the ILC.[22] There can be no doubt that conventions adopted in this way are no less law-making and no less enforceable than those adopted by a conference of plenipotentiaries held under the auspices of the United Nations.

GENERAL ASSEMBLY AND SECURITY COUNCIL RESOLUTIONS AS SOURCES OF LAW

Article 18(2) lists a number of "important questions" on which "decisions" of the General Assembly "shall be made by a two-

[20] U.N. Doc. TD/TRANSIT/9 and TD/TRANSIT/10 and Add. 1 (1965).

[21] See U.N. Doc. E/CN.4/L.610: The Use of the Terms 'Declaration' and 'Recommendation,' prepared for the Commission on Human Rights, at its request, by the Office of Legal Affairs of the United Nations Secretariat in 1962.

[22] By Resolution 375(IV) of December 6, 1949, the General Assembly adopted and proclaimed the Declaration on the Rights and Duties of States and referred it to the attention of member states and jurists *of all nations* as a substantial contribution to the development of international law, especially in its provision that every state has the right to independence, including the choice of its own form of government, and that it also has a duty, *inter alia,* to refrain from intervention in the internal or external affairs of any other state.

thirds majority of the members present and voting." Among such questions are recommendations regarding the maintenance of international peace and security, the election of the nonpermanent members of the Security Council, of the Economic and Social Council, and of the Trusteeship Council, the admission of new members, the suspension of the rights and privileges of membership, the expulsion of members, questions relating to the operation of the trusteeship system, and budgetary questions. Decisions on all other questions "shall be made by a majority of the members present and voting." Article 10 provides that the General Assembly "may discuss any questions or any matters within the scope of the present Charter" and may make "recommendations" to U.N. members, to the Security Council, or to both. It is in the light of these that Hans Kelsen has observed that "there is hardly any international matter which the General Assembly is not competent to discuss and on which it is not competent to make recommendations." [23]

The perennial question has been: What legal effects have the General Assembly resolutions? On the correct answer to this question must surely depend our assessment of the value of those resolutions in the development of modern international law. It seems clear that, as far as General Assembly recommendations in respect of the nine specifically enumerated matters in Article 18(2) are concerned, its "decisions" in the form of "recommendations" are binding upon all concerned once they have been adopted by a two-thirds majority. As regards all other matters within the competence of the Assembly, a simple majority is all that is required by Article 18(3) of the Charter. And, yet, despite these apparently clear provisions, problems have arisen in connection with their interpretation. For instance, it has been suggested that, in order to be

[23] *The Law of the United Nations*, 198–99 (1950). See also Goodrich and Hambro, *The Charter of the United Nations*, 152 (1949).

binding as a source of law, a General Assembly resolution should receive the *consent* of all members; another school has proposed that only a resolution supported by all the important groups in the United Nations Organization could be so regarded; while yet another school holds that the Assembly can only make recommendations, not decisions of a binding character, even in respect of the specific matters mentioned in Article 18(2).[24]

Certain Western lawyers tend to regard General Assembly resolutions as not binding, even in the case of the Uniting for Peace Resolution of 1950. Although both France and the USSR took the same line on this issue of 1950, the attitudes of the two countries seem to diverge in other respects. Nor are Soviet jurists in total accord with each other. G. I. Tunkin regarded General Assembly resolutions as only "subsidiary" sources of international law, while G. I. Morozov (now a Judge of the ICJ) has said that they are sources of international law only if they are adopted by states of the two socioeconomic systems (communist and capitalist) and of all the three main political groups (socialist, Western, and neutralist). To this, M. V. Yanovskii later added a proviso—that resolutions agreed to by the three main political groups should also have been adopted without any dissenting vote. This tangled web of Soviet theories has led Dr. E. McWhinney to observe:

In place of the old positivistic, law-as-command theories, therefore, we now have explicit recognition by Soviet jurists of a new law-as-consensus approach, in which the emphasis must be upon bilateralism, and on mutuality and reciprocity of interest, as the basis of international law norm-making in a pluralistic world community.[25]

[24] See, e.g., F. Vallat, "The General Assembly and the Security Council of the United Nations," 29 *Brit. Y. B. Int'l L.* 63; and also his "The Competence of the U.N. General Assembly," 97 Hague *Recueil des Cours* 203 (1959-II).

[25] McWhinney, "The Changing United Nations Constitutionalism: New Areas and New Techniques for International Law-Making," in 5 *Canadian Y.B. Int'l L.*, 68–83, at 83 (1967).

On the other hand, the other states in the socialist bloc regard
these resolutions as creating international law norms. V. Pech-
ota, a Czech, regards them as reflecting "the developing juridical conscience of people," giving as examples "the principle of
general disarmament" and "the principle of the final liquida-
tion of colonialism," both having been established by a series
of General Assembly resolutions. He also distinguishes between "simple recommendations" and "solemn declarations,"
the latter being binding upon states because they either create
new norms or change old ones. Manfred Lachs (now a Judge
of the ICJ), a Pole, takes a similar position, giving as examples
the right of self-determination of states, international trade exchanges, and general disarmament, producing "concrete and
imperative principles" of international law. He further cites
the Universal Declaration of Human Rights of 1948, the Declaration on the Granting of Independence to Colonial Countries and Peoples of 1960, and the Declaration of Legal Principles Governing the Activities of States in the Exploration and
Use of Outer Space of 1963 as General Assembly resolutions
which have interpreted U.N. Charter provisions and brought
them up to date, and which in the process have accomplished
"the shaping of new principles." Lachs realistically concedes:
"It is true that—with some exceptions only—they cannot be
viewed as creative of legal rights or obligations. But does this
imply that they are devoid of all legal value?" [26] This is certainly a pertinent question, the answer to which can hardly be
in the negative.

[26] See Lachs, "International Law of Outer Space," 113 Hague *Recueil des
Cours* 7, at 96 (1964-III). Lachs maintained that the principle of the non-or-
biting of nuclear weapons in space vehicles rests on General Assembly Resolution of October 17, 1963 (Resolution 1884 (XVIII). This principle has now
been embodied in the Treaty on the Exploration and Use of Outer Space the
text of which was agreed upon and finalized by the United States and the
USSR before being unanimously approved by Resolution 2222(XXI) of the
General Assembly of December 19, 1966. For a criticism of the manner of
achieving this treaty by big power influence, see Rosenbaum and Cooper,
"Brazil and the Non-Proliferation Treaty," 46 *International Affairs* 74–90 (January 1970).

Dr. Richard Falk's position [27] appears on the whole to be similar to Lachs's. He said:

In a world fraught with conflict and instability there is a widely felt need to find a way to adapt the international legal order to the changing character of social and political demands, to develop techniques of peaceful change as an alternative to violence and warfare. . . . If international society is to function effectively, it requires a limited legislative authority, at minimum, to translate an over-riding consensus among States into rules of order and norms of obligations despite the opposition of one or more sovereign States.[28]

This movement away from consent to consensus in the determination of international questions of a norm-making character has also been noted by Dr. C. W. Jenks, who contends that in the evolution of international law, "consent cannot be the ultimate source of legal obligation." [29] Oscar Schachter has suggested that the two main tests for the existence of an international obligation are legitimacy and effectiveness.[30] The problem surely is that most of the rules of customary international law were established in the last four centuries by only a handful of Western European states; the advocates of consent as the only basis of obligation for sovereign states are also the first to insist that the three-quarters of the world that took no part in its formation must be regarded as bound by it, consent or no consent.[31]

[27] See his interesting article, "On the Quasi-Legislative Competence of the General Assembly," 60 *Am. J. Int'l L.* 782 (1966); also O. Y. Asamoah, *The Legal Significance of the Declarations of the General Assembly of the United Nations* (1966).

[28] Falk, *id.*, at 788.   [29] *Law, Freedom and Welfare* 85 (1963).

[30] "Towards a Theory of International Obligation," in 8 *Virginia J. Int'l L.* 311 (1968). See also Tunkin, "Co-existence and International Law," 95 Hague *Recueil des Cours* 9 (1958-III).

[31] This has been expressed in political terms by Allan Bullock, Master of St. Catherine's College, Oxford, as follows: "In 1900 Europe stood at the height of her power and prestige. Geographically insignificant, the smallest but one of the seven continents, she enjoyed a primacy which had lasted so long that most Europeans simply assumed it would continue indefinitely. Only two nations outside Europe enjoyed real independence, the Americans and the Japa-

N. G. Onuf, in criticising Falk's distinction between consent and consensus as exaggerated, has suggested that there is now a trend away from consensus toward unanimity.[32] Onuf, however, ends with the observation: "Increasingly defensive, aware that its historic primacy in the making of international law is endangered, the West will almost certainly reject other such efforts in the future, thereby displaying the unwillingness of a major group to grant the General Assembly a real legislative competence. There is no world consensus without the West. . . ."[33] While there is force in the argument that a General Assembly resolution adopted without the West's participation would be unrealistic, it by no means follows that such a resolution may not be legally valid if the Charter provisions are duly met. As Dr. W. Friedmann has pointed out, "It is not only the codificatory work of the International Law Commission itself, but even more the law-making resolutions of the General Assembly that express new and different forms of the new development of international law."[34]

The traditional view that General Assembly resolutions, with certain exceptions, are only recommendatory and do not bind member states was expressed by the International Court of Justice in the *South-West Africa Cases (Second Phase)*.[35] While agreeing that "the accumulation of expressions of condemnation of *apartheid* . . . especially as recorded in the reso-

---

nese. The rest of the world was either parcelled out between the rival European empires or under the rule of governments too feeble or corrupt (or both) to withstand European political pressure or economic penetration." See his lecture, "Europe Since Hitler," 47 *International Affairs* 1–18, at 1 (January 1971).

[32] "Professor Falk on the Quasi-Legislative Competence of the General Assembly," in 64 *Am. J. Int'l L.* 349–55 (1970).

[33] Onuf had just referred (at p. 355) to the General Assembly's "Declaration on the Inadmissibility of Intervention in the Domestic Affairs of States and the Protection of their Independence and Sovereignty," adopted by means of Resolution 2131 (XX) of December 21, 1965.

[34] "The United Nations and the Development of International Law," 25 *International Journal*, 272, 274 (1970).

[35] [1966] *ICJ Reports* 6, at 50–51.

lutions of the General Assembly of the United Nations are proof of the pertinent contemporary international community standard," Judge Jessup did not subscribe to "the thesis that resolutions of the General Assembly have a general legislative character and by themselves create new rules of law." [36] What the learned judge is saying here amounts to what Falk, Friedmann, Tunkin, and Lachs have said, namely, that a certain category of decisions of the General Assembly are binding on member states, but that not every resolution has a binding character. If there is unanimity in the Assembly during the vote, all are bound, provided the subject falls within the Assembly's competence. If the vote is divided, then those states that vote for a particular resolution by the requisite majority are bound on the grounds of consent and of estoppel. Those that abstain are also bound on the ground of acquiescence and tacit consent, since an abstention is not a negative vote; while those that vote against the resolution should be regarded as bound by the democratic principle that the majority view should always prevail when the vote has been truly free and fair and the requisite majority has been secured.[37] To hold otherwise would be contrary to the democratic principle that, if every state has had its say, the requisite majority must have its way. It would be dangerous to mix up the question of the legal validity of such a vote with that of its desirability or wisdom in any given context; the one is an extralegal consideration, while the other is a matter of strict law. This is the *raison d'être* of the overwhelming trend toward consensus which is an expression of the juridical conscience of the world community. Jenks has warned: "The substitution of the principle of majority decision for that of unanimity as the basis of the functioning of international organizations marked a decisive stage

[36] *Id*. at 441.
[37] See Bleicher, "The Legal Significance of Recitation of General Assembly Resolutions," 63 *Am. J. Int'l L.* 445 (1969). See also Manno, "Majority Decisions and Minority Responses in the United Nations General Assembly," 10 *Journal of Conflict Resolutions*, 3–7 (1966).

in their development; no sane person would now wish to revert to the old order; but we have not yet learned how to operate the new order wisely." [38] The glorification of state sovereignty and the notion of consent as the only basis of customary international law should not be allowed to obtrude themselves into this sphere of international life in the General Assembly.

There is no provision in the U.N. Charter which either expressly or by implication requires that a vote in the General Assembly must be by affirmation of all member states, or of any particular state or group of states. The Charter merely requires that the subject matter be competent and the resolution or recommendation be adopted by the specified majority in accordance with the Charter. It is only in connection with the Security Council that the concurring votes of the five permanent members are required for a resolution on non-procedural matters to be validly adopted.[39] On procedural matters, all that is required is an affirmative vote of *any* nine members out of the fifteen; there is no stipulation for unanimity. There is no question that decisions of the Security Council bind all member states under Article 25 in respect of the exercise of its functions and powers in accordance with Article 24.

We would do well to bear in mind this observation of J. E. S. Fawcett:

The General Assembly has now adopted nearly two thousand five hundred resolutions, and the Security Council rather more than a tenth of that number. But the fact that, while certain decisions of the Security Council are mandatory for U.N. Members, all General Assembly resolutions are formal recommendations only, does not prevent a few resolutions from embodying directive principles or agreed standards, which may, by reason of their content, purpose and form of adoption, secure as great international observance as a treaty. That the provisions of such resolutions do not rank as legal obligations is then immaterial.[40]

[38] C. W. Jenks, *Law in the World Community*, 81–2 (1967).

[39] Article 27(3).

[40] "The Development of International Law," in *International Affairs*, Special Issue (November 1970), at 131.

JUDGMENTS AND OPINIONS OF THE
INTERNATIONAL COURT OF JUSTICE

Between April 1, 1946 and March 31, 1971, the International Court of Justice dealt with a total of 52 cases, including 31 judgments and 14 advisory opinions.[41] The last advisory opinion was requested by the Security Council on July 29, 1970 on "The Legal Consequences for States of the Continued Presence of South Africa in Namibia (South-West Africa), notwithstanding Security Council Resolution 276(1970)."

Through its judgments, opinions, orders, and other pronouncements, the ICJ performs or should perform an important role in the development of international law. Sir Gerald Fitzmaurice emphasized this when, in his separate opinion in *The Barcelona Traction, Light and Power Company, Ltd.* judgment,[42] he observed:

Although these comments can only be in the nature of *obiter dicta*, and cannot have the authority of a judgment, yet since specific legislative action with direct binding effect is not at present possible in the international legal field, judicial pronouncements of one kind or another constitute the principal method by which the law can find some concrete measure of clarification and development.

He added, however, that international tribunals should refrain from dealing with or commenting on points that lie outside the strict *ratio decidendi* of the case in hand.

This is in marked contrast to the attitude adopted by the very slight majority of the Court in the earlier *South-West Africa Cases* [43] in which it took the view that its duty is "to apply the law as it finds it, not to make it," and thereupon proceeded to give a legalistic, restrictive, and narrow ruling which said that, while Ethiopia and Liberia had a legal right to bring the case, they did not have the *locus standi* to receive judgment

[41] See [1969–1970] *ICJ Yearbook* 3–4 for the figures up to December 1970.
[42] [1970] *ICJ Reports* 3, at 64, para. 2.   [43] [1966] *ICJ Reports* 48.

on it. As McWhinney trenchantly remarked on this aspect of
the case,

Nevertheless, in the manner and form in which the decision was
rendered, it must be considered to be a major setback for the general cause of progressive development of world law to meet rapidly
changing political and social conditions in the world community.
For the actual, narrow procedural point on which the Court majority managed to decide the case, thereby avoiding ruling on the
substantive legal issues—including the burning issue of the compatibility of the Union of South African Government's *apartheid*
programme with international law—would surely have baffled the
intellectual ingenuity even of the medieval schoolmen.[44]

Judge Jessup, in his penetrating dissenting opinion, described
the majority judgment in the case as "completely unfortunate
in law." [45]

There are, however, a number of notable instances in which
the Court has rendered invaluable service to the progressive
development of international law. Thus, in its advisory opinion
in "Reparation for Injuries Suffered in the Service of the
United Nations," [46] the Court recognized a new type of international responsibility only because it decided to acknowledge
the existence of the independent legal personality of the
United Nations Organization and, by necessary implication,
that of the new international institutions.[47] The same kind of

[44] McWhinney, *supra* note 25, at 76–77. See also Higgins, "The International Court and South-West Africa: The Implications of the Judgment," *International Affairs*, p. 573 (October 1966); and Green, "South West Africa and
the World Court," 22 *International Journal*, 39, at 66 (1966).

[45] [1966] *ICJ Reports*, at 323. Another commentary on the South-West Af-
rica Cases" runs thus: "It [the Court] had already successively alienated the
Eastern *bloc* (*The Corfu Channel Case*), the Latin Americans (*Asylum* and
Haya de la Torre Cases), the Asians (*Temple of Preah Vihear* and *Rights of
Passage Cases*); it was perhaps inevitable that it should also alienate the African States. The International Court of Justice could properly be called the
'West European Court of Justice at this stage of its development.' " "Comment, The South West Africa Cases," 5 *Canadian Y. B. Int'l L.* 241, at 251
(1967).

[46] [1949] *ICJ Reports* 174.   [47] R. N. Swift, *International Law* 539 (1969).

novel situation in the field of state responsibility was dealt with similarly in its ruling against Albania in the *Corfu Channel* case [48] brought by the United Kingdom in 1947. An imaginative approach was adopted by the Court toward the "Conditions of Admission of a State to Membership in the United Nations" (1947–1948) [49] within the context of Article 4 of the Charter, while its opinions in the "Competence of the General Assembly for the Admission of a State to the United Nations" (1949–1950) [50] and the "Interpretation of the Peace Treaties with Bulgaria, Hungary and Romania" [51] show its readiness to give the basic instruments a teleological interpretation which ensures the principles of efficacy and legitimacy in the ordering of international affairs. These three last-mentioned opinions of the Court, as well as its brave pronouncements in "Certain Expenses of the United Nations," [52] have done much toward the development of an international constitutional law, while a solid foundation for the similar development of an international administrative law was laid in the "Effect of Awards of Compensation Made by the United Nations Administrative Tribunal" (1953–1954).[53]

When we look at the Court's judgment in the *Barcelona Traction (Judgment) case*, we see a hopeful appreciation on its part of the need to support the growing consciousness in the international community of the distinction between the obligations of a state toward the international community as a whole (*erga omnes*) and those arising *vis-à-vis* another state in the field of diplomatic protection. In a passage which is particularly significant because of its recognition of what others may be regarding as examples of *jus cogens*, the Court said:

Such obligations derive, for example, in contemporary international law, from the outlawing of acts of aggression, and of genocide, as also from the principles and rules concerning the basic

---

[48] [1949] *ICJ Reports* 4. [49] [1948] *ICJ Reports* 57.
[50] [1950] *ICJ Reports* 4. [51] [1950] *ICJ Reports* 65.
[52] [1962] *ICJ Reports* 151. [53] [1954] *ICJ Reports* 47.

rights of the human person, including protection from slavery and racial discrimination. Some of the corresponding rights of protection have entered into the body of general international law (Reservations to the Convention on the Prevention and Punishment of the Crime of Genocide, Advisory Opinion, I.C.J. Reports 1951, p. 23); others are conferred by international instruments of a universal or quasi-universal character.[54]

Of importance also is the Court's express pronouncement that, in modern international law at any rate, there is a need to realign the traditional relation between municipal law and international law, especially from the point of view of those who still hold it dangerous to draw upon municipal law analogies in considering international law questions. With reference to the legal character of municipal corporations, the Court observed:

In this field, international law is called upon to recognize institutions of municipal law that have an important and extensive role in the international field. This does not necessarily imply drawing any analogy between its own institutions and those of municipal law, nor does it amount to making rules of international law dependent upon categories of municipal law. All it means is that international law has had to recognize the corporate entity as an institution created by States in a domain essentially within their domestic jurisdiction. This in turn requires that, whenever legal issues arise concerning the rights of States with regard to the treatment of companies and shareholders, as to which rights international law has not established its own rules, it has to refer to the relevant rules of municipal law.[55]

The Court further deplored the fact that, despite the growth of foreign investments and the expansion of the international activities of corporations, which are often of a multinational character, "it may at first appear surprising that the evolution of law has not gone further and that no generally accepted rules in the matter have crystallized on the international plane," especially as "there has since the Second World War

[54] [1970] *ICJ Reports* 3, at 32, para. 34.   [55] *Id.*, at 33–4, paras. 37 and 38.

been considerable development in the protection of foreign investments." [56]

The importance of this case lies in the fact that, although the Court declined to go into the merits of the claims of Belgium, the plaintiff, it nevertheless touched upon a number of legal questions of general international law, some of which we have already considered. One or two others of relevance to the subject of this study may be referred to briefly here. The first is the argument of the traditionalists who insist that consent and not consensus continues to be the basis of international law—a facet of this being the assertion, to which we referred when considering the legal effect of General Assembly resolutions, that "there can be no consensus without the West." To which one may return the answer: there can equally be no consensus without Africa or Asia or Latin America or Eastern Europe, each considered as a group. But the difficulty about insistence upon consent in respect of General Assembly resolutions is that it raises the wider question as to the universal validity of customary international law for today's world. Judge Ammoun, in his separate opinion in the *Barcelona* case, put the point thus:

Among the treaties which have been in question, it is necessary to go back to those which organized international society in the eighteenth and nineteenth centuries, and at the beginning of the twentieth century. It is well known that they were concluded at the instigation of certain great Powers which were considered by the law of the time to be sufficiently representative of the community of nations, or of its collective interests. Moreover, the same was the case in customary law; certain customs of wide scope became incorporated into positive law when in fact they were the work of five or six Powers. . . . It thus becomes easier to understand the fears of a broad range of new States in three continents, who dispute the legitimacy of certain rules of international law, not only because they were adopted without them, but also because they do not seem to them to correspond to their legitimate

[56] *Id.*, at 46–47, paras. 89 and 90.

interests, to their essential needs on emerging from the colonialist epoch, nor, finally, to that ideal of justice and equity to which the international community, to which they have at last been admitted, aspires. What the Third World wishes to substitute for certain legal norms now in force are other norms profoundly imbued with the sense of natural justice, morality and humane ideals.[57]

Before we take leave of the *Barcelona* case, we may refer to a second question—that of the role of the new nations in the development of international law.[58] We may note this excerpt from the opinion of the World Court in the *Reparation for Injuries Suffered in the Service of the United Nations:* "Throughout its history, the development of international law has been influenced by the requirements of international life. That international life is being influenced by those States and their aspirations within the framework of the United Nations and outside it can no longer be denied." Judge Ammoun again observed:

In this connection, it is essential to stress the trends of Latin-American law and that of Asia and Africa, and their undeniable influence on the development of traditional international law. It seems indeed that among the principles and norms which have sprung from the regional law peculiar to Latin America are the norms and principles whose aim is to protect countries in that part of the world against the more powerful industrialised States of North America and Europe. An Afro-Asian law also seems to be developing as a result of the same preoccupations, springing from the same causes. In the field of the responsibility of States and of diplomatic protection, the same points of view have been adopted in the countries of the three continents, thus initiating a form of co-operation which will not be of slight effect on the renewal of law.[59]

Thus, the *Barcelona* case, the latest contentious matter before the Court, afforded it an opportunity to make worthwhile con-

[57] *Id.*, at 308–10.
[58] See my "The New States and the United Nations," 11 *Foro Internacional* (Oct.–Dec. 1970).
[59] Barcelona Traction Case, [1970] *ICJ Reports*, 290, para. 5.

tributions to the development of modern international law, especially in the areas indicated by the preceding analysis. It is not often that the Court does take occasion to deal with important but related issues outside the narrow point submitted to it. And yet, as H. Lauterpacht once remarked, "The development of international law is, in the long run, one of the most important conditions of their successful functioning. Their jurisdiction is largely dependent upon it." [60] Would that the International Court of Justice were always as resourceful and forthright as it has been in the *Barcelona* case. The cause of international judicial development of international law would be better served than hitherto.

INTERNATIONAL CUSTOM AS EVIDENCE OF LAW

It is common knowledge that modern international law has been developing not only by means of conventions but also by the accumulation of custom over a period of time. One may cite the instance of the modern doctrine of the continental shelf, which developed in the comparatively brief period of time between the Truman Declaration of 1945 and the two *North Sea Continental Shelf Cases*[61] (involving Denmark and the Netherlands, on the one hand, and the Federal Republic of

[60] *The Development of International Law by the Permanent Court of International Justice*, 3 (1934). The author later posed and answered (at 16 and 17) these questions: "Now, it will be asked: Is this variety of decided questions a necessary element in the work of the Court? Does not the Court wander away from the main point for the sake of *obiter dicta?* Does not the Court, in which the professorial element is not inconsiderable, indulge in little lectures and academic disquisitions which might well be avoided? Does it not perhaps happen that the judgment is not an organic whole but an artificial accumulation of individual opinions? All these questions—which have been discreetly asked here and there—must be answered in the negative. Admittedly, the pronouncements of the Court are long, but it is difficult to see how this can be avoided. And, for reasons to be stated, it is devoutly to be wished that they shall continue to be so."

[61] [1969] *ICJ Reports.*

Germany, on the other) in which it was given express recognition by the International Court of Justice. In this connection, I. A. Frowein has observed:

The General Assembly is not a world legislature but its resolutions can play a most important role in the development of general international law. . . . In the *Continental Shelf Cases* the court thought it possible that a conventional rule could become a general rule of international law without the passage of a considerable period of time if there was a very widespread and representative participation in the convention, "provided it included that of States whose interests were specially affected." [62]

Does one see in this a fourth requirement concerning the binding character of a resolution that it should have been adopted by "states whose interests were specially affected"? It will be recalled that the Soviet jurist, Morozov, had suggested that for a General Assembly resolution to be binding, it must have been adopted by the communists and the capitalists as well as by the West, the socialists, and the neutralists.[63] As we are here concerned only with evidence of custom, we need not go into that question further.

Modern international law has the great advantage that its source materials are many and varied, and evidence of this abounds. In a well-known remark, Higgins said:

The United Nations is a very appropriate body to look to for indications of developments in international law, for international custom is to be deduced from the practice of States, which includes their international dealings as manifested by their diplomatic actions and public pronouncements. With the development of international organizations, the votes and views of States have come to have legal significance as evidence of customary law.[64]

[62] In his article, "The United Nations and Non-Member States," 25 *International Journal* 333, at 342.
[63] See under General Assembly Resolutions, *supra*.
[64] "Development of International Law Through the Political Organs of the United Nations," 3 (1963).

The same trend has been noted and described for us by Dr. Clive Parry.[65] Friedmann admirably sums up the position thus:

An authoritative report, by the Commission or by another highly respected body of international lawyers, such as the *Institut de Droit International*, or a resolution of the General Assembly may be authoritative expressions of developing principles of international law. Often, although by no means always, they will presage the eventual adoption of a multilateral international convention on the subject (as in the case of the Space Law Resolution of 1962, which was followed, in January 1967, by a treaty of substantially the same content).[66]

Other notable evidence in the development of international law relates to the growing incidence of subsequent practice in the interpretation of treaty provisions. Let us take the case of Article 27(3) of the U.N. Charter, which provides that on non-procedural matters the Security Council is to take its decisions by "the affirmative vote of the permanent members." In "Certain Expenses of the United Nations," [67] the Court affirmed that it would not normally recognize the relevance of subsequent practice in the interpretation of the Charter. Sir Percy Spender in his separate opinion, however, made an exception to his generally negative view regarding the relevance of subsequent practice by organs of the United Nations, the exception being "a practice which is of peaceful, uniform and undisputed character accepted in fact by all current Members." [68] This exception clearly falls within the uniform and undisputed United Nations practice of not treating the abstention of a permanent member as a vote against a nonprocedural resolution. It does not matter whether we regard it as a rule of customary law or as a binding interpretation of the Charter. The practice has been well established since 1965, when the amendment to

---

[65] See his *The Sources and Evidences of International Law* (1965).
[66] Friedmann, *supra* note 34, at 275.
[67] [1962] *ICJ Reports* 151.   [68] *Id.*, at 195.

Article 27 enlarging the membership of the Security Council entered into force. The Court has also on a number of occasions stressed the importance which subsequent practice of the organs of international organizations has on the interpretation of its constituent instruments.[69] Of the numerous instances when resolutions of the Security Council have been adopted with the abstention of one or more permanent members, mention need be made of only these few: when more than 21 member states had been admitted; when the Security Council took its decision to establish a peace-keeping force in Cyprus, or to apply sanctions against Rhodesia, or to take measures to safeguard non-nuclear-weapon states; and when the Council decided on parties to the Treaty on the Non-Proliferation of Nuclear Weapons. In view of this evidence of an established custom or practice, the absence of a concurring vote of one or more permanent members does not offend against Article 27(3) of the Charter. Support for this position can be found in the Vienna Convention on the Law of Treaties (1969). Although the Conference decided to omit from the text of the Convention an ILC draft Article 38 which provided that a treaty might be modified by subsequent practice in its application establishing the agreement of the parties to modify its provisions, it nevertheless accepted Article 27 (which now appears as Article 31 of the Convention). Article 31 provides that in the interpretation of a treaty, there should be taken into account, together with the context, any subsequent practice in the application of the treaty which establishes the understanding of the parties regarding its interpretation.

[69] "Competence of the General Assembly for Admission of a State to the United Nations," [1950] *ICJ Reports*, 4, at 9; "Constitution of the Maritime Safety Committee of the International Maritime Consultative Organization," [1960] *ICJ Reports* 150, at 167.

THE CONTRIBUTION OF TEXT-WRITERS
AND PUBLICISTS

In modern international law there are discernible three broad categories of writers, all of whom have made and are making contributions. In the first category are those publicists who may be described as positivists, in the sense that they base their approach to international law on state practice, conventions, and decisions of international tribunals. They are largely orthodox and cautious about innovations. They are traditionalists because their writings, for the most part, reflect the customary mode of dealing with sovereignty, rights and duties of states, diplomacy, balance of power, war and peace, and neutrality as the main preoccupations of international law. Among the principal writers in this necessarily mixed group are Oppenheim-Lauterpacht, Guggenheim, and Schwarzenberger, although it must be said that the last-named has also been a pioneer in the opening up of new frontiers on the subject, as his *Expanding Frontiers of International Law* (especially his chapter on "Standards of International Economic Law") and his *Foreign Investments and International Law* show.

The second category embraces such various writers as Jessup, Jenks, Friedmann, and Falk, whose contributions lie in reshaping and remoulding customary law as well as in recognizing the need for wider horizons in our approach to both customary and conventional international law. Jessup's ideas were first set forth in 1948 when he wrote:

It is the purpose of this book to explore some of the possible bases for a modern law of nations. . . . Two points in particular are singled out as keystones of a revised international legal order. The first is that international law, like national law, must be directly applicable to the individual. . . . The second point is that there must be basic recognition of the interest which the whole international society has in the observance of its law.[70]

[70] *A Modern Law of Nations* (1948). In this book, much of the existing body of international law was not treated.

All this is but a short step to what he later expounded as
"transnational law" in his seminal book under that title.[71]
States now concede jurisdiction to try their nationals abroad,
and new institutions like the European Coal and Steel Community have power to adjudicate disputes between coal and
steel producers in the six states. Jenks broke out in a new
direction with his "Common Law of Mankind," advocating the
need to recognize that both interdependence and the development of international law require a wider and deeper knowledge of all cultures and all legal systems as worthy in themselves; he has since enlarged his initiative to encompass *Law,
Freedom* and *Welfare, Law in the World Community, The
World Beyond the Charter,* and, more recently, *A New World
of Law?* Equity, social justice, and universal law are the constant themes. Wolfgang Friedmann, after his epoch-making
Legal Theory on jurisprudence, has done it again in his
Changing Structure of International Law, which synthesizes
and analyses the principal trends, as well as indicating the
path of future advances in modern international law. Of somewhat similar vintage is Myres McDougal with his emphasis on
a sociological approach to international law.[72] Falk's *Law, Morality and War in the Contemporary World* sounded a liberal
note at a time when men were once more tending to lose their
heads over internecine strife. But it is through his "New Approaches to the Study of International Law" [73] that he has
made his contribution to the subject.

The third category of writers may be described as those who
are keen on breaking new ground in fields of modern international law that either are not treated in existing textbooks or
are the products of international commerce, science, and technology in our nuclear age. For example, Edward McWhin-

---

[71] P. Jessup, *Transnational Law* (1956).
[72] See P. E. Corbett, *From International to World Law,* 40 pp. (Lehigh Univ. Dep't
of Int'l Relations Monograph, (1969).
[73] 61 *Am. J. Int'l L.* 477, at 486–87 (1967).

ney,[74] in the *International Law of Communications,* which he edited, speaks of "the new international law of communications, with special reference to telecommunications and direct satellite broadcasting," in which there is as yet "no single, over-arching body of law, no one legally paramount international organization having jurisdiction over communications, no single code of principles or similar comprehensive enactment of positive law rules." [75] Jenks had preceded this with his *Space Law,* the first source of international law rules being the Space Treaty of 1967, which proclaims that the exploration and use of outer space should be "carried out for the benefit and in the interest of all countries, irrespective of their degree of economic or scientific development" and that outer space is "the province of all mankind," not subject to national appropriation. Thus, in this area of the new international law, claims to national sovereignty are discounted. Also, A. E. Gotlieb and C. M. Dalfen have observed:

Nevertheless, [norms governing direct satellite broadcasting] are at a significant stage, and, in view of the pattern of international legal development since 1945, most notably in respect of "new" law being developed to keep pace with the mastery of new environments made possible through the unprecedented technological developments of the era, we can safely foresee continued, on-going and marked progressive legal development.[76]

It is important to note the point they emphasize that the new law has not been developing by "attempting to forge out in entirely new directions, casting away previous precedents. Rather, the development has been a cumulative one, with a conscious concern being made to build on the principles and understandings of existing international law." [77] Let us under-

---

[74] See his development of the thesis in his *International Law and World Revolution* (1967).

[75] At 5, 11 (1970).

[76] See their article, "Direct Satellite Broadcasting," 7 *Canadian Y. B. Int'l L.* 33, at 56 (1969).

[77] *Id.,* at 59.

line this point in our assessment of the evolution of modern international law.

We would also do well to remember that post-1945 legal development has not only been cumulative, but has also been synthetic, in that "it has drawn where necessary upon relevant branches of existing law—usually international but sometimes domestic—for 'general principles of law recognized by civilised nations' . . . for analogies, and for legal precedents." [78] With regard to the phrase "general principles of law recognized by civilized nations," it is an anachronism in the context of a Charter expressly based upon the principle of the sovereign equality of all the member states of the United Nations Organization. The club of civilized nations idea of international law is now as dead as the dodo.[79] As J. E. S. Fawcett observed, "This vague notion of civilisation, which was supposed to mark them off from African and Asian communities in particular, led to the myth that international law was solely a European creation, and was still used to characterise international law in the statute of the Hague Court in 1920." [80]

Other important areas of modern international law have been covered by, for example, D. W. Bowett's *Law of International Institutions,* which treats of the United Nations organization, its subsidiary organs and specialized agencies, and non-U.N. organizations, governmental and nongovernmental, showing the emergence of a wholly significant development in the concept of a new international personality outside states as a subject of international law. Institutional pluralism, even in regional areas, has also taken place to strengthen the United Nations structures—for example, the EEC, the OAU and the OAS. Similarly, Friedmann and Kalmanoff's *Joint International Business Ventures* has heralded the arrival on the inter-

[78] *Id.,* at 60.
[79] See my "The Expanding Frontiers of Public International Law," *International Law in a Changing World* (1963).
[80] "The Development of International Law," in *International Affairs,* Special Issue (November 1970), 127.

national scene of the multinational corporations, "special interests instrumentalities," as Oscar Schachter has called them.[81]

It will have been observed that there is much overlapping between the three categories mentioned at the start of the present heading and that some publicists fit into more than one category.[82] The broad generalizations, however, remain true of the essential characteristics of modern international law as seen in the works of text-writers and publicists.

CONCLUSIONS

The foregoing analysis shows that there is now emerging a modern international law that is in many respects a reflection of contemporary social, economic, scientific, and technological needs. There has been a movement away from unmitigated state sovereignty, war and neutrality, and the old-world diplomacy of the League Covenant, toward equality, universality, fundamental human rights, and the promotion of social welfare, economic progress, and interdependence, which has been impelled by modern communications, transport, science, and technology and of which the guiding light is increasing emphasis on the interests of the community of nations as a whole. The general principles of international law, both customary and conventional, are undergoing a radical transformation through the work of the United Nations and its subsidiary organs and agencies by a process which ensures broadly universal participation. No longer is the law of nations made by only a handful of imperial powers; international law has ceased to be European law, and its institutions are now worldwide.

Leonine treaties are to be illegal under the Vienna Convention on the Law of Treaties from 1969 onward. *Jus cogens* has

---

[81] In his Presidential Address, "The Future of the United Nations," 64 *Am. J. Int'l L. Proceedings* 277, at 283 (1970).

[82] This is certainly true of Hersch Lauterpacht, who was a liberal editor in charge of a traditionalist, though notable, treatise.

set a new standard of international public policy and a new code of ethics. The twenty-one-year period between the Universal Declaration of Human Rights in 1948 and the Declaration on Friendly Relations and Peaceful Co-existence among States in 1970 has witnessed mankind's march of progress which has transformed the whole course of customary international law no less than the traditional concepts of interstate relations and man's relation to the cosmos. Treaties are now made not only between states but also between one international institution and another. International conventions now provide for settlement of disputes between states and individuals, and violations of human rights can be impleaded before international tribunals. We are indeed in the era of transnational law.

It is not to be supposed, however, that modern international law has been firmly established or generally accepted. On the contrary, there are some traditionalists who are still opposed to any form of "contemporary" international law and who are fighting a rear-guard action for the maintenance of the *status quo ante*. As we have shown, modern international law has not broken away entirely from its roots, nor has it cast aside precedents and well-tried techniques of legal development. Its evolutionary process is both cumulative and synthetic, borrowing from the past while at the same time striving to keep in step with the current as well as the future requirements of international life. In this way such new branches as international constitutional law, humanitarian law, the law of the sea and of the air, and the international law of communications have grown up and continue to evolve—in fact, a wholly new range of specialized fields has recently been brought within the ever-expanding frontiers of international law.

Without a doubt, most existing textbooks on the subject are already out of date. Can the explosion ever again be contained within the covers of a single textbook of moderate size? Something has certainly happened to a subject which, until recently, it was fashionable in some quarters to deride as being on thin ground.[83] The truth is that modern international law, for all its lack of enforceability, has developed and will continue to develop to meet the constantly changing needs of the world of today and of tomorrow, a world of growing interdependence and indivisibility that is also committed to the achievement of peace and happiness for all mankind.

[83] Given its present momentum, modern international law, especially as it is evolving in the practice of the United Nations, will have become by 1980 almost as adequate a system of law for international purposes as is the municipal law of a state for national purposes.

C. WILFRED JENKS

Multinational Entities in the Law of Nations

SOCIAL EVOLUTION in different phases of development tends to proceed sometimes from complexity to simplicity and sometimes from relative simplicity to greater complexity. The general trend of legal development at any particular time naturally reflects the tendency of social evolution at the time.

On the international plane the present tendency is toward a much greater complexity in social organization. New types and forms of collective action and new institutional arrangements for such action are emerging constantly. We find them in the political, economic, financial, social, cultural, scientific, and humanitarian fields alike.

The future of the law of nations, the growth of an organized world community, and the prospects of a world rule of law will inevitably be profoundly influenced by this increasingly complex pattern of social organization. At one time it was much argued whether the law of nations was a "law between

C. WILFRED JENKS is Director General of the International Labour Organisation; a Member of the Institute of International Law; and a Member of the International Academy of Comparative Law.

States only and exclusively" [1] or a law of which states are the "immediate" but men the "ultimate members." [2] Neither conception is comprehensive enough to embrace our present needs. The law of the world community is the common law of mankind; its ambit extends to all the varied activities and forms of social organization in which the life of man has overleaped the boundaries of the state and now defies any possibility of effective national regulation or control. No lesser concept of the scope and function of the law can give us a world rule of law. In none of the main areas in which we are seeking a new world of law, the preservation of peace with justice, the protection of human dignity, the promotion of economic stability and growth, and the social discipline of scientific and technological development can the rule of law be made effective if the law limits its horizon to the obligations of states and the rights of individuals and fails to control the innumerable multinational entities which play so increasingly important a part in the life of our growing world community.

Every legal system as it develops must grapple with the problem of placing an effective restraint upon power and insuring responsibility; this is the essence of the whole concept of due process of law. The forms and types of power which the law seeks and needs to control become more varied and complex, and the standards of responsibility which it seeks and needs to enforce more exacting, as society develops. As the province of government expands from the maintenance of law and order to embrace, even in the freest of the free economies, virtually the whole life of the community, the scope of the law expands with the expanding province of government. This is no less true internationally than nationally. The reach of the law increasingly extends beyond what was called of old "lawyers' law," and political and military matters, to economic and scientific matters. The law can be effective in relation to these

---

[1] L. Oppenheim, *International Law* 341 (1905).
[2] J. Westlake, *Collected Papers* 78 (1914).

matters only if it applies effectively to the forms of social organization which in practice control them.

It is in the light of these fundamental considerations that we must consider the present status in the law of nations of multinational entities.

Without attempting any exhaustive enumeration of the possible types of multinational entity, existing and conceivable, we may distinguish some of the more significant. We may divide these into three groups.

The first group consists of international organizations of states or governments, official international trust funds, and international public services constituted by and responsible to states or governments. These are the creation of, and now have a relatively clear status in, public international law.

The second group consists of privately established multinational associations and foundations of a non-profit-making character. For the most part, these are neither highly law-conscious nor a major practical problem for the law. They often have little or no defined legal status; and when they have sought to clarify their legal status, they have generally, in the absence of a recognized international status for which they could qualify, been constituted in accordance with the law of a particular country and are governed by that law and the rules of conflict of laws applicable when a matter arises.

The third group consists of multinational corporations, consortia, and cartels. These, by their nature and the nature of their operations, come into contact and may come into conflict with the law at many points, whether law-abiding or less law-abiding; they tend to be highly law-conscious; the relationship of their operations to the law is one of the largest questions to be resolved to create an effective world rule of law. But they are not the creation of any one legal system and are not, and cannot be, effectively controlled in the public interest by any existing legal system or combination of legal systems. They are a triumph of economic power and legal ingenuity operating on a scale which transcends and at times dwarfs the authority of individual states, and for which the existing legal order makes no appropriate provision. It is inevitable that in such a situation so much economic power and so much legal ingenuity should sometimes be tempted to take advantage of the complexity of political and legal systems to create a world of their own which must accommodate itself in the conduct of its operations to many legal systems but is not in any real sense subject to any of them.

In considering the present legal status, or lack of legal status, of entities falling into the second and third of these groups, we do well to recall how recent is the explicit recognition of the present legal status of entities falling into the first group.

A quarter of a century ago the status as legal entities of international organizations of states or governments remained highly debatable and was still much debated. The legal capacity of the League of Nations had remained equivocal everywhere outside Switzerland, and clear authority and precedent relating to other international organizations was sparse. The San Francisco Conference, when drafting the Charter of the United Nations, preferred to deal with the matter in somewhat tentative and indecisive terms. Within little more than months there was a decisive breakthrough, subsequently consolidated by a whole series of provisions in the constitutional instruments of international and regional organizations, conventions and agreements defining their status, privileges, and immunities, and national laws and regulations giving effect to these international arrangements, the general effect of which has been to give international organizations of states and governments a clearly recognized legal personality for international and municipal law purposes alike.

Doctrinal arguments concerning the general significance and effect of these arrangements there may still be, and questions concerning their precise interpretation and application will inevitably continue to arise, but the point of departure has been completely changed. The law of nations as "a law between States only and exclusively" now belongs wholly to the past. The position of international organizations has become so unequivocal in international law that their status as legal entities is no longer open to question in municipal law. By and large, municipal law, while still hesitant as to how much recognition it should give international organizations, accepts them among the facts of life in the same manner in which it accepts the existence of foreign states, though not necessarily with the same consequences (sometimes rightly, sometimes more questionably).

There has been no comparable breakthrough in the formulation of the legal status of official international trust funds. The innovative legal minds which created such funds as autonomous entities with legal personality by the Paris Agreements of April 28, 1930 relating to the obligations resulting from the Treaty of Trianon [3] have had no worthy successors. What are in essence official international trust funds have become common; but, perhaps because there have not been significant occasions for charging against them liabilities enforceable by legal proceedings, they have generally taken the form of special accounts administered by international organizations, and the question of their legal nature and status has remained relatively dormant. It remains, however, potentially an important question how far legal capacity, obligations, and immunities distinct from those of the organization administering it can be conferred on such a fund, or to what extent a fund created independently of a recognized international organization can be invested with legal capacity, obligations, and immunities. The answer can hardly be doubtful. The law of nations permits the creation of any new legal entity which the needs of international society require, provided the will to create it is clearly expressed and what is created is tangible and workable. Nov-

[3] See 25 *Am. J. Int'l L.* 19 (Supp. 1931).

elty as such is no bar in international law to any form of innovation. The principles which have been evolved in respect of international organizations of states and governments can therefore reasonably be regarded as fully applicable in principle to official international trust funds whenever occasion arises for their application and provision for such application is made in the legal instruments or decisions creating and governing the fund.

There has also been a near stalemate in the development of the law relating to the status as legal entities of international public services. A quarter of a century ago the classical illustration of an international public service was the international canal; some years hence it may be the communications satellite corporation or some other collective space venture. Meanwhile, the most characteristic form of such a service is a more modest arrangement whereby a relatively small number of governments, sometimes only two, operate together some public utility or analogous service of common interest; a large proportion of these arrangements are in Western Europe, but some of great interest are now developing in Africa. These arrangements provide for varied combinations of recognition as an international legal entity, recognition as a legal entity constituted under the law of one of the participating countries but with some special international status (both its constitution as a legal entity under the law from which it derives that character and its special international status being recognized by the other participating countries) and complementary incorporation under the laws of two or more of the participating countries (either by multiple incorporation of the same entity, consisting of the concern as a whole, or by the incorporation in each country of the part of the concern localized or regarded as localized therein). These varied combinations and the complications which they imply emphasize that the law on these matters remains experimental and tentative, but as with international trust funds, there appears to be no barrier to a less inhibited use in respect of international public services owned and controlled by governments of the principles now generally accepted in respect of international organizations of states and governments. It is when governments choose to act through autonomous corporations, or international public services are entrusted to mixed corporations in which there is both a public and a private interest or to private corporations which constitute an element in some special international regime, that the matter becomes more complex, and the extent to which the principles which have been evolved for international organizations of states and governments can be regarded as applicable needs fuller consideration.

When we pass from the consideration of international organizations of states or governments, and of trust funds and public services assimilable thereto, to consider the position of privately constituted multinational associations and foundations of a non-profit-making character, we find the law as amorphous and unhelpful as it was in respect of international organizations of states and governments prior to the breakthrough of the mid-1940s.

A number of proposals for giving such associations a recognized international legal status have been put forward during the last fifty years. The Politis proposals approved by the Institute of International Law in 1923 [4] provided for a combination of the grant of legal personality to international associations by countries to which they apply for the grant of such personality, the recognition of the legal personality so granted by other countries, and an international regime administered by an international commission in virtue of which associations complying with certain registration requirements were to become entitled to all the advantages of legal personality, subject to a right of each country to refuse recognition of such registration, which was itself subject to an appeal to the Interna-

[4] See 30 *Annuaire de l'Institut de Droit International* 97 (1923).

tional Court. The Bastid proposals [5] approved by the Institute of International Law in 1950 were designed to give international associations an international legal status conferring certain rights and privileges, irrespective of the legal regime of the association. The Niboyet proposals of 1948 for a convention empowering the Economic and Social Council to grant international juridical personality to associations accepting a measure of supervision by it in accordance with rules laid down by the General Assembly were rejected by the associations themselves because they were unwilling to accept the measure of public control involved. None of these proposals have borne fruit in practical results.

The continued stalemate in the matter appears to have been due to three main reasons. While the number, importance, and influence of international associations have continued to increase, the problem of their legal status has not become of such acuteness and urgency as to make a comprehensive solution of it imperative. International associations vary widely in their purposes, membership, and responsibility; in the extent to which they command general approval or are highly controversial, either because their purposes are controversial or because there are rival associations for the same purpose; in the extent to which their activities have political implications or involve economic interests or security considerations; and in the nature of their relations with governments, political parties, economic groups, and religious bodies. In these circumstances, the creation of any uniform international legal status for such associations presents intrinsic difficulties of great complexity. Given these difficulties, the most promising approach would surely be to break the problem down into manageable segments and deal separately and somewhat empirically with a limited number of segments chosen on the basis of their importance and the prospect of doing something worthwhile in

[5] See 43 *id*. 547 (1950).

respect of them; but no serious attempt has been made to approach the problem systematically in this way. Such an approach would make it possible to deal separately with such essentially different types of international association as associations for humanitarian purposes which command general assent, cultural and scientific associations, religious bodies, professional bodies, non-profit-making associations dealing with economic matters and interests, and associations dedicated to controversial causes. It would also permit a clear distinction between such associations and privately established multinational foundations, endowments, and educational and scientific institutions.

None of the philanthropic foundations with worldwide interests and activities whose names have become household words has been constituted multinationally with a recognized international status, and the desirability of thus constituting such a foundation has attracted curiously little attention. This may be primarily because the large philanthropic foundation dedicating its resources to educational, cultural, and scientific purposes is widely regarded as essentially an American institution made possible by the wealth and tax laws of the United States; it is not, however, an exclusively American device and has become increasingly common in Britain and Western Europe. Should it be made possible to constitute such foundations on a multinational basis with a recognized international status?

Could we perhaps conceive of the United Nations or the Organization for Economic Cooperation and Development (OECD) maintaining a register of such foundations, of a host agreement with an appropriate country, preferably Switzerland, guaranteeing them a base of operations, of the Bank for International Settlements acting as their financial agent under a trustee agreement, of their investing in World Bank bonds or a representative multinational portfolio, and of their operating wherever their international status is recognized by virtue of a general international agreement or, without participation in any such agreement, by national law or practice? Certain conditions of registration would, of course, have to be fulfilled to the satisfaction of the registering authority, such as that the purposes of the foundation be international in character and consistent with the purposes and principles of the United Nations, that the control of the foundation be effectively multinational, that the foundation comply with prescribed audit rules and standards and publish regularly reasonably detailed and informative reports of its activities, that the foundation recognize its obligation to respect the law in force wherever it operated, and that it accept the authority of an appropriate supervisory body to verify and enforce its continued compliance with these conditions.

Such a scheme, it is submitted, would be in the interest of all the parties whose cooperation in launching it would be necessary to make it effective. From time to time donors would find it convenient to entrust funds for philanthropic purposes to foundations constituted in this manner, and the habit of so doing could develop gradually as its advantages were demonstrated. The adoption and development of the scheme would therefore not require the degree of simultaneity of action by a large number of governments which proposals of this kind can rarely hope to enlist.

A recognized international status for multinational educational and scientific institutions could perhaps be evolved in a similar way through an experimental approach in which UNESCO might play a catalytic part in conferring such a status, formulating its legal consequences, and negotiating its recognition.

There remains the hard core of the problem, that currently known as the question of the multinational corporation. This has become the subject of so much political and economic discussion, some of it with a strong emotional tinge, that the legal issues tend to be overshadowed and at times obscured. The fundamental issue is the relationship between the public interest and the economy when the scale of the economy dwarfs the representation of the public interest and the complexity of economic structures escapes the control of any government or legal system. This is an issue on the same order of importance for the future of international law as the control of force, the peaceful settlement of international disputes, the protection of human rights, the provision of an adequate legal framework for a buoyant and expanding economy, and the social discipline of science and technology. It poses in an acute form the international analog of the question of the place of the state in the complex modern community, a question the difficulty of which in political philosophy and constitutional law becomes still more difficult when transposed to the world scene and scale.

The essence of the multinational corporation is that it has no coherent existence as a legal entity; it is a political and economic fact which expresses itself in a bewildering variety of legal forms and devices. It is the complexity of its legal structure, or rather of the interplay of legal entities and relationships constituting that structure, no less than the size of its resources or the scale of its operations, which makes its power so elusive and so formidable a challenge to the political order and rule of law. It is therefore inherent in the nature of the multinational corporation that there is no simple solution for the problem of its relationship to states, the world of states, or an organized world community; but some of the principles which must govern any rational approach to the matter are already becoming apparent.

We need far more and far more reliable facts. Much of the current discussion is based on assumptions, and prejudices for and against, rather than facts. We cannot evolve a satisfactory legal regime for multinational corporations until we know much more about the facts. We are certainly entitled to adequate disclosure of the facts, without which we cannot judge the reality of problems which are alleged to be acute. The most objectionable feature of the present situation is that essential facts on matters which may vitally affect the public interest are available, or conveniently available, only to interested parties, whose interests may diverge sharply from the public interest. The facts can be made readily available only by organized international cooperation in assembling and analyzing them, backed by such legal obligations of disclosure as may prove practically necessary to make it effective. At least the germ of what is required is not developing in OECD.

We must regard the public interest as the overriding consideration. The claim that the greatest service which the law can render to the economy is to leave it alone, or at most to give legal effect to the customary practice and mutual expectations of men of business, is no longer accepted by public policy anywhere. The multinational corporation is no more immune from the rule of law than its constituent elements or the state itself, and the law must therefore be so developed as to embrace effectively the complexity and range of its structure and transactions.

No international status for multinational corporations is conceivable unless it represents a nice balance of advantages and responsibilities for governments and corporations alike. Corporations will not seek or willingly accept such a status unless the obligations of registration, audit, disclosure, and respect for law which it involves are reasonable, and the general effect of the status is to enhance their public position and facilitate their operations rather than subject them to tiresome restraints inconsistent with efficient and economical operation. Governments will not recognize or concede such a status unless it permits them to protect the public interest more effectively than is possible in the present legal jungle. The working out of the details will require a judicious weighing of alternatives, tedious negotiation, and meticulous drafting, but this must be the spirit of the thing.

No international status for multinational corporations can be created in any foreseeable future by a mandatory decision. It must commend itself by its merits to governments and corporations alike and rely for widening acceptance on its merits becoming increasingly apparent. The initial decision creating such a status could be taken by the United Nations or OECD without recourse to an international convention, which it might be difficult to get sufficiently widely ratified to make its provisions effective; but the status would become a significant reality only insofar as corporations sought it and governments recognized it. In course of time, it might become a requirement for and confer a right to the enjoyment of valuable privileges and facilities under international conventions and national laws. The internationally recognized multinational corporation might gradually supersede earlier arrangements, in the manner in which different types of corporate structure have so often superseded each other as corporate law and practice have evolved.

There is therefore little prospect of a breakthrough comparable to that which established the legal status of international organizations of states and governments a quarter of a century ago. Only by focusing attention on the question in the broad context of the changing pattern of world society in every sphere of life can we hope to contribute to its ultimate solution. The world community is, and must by its nature be, a pluralistic society. It is because it is a pluralistic society that the doctrine of sovereignty is so unhelpful to the progress of world organization. It is because it is a pluralistic society that the status within it of a wide range of varied types of multinational entity constitutes one of the central problems of the future of international law. As Philip Jessup has so cogently shown,[6] it is the universality of human problems and the vital importance of effective power to deal with these problems which must provide the key to the choice of law governing

[6] *Transnational Law* (1956).

them, and this law will have increasingly less resemblance to the law limited to the mutual relations of states, which constituted for some of our forerunners the whole of the law of nations but now falls into perspective as only a part of the common law of mankind.

ABDULLAH EL-ERIAN

International Law and the

Developing Countries

IT IS particularly fitting in a volume dedicated to Judge Philip C. Jessup to describe the contribution of the non-aligned countries to the elaboration of principles of international law pertaining to friendly relations and cooperation between states. For no one has done more than Professor Jessup to create awareness of the need for the development of international law and to chart the direction in which this development should proceed. As early as 1946 and in the immediate aftermath of the Second World War, during which the international legal order was shaken to its very foundations, Professor Jessup indicated the need and opportunity for the development of "a modern law of Nations." [1] With his concern for the individual and for the community interest on the international level,[2] Professor Jessup paved the way for the advent of an international legal order of a truly universal character, based on "the universality of human problems" [3] and in which the

ABDULLAH EL-ERIAN is Ambassador to France for the United Arab Republic and an Associate of the Institut de Droit International.

[1] See *A Modern Law of Nations* (1946).   [2] *Id.* at p. 2.

[3] This is the title of the first chapter of his work, *Transnational Law* (1956).

newly independent states of Asia and Africa can find an equal and rightful place.

Professor Jessup's influence cannot be measured, however, only by the impact of his pioneering written work, much of which covered with amazing speed the rough and lengthy road from vanguard ideas to positive law. His impact as a teacher, imparting both techniques and principles, and his humane approach to law have left their imprint on generations of students in all parts of the world. Many of his former students, including the writer, have participated as representatives of their respective countries in the work of the Sixth Committee and the special committee established by it to study the principles of international law concerning friendly relations during the several years in which the General Assembly of the United Nations was seized with that subject.

THE DECLARATION

On October 24, 1970, during its commemorative session of the twenty-fifth anniversary of the United Nations, the General Assembly adopted the "Declaration on Principles of International Law concerning Friendly Relations and Co-operation among States in accordance with the Charter of the United Nations." [4]

The seven principles contained in the declaration concern the nonuse of force, peaceful settlement of disputes, nonintervention, sovereign equality, duty to cooperate, equal rights and self determination, and fulfillment of obligations under the United Nations Charter. The Declaration is essentially an elaboration of the rights and duties of states under the main principles that form the basis of the Charter and correspond to the fundamental purposes of the United Nations. In the

[4] Document submitted by the Sixth Committee (Doc. A / 8082 para. 8) and considered by the General Assembly at its 1860th plenary meeting, Oct. 6, 1970.

preamble to the Declaration, the General Assembly notes that the great political, economic, and social changes and scientific progress which have taken place in the world since the adoption of the Charter give increased importance to these principles and to the need for their more effective application in the conduct of states everywhere. It further emphasizes that, in elaborating these principles, it has considered the provisions of the Charter as a whole and has taken into account the role of relevant resolutions adopted by the competent organs of the United Nations relating to the content of the principles.

It further declares that nothing in the Declaration shall be construed as prejudicing in any manner the provisions of the Charter, the rights and duties of member states under the Charter, or the rights of peoples under the Charter, taking into account the elaboration of these rights in the Declaration.

From the outset and throughout the consideration by the General Assembly of the item relating to the principles of international law concerning friendly relations, which spanned a period of almost ten years, the delegations of the nonaligned countries played an active role. They exerted concerted and continuous efforts for the activation of the item and in charting the course toward the adoption of a declaration. They defended their views, stated their interpretations, and expounded their method of approach to the different questions of doctrinal, practical, juridical, and political character raised during the consideration of this item. The debates, whether in the Sixth Committee or the special committee it set up to carry the work further between sessions of the General Assembly, ranged over a wide spectrum of subjects. These subjects include:

(1) the relationship between the Sixth Committee and the International Law Commission and the constructive role to be played by the Sixth Committee in a manner not duplicating or interfering with the work of the International Law Commission;

(2) the impact of the United Nations Charter on traditional international law and the transformation of the latter in order to reflect the needs of the times and the requirements of a new community of nations based on equality and cooperation;

(3) the interaction between law and politics as two of the social phenomena closely connected with other aspects of social structure;

(4) the close relationship between the progressive development of international law and the ultimate establishment of conditions under which justice and the respect for obligations could be maintained;

(5) the prerequisites essential for the creation of conditions of stability necessary for the achievement of peaceful and friendly relations among nations; and

(6) the proper method to be applied—whether it consists of the formulation of a declaration of general principles or an empirical study of specific areas of international law.

A number of delegations from the nonaligned countries submitted to the Sixth Committee draft proposals embodying their approaches to the item. They also submitted draft resolutions at successive sessions of the special committee containing an elaborate statement on the seven principles. No attempt shall be made here to expound the views of the nonaligned delegations on the substantive issues relating to the seven principles.[5] The purpose of this paper is rather to give a brief

5 The role of the newly independent and nonaligned countries in the development of international law and their place in the contemporary international order have been accorded on ever-increasing attention in the literature of international law during the last decade. See G. Saab, "The Newly Independent States and the Rules of International Law: An Outline," 8 *Howard Law Journal* 95 (1962); "Peaceful change and the integration of the newly Independent States in the International Community," 32 / 33 *Annuaire de l'A.A.A.* 172 (1962 / 1963); *The Newly Independent States and International Law: Some Reflections and a Selected Bibliography* (1963); R. Anand, "Role of the 'New' Asian-African Countries in the Present International Legal Order," 56 *Am. J. Int'l L.* 383 (1962); J. Castañeda, "The Underdeveloped Nations and the Development of International Law," 15 *International Organization* 38 (1961); R.

account of the role of the nonaligned countries on the general questions of: (1) activation of the item; (2) basic issues of approach; (3) method of interpretation.

Before turning to these remarks of a general character, reference should be made to the importance accorded to the item by the heads of state or government of the nonaligned countries in their second conference held in Cairo in 1964 and their third conference held in Lusaka in 1970.

The Cairo Conference adopted a Declaration entitled "Programme for Peace and International Co-operation." It devoted part IV of the Declaration to "Peaceful co-existence [6] and the codification of its principles by the United Nations." In this part of the Declaration, the Conference reaffirmed its deep conviction that, in the present circumstances, mankind must regard peaceful coexistence as the only way to strengthen world peace, which must be based on freedom, equality, and

---

Falk, "The New States and International Legal Order," 118 Hague *Recueil des Cours* 7 (1966-II); O. Lissitzyn, *International Law Today and Tomorrow* (1965), first published as "International Law in a Divided World," 542 *International Conciliation* (1963); B. Roling, *International Law in an Expanded World* (1960); J. Syatauw, *Some Newly Established States and the Development of International Law* (1961); Q. Wright, "The Influence of the New Nations of Asia and Africa upon International Law," 7 *Foreign Affairs Reports* 33 (India, 1958).

[6] When the Sixth Committee was working on the title of the item, the term "peaceful co-existence" was suggested. Several delegations, including the nonaligned delegations, supported this suggestion. Some delegations, however, took issue on the use of the term on the ground that it invoked certain political connotation. General agreement was sought through the use of the Charter terms "friendly relations and co-operation." For the varying meanings given to the concept of peaceful coexistence by international lawyers of different schools of thought see J. Hazard "Co-existence Codification Reconsidered" 57 *Am. J. Int'l Law* 88 (1963); and "The U.N. Sixth Committee and New Law" I 57 *Id*. p. 604. In his statement before the Sixth Committee on Nov. 23, 1966, the writer pointed out that "co-existence" was a legal term which had been used in 1928 by Max Huber in the Island of Palmas Case, Hague Court Reports 130 (2d series), 2 U.N.R.I.A.A. 829; and in 1944, by J. L. Brierly in his book, *The Outlook for International Law*, p. 4. He also referred to a book by W. Friedmann, *The Changing Structure of International Law* (1964), where international law had been divided into two branches: the international law of coexistence and the international law of cooperation.

justice between peoples within a new framework of peaceful and harmonious relations between the states and nations in the world. It proclaimed the following fundamental principles of peaceful coexistence:

(1) the right to complete independence;

(2) the right to self-determination;

(3) the possibility and necessity of peaceful coexistence between states with differing social and political systems;

(4) the recognition and respect of the sovereign equality of states, which includes the right of all peoples to the free exploitation of their natural ressources;

(5) the nonuse of force and the nonrecognition of situations brought about by the threat or use of force;

(6) respect for the fundamental rights and freedoms of the human person and the equality of all nations and races;

(7) settlement of international conflicts by peaceful means, in a spirit of mutual understanding and on the basis of equality and sovereignty;

(8) cooperation of all states with a view to accelerating economic development in the world, and particularly in the developing countries;

(9) necessity of states to meet their international obligations in good faith in conformity with the principles and purposes of the Charter.

The conference recommended that the General Assembly of the United Nations, on the occasion of its twentieth anniversary, adopt a declaration on the principles of peaceful coexistence. It expressed the view that "this declaration will constitute an important step towards the codification of these principles."

The Lusaka Conference includes a "Statement on the United Nations (Resolution 12) in its Declaration on Peace, Independence, Development, Co-operation and Democratization of International Relations." Paragraph 8 of this statement reads as follows:

"On the occasion of the 25th Anniversary of the United Nations, the non-aligned countries participating in the Conference are determined to co-operate among themselves and with other countries, to strengthen the functions of the United Nations for the purpose of strengthening peace, consolidating independence, promoting development and bringing about greater co-operation on the basis of equality of all states. With this end in view, the participating countries agree to specifically exert efforts on the following issues during the current session.

(1) Adoption of the Declaration on Principles Governing Friendly Relations among States as approved by the 1970 Special Committee on Principles of International Law concerning Friendly Relations and Co-operation among States. The Conference urges all countries to co-operate actively with a view to ensuring that the General Assembly adopts this Declaration at its commemorative session.

ACTIVATING THE ITEM

The item of principles of international law concerning friendly relations emerged from the discussion which took place in the fifteenth session of the General Assembly in 1960 on the role of the Sixth (Legal) Committee in the activities of the United Nations. Concern was expressed over the decline in the activities of the United Nations in the legal field, and a great number of delegations pointed out that the most disturbing aspect of the decline in the Sixth Committee's importance was the fact that it reflected the rather subordinate place to which international law had been relegated within the general activities of the United Nations.[7] In their opinion, the decline of international law in the United Nations was all the more serious at a time when the conditions prevailing in the world gave increased importance to the role of international law in strengthening

[7] The discussion in the Sixth Committee was preceded by informal consultations by some delegations, mostly from nonaligned countries, which focused on the problem of the decline in the work of the Sixth Committee and the means of reversing such a trend.

peace, developing friendly and cooperative relations among nations, settling disputes by peaceful means, and advancing economic and social progress throughout the world.

The paucity of the Sixth Committee's agenda for the fifteenth session and the sessions preceding it was in sharp contrast to the active role which that committee played in the early days of the United Nations in initiating legal programs and framing basic legal documents. Among these were: the establishment of the International Law Commission, the preparation of the Convention on the Privileges and Immunities of the United Nations and of the Rules of Procedure of the General Assembly, the confirmation of the Nuremberg principles, and the drafting of the Genocide Convention.[8]

The discussion in the Sixth Committee during the fifteenth session arose in connection with the consideration of the report of the International Law Commission. It took on, however, a more general character and dealt with different aspects of the state of law in the United Nations. The outcome was the adoption of Resolution 1505(XV) which is considered in retrospect as the marking of a new phase in the activities of the Sixth Committee. The resolution noted that many new trends in the field of international relations have an impact on the development of international law. It emphasized the necessity of reconsidering the International Law Commission's program of work in light of recent developments in international law and with due regard to the need for promoting friendly relations and cooperation among states.

[8] Commenting on this question and the contrast between the activities of the Sixth Committee in its formative years and its activities in the period preceding the fifteenth session in 1960, the Legal Counsel of the United Nations stated, "After this initial period of activity an interlude followed in which the work of the Sixth Committee was devoted primarily to the examination of reports of the International Law Commission. However, beginning with its fifteenth session in 1960, the Sixth Committee has embarked on a bold new program for the development of International Law." See G. A. Stavropoulos," The United Nations and the 'Rule of Law,' " 16 *Revue Hellénique de Droit International* 32 (1963).

A thorough discussion took place thereafter, in both the Sixth Committee and the International Law Commission, in relation to the "future work in the field of the codification and progressive development of international law." It revealed general agreement on two important facts: first, the difference between the work to be entrusted to the Sixth Committee and that to be entrusted to the International Law Commission; second, the need for reinvigorating the Sixth Committee as the most appropriate forum for enunciating and formulating general principles which, because of their stage of development, were not yet ripe for codification by the International Law Commission. This discussion resulted in the adoption of General Assembly Resolution 1815(XVII). By this resolution, the General Assembly recognized the paramount importance, in the progressive development of international law and in the promotion of the rule of law among nations, of the principles of international law concerning friendly relations and cooperation among states and the duties deriving therefrom as embodied in the Charter of the United Nations, which is the fundamental statement of these principles; and it resolved "to undertake, pursuant to Article 13 of the Charter, a study of the principles of international law concerning friendly relations and co-operation among states, in accordance with the Charter, with a view to their progressive development and codification, so as to secure their more effective application." Operative paragraph 1 of the same resolution listed those principles as being "notably" the following seven:

(1) the principle that states shall refrain in their international relations from the threat or use of force against the territorial integrity or political independence of any state, or in any other manner inconsistent with the purposes of the United Nations;

(2) the principle that states shall settle their international disputes by peaceful means, in such a manner that inter-

national peace and security and justice are not endangered;

(3) the duty not to intervene in matters within the domestic jurisdiction of any state, in accordance with the Charter;

(4) the duty of states to cooperate with one another in accordance with the Charter;

(5) the principle of equal rights and self determination of peoples;

(6) the principle of sovereign equality of states;

(7) the principle that states shall fulfill in good faith the obligations assumed by them in accordance with the Charter.

SOME BASIC ISSUES OF APPROACH

During the consideration of the subject of principles of international law concerning friendly relations, two main trends of thought on the approach to the subject were apparent. One group of delegations favored the adoption by the General Assembly of a declaration of principles of international law concerning friendly relations and cooperation among states. Another group of delegations preferred that the General Assembly direct itself to an empirical and more detailed study of a few essential principles, rather than to the adoption of a declaration covering the entire field.

Underlying these opposing trends were differences of approach to two basic issues. The first relates to the nature of the work of the Sixth Committee, and to what extent it should involve itself in questions which, although admittedly legal questions, are nevertheless of a political and controversial nature. The second concerns the criteria for determining what constitutes legal principles in the Charter. Some delegations appeared to maintain a sharp distinction between legal principles and political propositions, with the implication that the work of the Sixth Committee should be confined to the enunciation of what they termed "strictly legal principles." This restrictive approach was opposed by a great number of delegations who stated that such a sharp distinction was unrealistic. Dr. Nincic, the Representative of Yugoslavia, articulated the approach of the nonaligned countries when he stated: [9]

Much had been said about the need of confining the commission's activities to purely legal, as distinct from political, subjects and of avoiding what were considered to be controversial political questions. Such an approach was unrealistic. To attempt to divorce international law from the broader political context within which it necessarily had to evolve would, even if it were feasible, prove the surest way to stultify the growth of international law and to deprive it of any real possibility of affecting the course of international affairs. Indeed, the very tendency to insulate international law from politics seemed to reflect an outlook which was itself manifestly political.

In its advisory opinion on *Certain Expenses of the United Nations,* the International Court of Justice noted: "it has been argued that the question put to the Court is intertwined with political questions and that for this reason the Court should refuse to give an opinion. It is true that most interpretations of the Charter of the United Nations will have political significance, great or small; in the nature of things it could not be otherwise." [10]

Professor Jessup, in his lectures at the Hague Academy, stated: "A line between political and economic or social affairs, or even technical affairs like atomic energy, can no longer be drawn in the conduct of foreign relations. This fact is reflected in the modern development of international law as well." [11]

Another difference of approach arose in connection with the

[9] 16 U.N. GAOR 123, at 124 (1961), Sixth (Legal) Committee, Records of the 714th meeting, Nov. 15, 1961; Doc. A / C.6 / SR. 714.

[10] [1962] *ICJ Reports* 151, at 155.

[11] "Parliamentary Diplomacy," 89 Hague *Recueil des Cours* 185, at 188 (1956-I).

definition of "legal principles" within the meaning of the Charter. Some statements made in the Sixth Committee during the debate echoed the restrictive interpretation applied by some writers. It has been argued that principles like self-determination or international cooperation are not legal principles but standards of achievement, "general statements of policy," or "purely political principles devoid of any legal basis." [12]

This view seems to suggest a sharp differentiation between Article 2 of the Charter on the one hand and the Preamble and Articles 1 and 55 on the other, reserving for those principles enumerated in Article 2 the character of legal principles. The discussions at the San Francisco Conference and the practice of the General Assembly of the United Nations do not warrant such a distinction. It was recognized in the discussion of Committee I/I of the San Francisco Conference, that "it was difficult, in fact impossible, to draw a clear-cut distinction between the Preamble, the statement of 'Purposes' in Article 1, and the enumeration of governing 'Principles' in Article 2 . . . The Committee was forced to admit that the distinction between the three parts was not particularly profound." [13] In a number of resolutions, the General Assembly and other organs of the United Nations have recognized "the right of peoples and nations to self determination as a fundamental human right," for instance, Resolution 545(VI), Resolution 637A(VIII), and Resolution 1514(XV). As early as 1946, the view advanced by the Government of the Union of South Africa on the question of the treatment of Indians in South Africa, to the effect that no relevant legal obligations existed under the Charter, was rejected by the General Assembly, which adopted a resolution recording the opinion that the treatment of Indians in South Africa should be in conformity

[12] See C. Eagleton, "Excesses of Self-determination," 31 *Foreign Affairs* 592 (1953), where it is contended that "the text books of international law do not recognize any legal right of self-determination." (593).

[13] Goodrich and Hambro, *The Charter of the United Nations* 88 (2d ed. rev. 1949).

with the relevant provisions "of the Charter." This suggests that the general provisions of the Charter relative to human rights have a certain obligatory force even before their explicit formulation.[14]

METHOD OF INTERPRETATION

Another issue which gave rise to opposing concepts in the Sixth Committee during its consideration of principles of international law concerning friendly relations was the scope of the contemplated declaration, which would be determined by the mode of interpretation to be given to the Charter of the United Nations and the factors to be taken into account in undertaking such a task. Some delegations were inclined to give the declaration a rather restricted character. They favored a restrictive interpretation of the Charter and voiced apprehensions concerning what they termed attempts to "rewrite the Charter" or "to revise some of its provisions under the disguise of interpretation."

A number of delegations from nonaligned countries expressed themselves in favor of "effective interpretation" of the provisions of the Charter. Their approach can be summed up as follows: The task of the Sixth Committee as defined by the resolutions of the General Assembly is the enunciation of the principles of international law on peaceful coexistence in accordance with the Charter of the United Nations. This task entails the interpretation of the Charter in an effective manner, inspired by its general philosophy and underlying bases and directed toward the fulfillment of its fundamental purposes and declared objectives. It further entails an investigation of the impact of the Charter on the traditional fragmentary rules of international law.

First, the interpretation of the Charter should be effective. The case law of the International Court of Justice abounds

14 Jessup, *A Modern Law of Nations* 88 (1946).

with many clear statements sustaining effective interpretation. In its advisory opinion on *Reparation for Injuries Incurred in the Service of the United Nations* [15] in 1949, the Court stated that "the Organization must be deemed to have those powers which, though not expressly provided in the Charter, are conferred upon it by necessary implication as being essential to the performance of its duties. The capacity of the organization to exercise a measure of functional protection of its agents arises by necessary intendment out of the Charter."

Second, the Charter should also be interpreted in the context and in light of its objects and purpose. Reference was made to the general rules of interpretation as laid down in Article 27, paragraph 1 of the International Law Commission's draft articles on the Law of Treaties (Doc. A/6309), which reads as follows: "A treaty must be interpreted in good faith in accordance with the ordinary meaning to be given to the terms of the treaty . . . their context and in the light of its object and purpose." [16]

Third, the interpretation of the Charter should be inspired by its general philosophy and should be in keeping with its fundamental bases. The Charter is not merely an institutional instrument which sets up an organizational machinery and defines the functions and powers of its various organs; it is the greatest law-making treaty of modern times. It has replaced the fragmentary and mainly prohibitive rules of international law by an integrated system of more positive standards and cooperative norms which might be called the "law of the United Nations." Moreover, it has created an organ of collective action. Member states have agreed to transfer to the United Nations certain functions which previously come within their own exclusive competence, and have undertaken

[15] [1949] *ICJ Reports* 174, at 182.
[16] This Provision has become Art. 31, para. I of the Vienna Convention on the Law of Treaties, not yet in force; *done* at Vienna May 23, 1969; text at U.N. Doc. A / CONF. 39 / 26 and corrigenda 1 and 2, May 23, 1969; also at 63 *Am. J. Int'l L.* 875 (1969) and 8 *Int'l Legal Materials* 679 (1969).

to act together in many fields. It is only on the basis of such underlying principles that the principle of cooperation as stated in Article 55 of the Charter can be seen in its true perspective.

Fourth, the Charter as a constitution should be interpreted on the basis of the practice of the United Nations in applying it. General Assembly resolutions such as the Universal Declaration on Human Rights, the Resolution on Permanent Sovereignty on National Resources, and the Declaration on the Granting of Independence to Colonial Countries and Peoples are significant elements of that practice.

Of significance in ascertaining the interpretation of the Charter as given in international practice are some basic documents of contemporary international relations, which though adopted outside the framework of the United Nations are nevertheless greatly inspired by its Charter and deeply concerned with its progress and problems. They include the Declaration of the Bandung Conference on the Promotion of World Peace and Co-operation of 1955, the two Conferences of Heads of States or Government of Non-aligned Countries of 1961 and 1964 and the Charter of the Organization of African Unity of 1963.[17]

[17] This concept is reflected in the first paragraph of the preamble to Resolution IV on "Peaceful Co-Existence and the Codification of Its Principles by the United Nations" of the Declaration of the Cairo Conference of Heads of State or Government of Non-aligned Countries, 1964. This paragraph reads: "Considering the principles proclaimed at Bandung in 1955, Resolution 1415 (XV) adopted by the United Nations in 1960, the Declaration of the Belgrade Conference, the Charter of the Organization of African Unity, and numerous joint declarations by Heads of State or Government on peaceful co-existence."

MANFRED LACHS

Some Reflections on Substance
and Form in International Law

IN CHOOSING this subject for my contribution to a
volume in honor of Philip Jessup, I have had in mind the notable contribution to its clarification which he himself has made,
not only in his writings but also in the opinions and dicta he
expressed when on the bench of the International Court of
Justice: these contained a wealth of stimulating reflections on
a wide range of issues covering many fields.

What I here propose is no more than a brief outline of some
of the problems involved in the question of substance and form
in international law, a question which calls in reality for much
more searching analysis. The interrelation of substance and
form is an ever-recurring theme in every field of law. This has
been particularly so in the law governing relations between
states. Small wonder, therefore, that this theme has played an
important part in the formation of rights and obligations in
the day-to-day intercourse among subjects of international law
and in their efforts toward its progressive development and
codification. The growing pattern of links between them, the

MANFRED LACHS is a judge on the International Court of Justice and an Associate of the Institut de Droit International.

expanding chessboard on which permanent or temporary relationships are established between states, has given rise to a
host of problems.

Whenever states agree on a common course of action, conferring rights and accepting obligations, they are obviously
prompted by interests which have produced a combined will
to attain the concrete end in view. So long as these interests
remain the same, retain similar proportions, or are not subjected to considerable change, the underlying motivations, be
they common or complementary, continue to sustain the relationship thus established. This, therefore, may be maintained
even without special legal bonds between the parties. The interests continue, and they may even be reinforced by added
benefits arising out of the relationship or further accentuated
by the expectation that whatever is done by one state will be
emulated by the others concerned. So long as the stage of mutual interest continues relatively undisturbed, the legal aspects
of the relationship may seem of minor importance. In the
main, it is only when the balance shifts and the interest of one
of the parties starts to fade that problems arise. It is then that
the essential issue of the "legitimacy and effectiveness" [1] of
rights and obligations comes to a head.

However, it is not only in this limited sphere that such problems have to be faced. They frequently arise at the very outset,
when a legal relationship has to be established. They are latent
in the wider sphere of both the theory and application of the
law, and courts must be sure of their ground when called upon
to determine the validity or legal effects of an allegedly binding obligation arising from an agreement arrived at by states.
This means that they must be prepared to ascertain the bonds
between states, uncover what may be concealed, clarify what
looks complicated, and search for the one legal situation where
there is an appearance of dichotomy: in short, seek whether a

[1] O. Schachter, "Towards a Theory of International Obligation," 8 *Va. J. Int'l L.* 311 (1968).

substantive right and a corresponding obligation have come into existence, in the light of the formal requirements for their establishment and effectiveness.

At first sight, the international legal order gives the impression of one in which form plays an important part. To a student of international law who tries to trace the ways and byways of its development, all those formal documents, treaties, and other instruments constitute, of course, indispensable evidence. It is through them that he may hope to discover the essence of interstate relations and the trends in their development. Nor will he fail to note that, from time immemorial, treaties, the oldest of those instruments by which states have created mutual bonds, have been expected not only to *give* but also to *have* form, the form of the document being sensed, sometimes even to a superstitious degree, as the mirror and guarantee of the pledges: indeed an essential diplomatic concept, in both senses of the word. Formality and solemnity are, of course, virtually synonymous in this context, and they originated in the need to emphasize the seriousness of words not given lightly. From ancient times, moreover, divinities were called to witness, thus bestowing on treaties a sacral character which served to accentuate still further the importance of form. The earliest treaties known—those of the Hittites, of Egypt, of Delphi, or of Rome—all share this character. For centuries religious ceremonies were the inseparable concomitant of the signing of treaties, and so it continued until nearly 1800. Remnants of this association can be found in the solemn invocations of the preambles preceding substantive provisions.

However, that is history. Gradually, international practice has manifested a marked decline of form: states began to reach agreements, acquire rights, and accept obligations in the most varied ways. Documents have become more workmanlike, and if they still employ stereotyped formulae, that is more for reasons of facility and interpretative surety than out of a search for talismans—though doubtless some would prefer to view this development as a mere shift in emphasis. At all events, the limelight of solemn ceremonies is ever more rarely employed, the discreet atmosphere of chancelleries ever more preferred, while the rank of those acting on behalf of states is undergoing a wide extension, both horizontally and, even more, vertically.

Nowadays, then, Philip Jessup's conclusion that "International law, not being a formalistic system, holds States legally bound by their undertakings in a variety of circumstances . . ." [2] reflects the reality of the law.

Evidence of this trend abounds, and the extent to which it has gained ground is particularly reflected in a recent, most important instrument dealing with the law of treaties.[3] To begin with, it is worth recalling that there has been a simplification of the treaty-making process. The rules concerning full powers to represent states in the conclusion of treaties have become less rigid, and some presumptions have been accepted to facilitate such conclusion.[4] The possibilities for states to become parties to treaties by the sole signature have been widened; this is envisaged not only in cases when the treaty provides for the signature to have this effect, but also if "it is otherwise established" that the negotiating states agree that it "should have that effect," or that the same intention "appears from the full powers" or "was expressed during the negotiation." [5] Thus states are in fact encouraged to apply this simplified method of entering into binding international agreements.[6]

[2] South West Africa Cases, [1962] *ICJ Reports* 319, at 411 (sep. opin. Judge Jessup).

[3] Vienna Convention on the Law of Treaties, done at Vienna May 23, 1969, not yet in force; see U.N. Doc. A/CONF. 39/27.

[4] Art. 7 of the Vienna Convention. See also the Commentary to what was Art. 6 of the Draft Articles prepared by the International Law Commission, particularly paras. 3–6. Int'l L. Comm'n, Report, 21 U.N. GAOR, at 26, Supp. 9, U.N. Doc. A/6309/Rev. 1 (1966).

[5] Cf. Art. 12, para. 1 (a), (b), and (c).

[6] Cf. also the provisions concerning consent to be bound by instruments exchanged between states, Art. 13 of the Convention.

The same tendency is reflected in the abandonment of the presumption that ratification is necessary whenever it is not provided for, and its requirement only when the treaty or full powers so stipulate or the intention of the parties to this effect is otherwise established.[7]

These are but a few illustrations of how treaty-making procedure has been simplified. However, form concerns wider aspects. Besides the treaty in its traditional form, exchanges of notes, correspondence, letters or even telegrams now constitute a considerable proportion of the body of diplomatic law; they may soon constitute almost one-half of the total number of instruments recorded in our times. Then there are, of course, those documents which reflect agreements reached at international conferences: the *acte final* or even the communiqué which is sometimes the only written evidence of decisions of far-reaching significance, whose consequences range far beyond the interests of the participants.

---

[7] Cf. Art. 14 of the Convention and also the Commentary to what was Art. 11 of the Draft of the International Law Commission, which indicated the evolution of the rule from the first draft of 1962 to that of 1966. Int'l L. Comm'n, Report, *supra* note 4, at 30–31. Cf. also Art. 7 of the Harvard Draft Convention on the Law of Treaties, 29 *Am. J. Int'l L.* 710, at 756 (Supp. 1935).

The general trend toward abandonment of the requirement of ratification is reflected in a comparison between treaties concluded in the days of the League of Nations and about 1,300 instruments published in the United Nations *Treaty Series;* only 23 percent of the latter, as compared with 53 percent of those published by the League, required ratification; see Blix: "The Requirement of Ratification," 30 *Brit. Y. B. Int'l L.* 352–80 (1953). One of the important factors which prompt states to dispense with ratification is no doubt the considerable delay with which this process is completed, a delay caused by factors frequently unrelated to the substance of the treaty. See the very valuable study, "Wider Acceptance of Multilateral Treaties," *Unitar Series*, no. 2, 19–156 (1969).

One of the new methods facilitating the participation of states in treaties is the so-called "triple option clause": (1) signature alone, (2) signature subject to "acceptance," and (3) "acceptance" without previous signature. It was applied in the Narcotic Drug Protocol, 1946, Art. V and several other United Nations instruments. See also Art. 79 of the Constitution of the World Health Organization 14 U.N.T.S. 185, and "Wider Acceptance of Multilateral Treaties," *supra*, at 144–45.

In sum, the catalog of instruments by which states express their will and establish mutual relations is being continuously enriched by additions bearing the most varied labels. Instruments of similar or identical substance are clothed in various forms and bear different denominations. This situation has frequently been described as reflecting anarchy in this field. There is little doubt that greater uniformity could not but benefit both the practice and the theory of international agreements. Yet, while all attempts to this end have failed, it has become manifest that the various appellations do not in principle affect the legal nature of the agreements.[8] Here again, the subordinate character of form has had to be stressed; it has even been termed irrelevant.

No less significant is the confirmation that while the law of treaties covers agreements "in written form," the exclusion of international agreements concluded "not in written form" cannot affect their legal force.[9]

Oral agreements are known to have been concluded even at a time when the requirements of form were held to be more stringent than they are today. Textbooks of international law list a number of telling illustrations. That they are ever more frequently resorted to in our time is obviously the result of

[8] Cf. Arts. 4 and 5 of the Harvard Draft Convention on the Law of Treaties, 29 *Am. J. Int'l L.* 710, 722 (Supp. 1935); Art. 2(a) of the Draft Articles of the Law of Treaties prepared by the International Law Commission, Report, *supra* note 4 at 21, and the same text adopted by the Vienna Convention of the Law of Treaties. The Commentary of the Commission significantly stresses: "The law relating to such matters as validity, operation and effect, execution and enforcement, interpretation and termination, applies to all classes of international agreements. In relation to these matters there are admittedly some important differences of a juridical character between certain classes or categories of international agreements. But these differences spring not from appellation, nor any other outward characteristic of the instrument in which they are embodied: they spring exclusively from the content of the agreement, whatever its form."

[9] See Art. 3 of the Vienna Convention. Nor does it exclude "the application to them of any of the rules set forth in the . . . Convention to which they would be subject under international law independently of the . . . Convention."

practical requirements. It should not be open to question that the mere fact that they were unwritten cannot deprive them of binding force. Some oral declarations have even acquired the value of *causes célèbres,* while others, having been made in specific circumstances—for instance, before a court—could be immediately established as binding by the court.[10]

In addition to all the above processes whereby states may enter into international obligations there are others created by modern institutions. It is, of course, the phenomenon of the international organizations which opens these possibilities.

Some organs of such organizations are vested with rights to adopt decisions binding upon member states; thus they create rights and obligations embodied in their resolutions. Some of these are in principle recommendations only. Their legal effect has been the subject of a wide-ranging and lively discussion, but there is no need to dwell upon this issue, as for present purposes only one aspect is of interest. While in principle *leges imperfectae,* some of them take us into the legal realm and indeed may constitute an important contribution to the development of the law. Sometimes they are followed by the eventual conclusion of a more general instrument, the binding force of which is unquestionable.[11]

Sometimes the document in question passes through several stages or through several organs of the organization prior to reaching the stage of a declaration or decision. In the process the representatives of states have an opportunity to express the attitudes of their governments not only by a vote but also by statements made before or after the vote. Thus, they may de-

[10] Declarations by Agents before the Permanent Court of International Justice, Case of the Mavrommatis Jerusalem Concessions, [1925] P.C.I.J. ser. A, No. 5. See also the Case of the Free Zones of Upper Savoy and the District of Gex, [1932] P.C.I.J., ser. A/B, No. 46, 96, at 170–72.

[11] Here are some examples: The Universal Declaration of Human Rights (1948) was followed by two Covenants on Human Rights (1966); the Declaration on the Elimination of All Forms of Racial Discrimination (1964), by a Convention on the subject (1966).

clare that their governments consider the instrument they
voted for as reflecting the law on the subject and therefore
hold themselves bound by its provisions. If this is done, no
problem should arise. The form is of little importance, provided the intention is made clear. The will of the governments
to be bound having been declared, they can be held to it.[12]

However, this is only one of the methods by which a resolution of a recommendatory character may be transformed into a
binding international instrument. There may be other ways
through which the intentions of states are made manifest. Such
a resolution may be a vehicle for recording an agreement and
for giving it a much more general scope. This was so when the
General Assembly of the United Nations, by one of its resolutions, "welcomed" "the expression" by two powers "of their intentions" not to proceed with certain activities and called
upon all other states "to refrain" from similar activities. The
case is of interest, since it was through the United Nations that
what was described as a "declaration of intentions" and later
as an "agreement" between two states became known, the
form, time, and place of its elaboration not having been revealed. Subsequently, by voting for the resolution the two
states in question confirmed the conclusion of the agreement
and its binding character.[13] Moreover, they thus became

[12] See the Declaration of Legal Principles Governing the Activities of States
in the Exploration and Use of Outer Space, adopted unanimously by the General Assembly, G. A. Res. 1962, 18 U.N. GAOR Supp. 15, at 15, U.N. Doc.
A/5515 (1963). Following the vote the representatives of the United States
and the Soviet Union declared that their governments would "respect" the
principles of the Declaration. Many other representatives, made similar statements. See Verdross, "Les Principes Généraux de Droit dans le Système des
Sources du Droit International Public," *En hommage à Paul Guggenheim*
525–526 (1968); Lachs, "The Law-Making Process for Outer Space," *New
Frontiers in Space Law* 21 (1969).

[13] G. A. Res. 1884, 18 U.N. GAOR Supp. 15, at 13, U.N. Doc. A/5515
(1963). The events which led to the adoption of the resolution may be worth
recalling. In the General Assembly, President Kennedy and Foreign Minister
Gromyko, on September 19 and 20, 1963, stated that their governments were
willing to take steps in order to reach an agreement to keep nuclear weapons
out of space. The representatives of the two powers referred to it in the

bound by it not only in their mutual relations but also vis-à-vis other member states of the United Nations. This example may serve as an illustration of how such resolutions may become an important and sometimes the only source of evidence of an agreement concluded.

Then there is the wide area of unilateral acts through which states may become legally bound: whether expressly or by implication, whether by recognition, notification, or acquiescence. International practice is rich enough in illustrations indicating that their forms vary from situation to situation, and the real test remains the intention of the state to commit itself, either by the exercise of rights or by the recognition of rights exercised by other states. In the latter respect, even silence, "toleration," or "prolonged abstention" may be held to produce such effects.[14]

Flexibility and dispensation with traditional forms of decision-making can also be illustrated in regard to some provisions of treaties. It may suffice to recall how the Council of the League of Nations was requested to perform certain important functions arising out of the Treaties of St. Germain, Trianon, and Neuilly. Even the delimitation of a boundary was left to the Council, in case the states concerned proved unable to reach agreement.[15] Similar provisions were made in the Peace Treaty with Italy (Paris 1946) concerning the future of Italian colonies. It was laid down that, in case no direct agreement was possible, a recommendation of the General Assembly of

course of the later discussion. On October 17, the representative of the USSR stated that they "agreed on the matter" and that "the agreement is embodied in the draft resolution." The Report of the Political Committee spoke of "the agreement arrived at" (Doc. A/5571), while the representative of Mexico, Mr. Padilla Nervo, used the words "the solemn acceptance on the part of the nuclear Powers of an agreement . . ." (Doc. A/PV. 1244, Oct. 17, 1963, p. 8).

[14] The Anglo-Norwegian Fisheries case, [1951] *ICJ Reports* 116, at 139. However there are obvious limits to the effects of such unilateral acts.

[15] Art. 3(2) of the Treaty of Lausanne concerning the boundary between Turkey and Iraq, July 24, 1923.

the United Nations would "decide" the issue—finally and with binding effect.[16] At first sight, this was an unusual procedure. Yet in specific circumstances it may be the most advisable of procedures when the parties to a treaty wish to avoid a serious dispute, and some of them also wish to evade the final responsibility for a decision. Thus the burden is transferred to an international organ, representative of the international community.

These organs are also resorted to in order to confirm existing law and by so doing lend it greater precision.[17] Such action may eventually result in a convention. However, in some cases, legal effects as authoritatively stated would remain the same even without such a sequel.[18]

I now turn to the least formalistic of all sources of international rights and obligations: the "general practice of States, accepted as law." Within the compass of the present article it is impossible to do justice to this aspect of the subject. I will therefore limit myself to mentioning practice influenced by an international instrument that is not binding on the states concerned because, for whatever reason, they are not parties to it,[19] or by unratified treaties.[20]

[16] So it was decided. See G.A. Res. 289, U.N. Doc. A/1251 at 10 (1949).

[17] G.A. Res. 96, U.N. Doc A/64 (1946).

[18] In regard to the provisions of the Convention of the Prevention and Punishment of the Crime of Genocide, it was held that "the principles underlying the Convention are principles which are recognized by civilized nations as binding on States, even without any conventional obligation." Reservations to the Genocide Convention, [1951] *ICJ Reports* 15, at 23. This is how the Court interpreted "the objects" and "the will" of the General Assembly. See also J. Castañeda, *Legal Effects of United Nations Resolutions* (1969), and his views on the legal force of similar pronouncements, pp. 121 ff.

[19] The Convention on Certain Questions relating to the Conflict of Nationality Laws, 1930. Only 14 states were parties to it after a lapse of almost forty years, yet some of its provisions were relied on vis-à-vis states which were not parties to it. Nottebohm Case, Second Phase, [1955] *ICJ Reports* 4, 22 ff. Also Italian–United States Conciliation Commission, Merigé Claim, 22 *International Law Reports*, 450 (1955). See also the fourth Hague Convention Concerning the Laws and Customs of War on Land, *Judgment of the International Military Tribunal for the Trial of German Major War Criminals* p. 65 (Nuremberg, 1946).

[20] Suzanne Bastid quotes the Declaration of London of 1909 and the Code on Air Warfare of 1923 as illustrations of "une étape vers l'établissement du

Here again, resolutions of organs of international organizations constitute a similar category.

Through the conduct of states which comply with them or cooperate in the implementation of their provisions, these instruments sometimes acquire binding force. Thus the lack of the traditional formal consent (ratification) or an inherently inchoate character (recommendatory nature) is subsequently remedied by other acts such as active implementation or acquiescence, and a process is set in motion which, without formal concretization, leads to the creation of rights and obligations for states.

In yet other cases, states may by their conduct accept obligations, while others acquire correlative rights in bilateral or multilateral relations.[21] To produce legal effects, this conduct need not be active or explicit: mere silence may suffice— especially when explicit reaction in the form of dissent could have been expected.[22] Thus the process of the formation of customary international law may pass through various stages, and the law may mature "in a variety of circumstances." The well-known criteria of frequency, continuity and uniformity are not always applicable, and if they are they may themselves be subject to differing tests.[23] In the light of modern develop-

droit international." "Observations sur une 'étape' dans le développement progressif et la codification des principes du droit international," *En Hommage à Paul Guggenheim*, 143 ff. (1968).

[21] See Cahier, "Le Comportement des Etats comme Source de Droits et Obligations," *En Hommage à Paul Guggenheim* 237 ff. (1968). See also The Minquiers and Ecrehos Case, [1953] *ICJ Reports* 47, at 71; Case Concerning the Temple of Preah Vihear, [1962] *ICJ Reports* 6, at 30.

[22] This may lead to the conclusion of a "general toleration" by other states of a certain practice by one state. Cf. Anglo-Norwegian Fisheries Case, [1951] *ICJ Reports* 116, at 138, that "an acknowledgment by conduct was undoubtedly made in a very definite way" or that the state in question "must be held to have acquiesced," Temple of Preah Vihear, [1962] *ICJ Reports* 6, at 23. Hence it is clear that "knowledge is a prerequisite of acquiescence," MacGibbon, "Customary International Law and Acquiescence," 33 *Brit. Y.B. Int'l L.* 115 (1957). See also Schwarzenberger, "The Fundamental Principles of International Law," 87 Hague *Recueil des Cours.* 200, at 256 (1955-I).

[23] See my comments on the formation of customary law, North Sea Continental Shelf Cases, [1969] *ICJ Reports* 4, at 230–31 (diss. opin. Judge Lachs).

ments the dimension of time, to which so much importance was attached in the past, has taken on a different and less decisive significance. What used to be considered in terms of decades or centuries now has to be telescoped into very short periods. Here too, law has undergone changes under the impact of the revolutions of science and technology: to use the language of a dictionary of science, "space and time are considered as being welded together in a four-dimensional space-time continuum."

In the light of these brief and very general reflections, "form or formlessness"—to use Philip Jessup's words—cannot *in principle* be held to be decisive in establishing the existence or nonexistence of a right or obligation.

It is the will of states, their consent or consensus, which has to be ascertained, revealed, or discovered. In this process there can, of course, be no question of imposing rules of conduct upon them against their will. Nor is this tantamount to questioning the binding force of a peremptory rule of international law, "from which no derogation is permitted and which can be modified only by a subsequent norm of general international law having the same character." [24]

The reasons which justify these developments are compelling. As indicated, they are to be sought in the complexity of political, economic, and other relations, in the imponderables of international life. The rapid rise in the level of interstate activity and the multiplication of international contacts have meant that the forms such activity takes are undergoing continuous change. With so many representatives acting in so many capacities, formal requirements have had to be increasingly dispensed with. It is they which prompt states to seek ever new methods by which to establish new forms for the links thus created. Very frequently the reason lies in the dis-

---

[24] See Art. 53 of the Vienna Convention on the Law of Treaties.

cretion necessary either to avoid too-formal bonds or to ensure their relative flexibility, to permit an indirect rather than a direct relationship. Circumstances may, of course, change, and within a short period of time and with changed conditions the adoption of more formal links may become possible and expedient.

However, not infrequently owing to the swift change of circumstances, the opportunity to establish a relationship does not reappear: a chance, once missed, may not recur. In matters of great importance, when conflicts and disputes arise and the opportunity to arrest a dangerous process is missed, an irreversible trend may be set in motion. In such circumstances a less rigid approach may open the door to the resolution of many vital issues by unorthodox methods. In such cases it is not only the "agreement" but also the "disagreement" which produces far-reaching consequences. Thus, the higher the requirements for a formal and binding agreement, the more difficult it becomes to bridge a gap, to find a compromise. It is here that the wealth of situations in modern international relations calls for the selection of adequate forms, which do not fit the traditional pattern of forms of legal arrangement: either for an *ad hoc* relationship or for a long-term arrangement, both in bilateral and multilateral relations.

It is therefore of the utmost importance that the forms of law should facilitate the passage from confrontation to cooperation. Here, then, we are at the heart of the problem. With this process in mind, even more emphasis must be laid on the real dynamic of international law, the intention of states to seek mutually acceptable arrangements in forms adapted to individual situations.

It is in this context that one of the most important functions of international law should be recalled. If it is to perform its paramount tasks of safeguarding the vital rights of nations and of states and protecting international peace and security, it must assist in the creation of legal instruments by which friendly relations between states can be forged, thus bringing these relations more and more effectively within the legal framework. In this process the traditional formal tests of perfection may not be conducive to strengthening legal ties among nations.

The trend is clear. International law is treating matters of form with ever growing tolerance and flexibility. If it continues to do so, far from adding to its "glorious uncertainty," [25] it will prove better able to extend its protective wings over the rights of all its subjects. It is therefore significant—and perhaps encouraging—that the decline in formality has run parallel to the substantive expansion and consolidation of international law. It may therefore, perhaps, further contribute to an increase of confidence in law.

[25] Joseph C. Hutcheson Jr., Sole Arbitrator in Edward J. Ryan v. the United States of America, 3 U.N. R.I.A.A. 1767, at 1787 (1927). See Karl Zemanek, "Die Bedeutung der Kodifizierung des Voelkerrechts für seine Anwendung," *Internationale Festschrift fuer Alfred Verdross,* 565 (1971).

WOLFGANG FRIEDMANN

Human Welfare and International Law—

A Reordering of Priorities

OVER THE last few decades, a number of international lawyers have begun to outline and develop a basic shift in the dimensions and functions of contemporary international law. We may briefly describe the new developments and challenges as "an international law of welfare," a term used by Professor Roling in his remarkable essay on *International Law in an Expanded World*, published in 1960. Dr. Roling characterizes the international law of welfare as a body of laws concerned with conditions of well-being and the promotion of higher standards of living, full employment, economic and social progress, and the development of all the members of the international community. Professor Roling was not, however, the first to note this vital evolution in the tasks and dimensions of international law.

Shortly after the last world war, Professor Bourquin, in a notable series of lectures delivered at the Hague Academy,[1] had

WOLFGANG FRIEDMANN is Professor of International Law and Director of International Legal Research, Columbia University Law School.

[1] Bourquin, "Pouvoir Scientifique et Droit International," 71 Hague *Recueil des Cours* (1947-II) 331, 359 *et seq*.

emphasized that the subject matter of international law was not enclosed in "immovable boundaries." Among the fields increasingly affected by international regulation, Bourquin mentioned human rights, labor, education, science, communications, agriculture, and international money matters. In *The Common Law of Mankind* (1958), Wilfred Jenks—one of the principal architects and now Director-General of the first of the international welfare organizations, the International Labour Organisation (ILO), established in 1919—said that the emphasis of international law was "increasingly shifting from the formal structure of the relationship between states and the delimitation of their jurisdiction to the development of substantive rules on matters of common concern vital to the growth of an international community and to the individual well-being of the citizens of its member states." And Philip Jessup, who had earlier pleaded for a reassessment of the scope and objectives of postwar international law,[2] pointed out in his book *Transnational Law* that "some of the problems that we have considered essentially international . . . are, after all, merely human problems which might arise at any level of human society—individual, corporate, inter-regional, or international." [3]

I have sought to rationalize this new phase of international law by distinguishing the traditional, essentially "horizontal" international law of coexistence from the newer, "vertical" international law of cooperation. The former is essentially concerned with the regulation and formalization of interstate diplomatic relations; the latter with the elaboration of common objectives and rules in matters vitally affecting human welfare in our time.[4]

The growing importance of this steadily expanding network of international institutions and arrangements concerned with

[2] Jessup, *A Modern Law of Nations* (1948).

[3] Jessup, *Transnational Law* (1956), 15 ff.

[4] See, e.g., W. Friedmann, *The Changing Structure of International Law* (1964), 64 ff., and "General Course in Public International Law," 127 Hague *Recueil des Cours* (1969-II), chap. V.

matters of human welfare is now obvious. What is far less clearly recognized is the need for a reordering of priorities. The League of Nations Covenant of 1919—the first major breakaway from the traditional system of interstate relations which left control over the use of force in the hands of states —placed its principal emphasis on collective security. It also established, in the International Labour Organisation, the first worldwide institution concerned with the regulation and improvement of conditions of labor and social welfare on an international level. Nevertheless, it was the attempt to transfer the use of force from the nation states to the League—an attempt that finally collapsed with the failure of the League of Nations to stop Mussolini's invasion of Abyssinia in 1935—that dominated not only the structure of the Covenant but international legal thinking in the interwar period.

While the United Nations Charter shows many significant differences from the League of Nations Covenant, it basically retains the same order of priorities. Its main emphasis is on the attainment of collective security, with primary responsibility given to the Security Council—of which the principal pillars were supposed to be the five major powers emerging from the postwar world. While less elaborate on the types and incidences of sanctions to be imposed upon an aggressor, the U.N. Charter went further than the Covenant in prescribing the establishment of a permanent international military force based on the collaboration of the major powers. The evolution of an international welfare law was expressed in the creation of a considerable number of specialized U.N. agencies, which were added to the ILO: from the Bretton Woods Organization, established in 1944 (World Bank and International Monetary Fund) to the various organizations concerned with food and agriculture, health, education, atomic energy, communications, and transport. More recently, several organizations primarily concerned with economic development problems have been added: the U.N. Conference on Trade and Development

(UNCTAD), the U.N. Industrial Development Organization (UNIDO) and the U.N. Development Fund.

After two years of fruitless labor, the plan to establish an international military force as the principal instrument of U.N. authority in matters of international security collapsed in 1949, with little prospect of resurrection in our time. Some of the new international welfare agencies—notably the Bretton Woods organizations—developed into effective although far from adequate instruments of international economic development and currency stabilization. Most of the other agencies, lacking an independent financial basis and confined to advisory powers, have remained important but essentially secondary adjuncts to the United Nations, dependent for their effectiveness upon the fluctuating policies of the member states and generally hampered by inadequate powers and financing. A recent illustration of this structural weakness was the refusal in 1970 of the United States, the largest contributor, to contribute its share to the oldest of the international welfare agencies, the ILO, because the new Director General had appointed as one of the Assistant Directors General a citizen of the USSR, one of the major members of the organization. The United States' action was a clear breach of an international obligation and contrary to the U.S. position taken in the ONUC Expenses Case.[5]

Despite the proliferation of international welfare concerns (some expressed in permanent international organizations, others—like the GATT or the international agreements concerning the pollution of the seas—expressed in international conventions with little or no institutional structure), the primary emphasis has remained the concern with international military security. This is understandable enough. At a time when the two major nuclear powers—with a number of others following on their heels—are capable of destroying each other,

[5] For a fully documented account of this action, see Schwebel, "The United States Assaults the ILO," 65 *Am. J. Int'l L.* 136 (1971).

killing or maiming hundreds of millions within hours, and generally destroying civilized existence for an indefinite period, and when conflicts between minor powers can rapidly escalate into destructive wars of worldwide dimensions, physical survival is naturally the issue overshadowing all others. Yet it is submitted that we are in danger of losing sight of the most urgent priorities, and of failing to realize what international law can and cannot do, if we continue to be preoccupied with a system of worldwide collective security that is presently unattainable. Nobody seriously contemplates the organization of a permanent international military force, within or outside the United Nations. Special task forces formed for specific purposes and manned by contingents of smaller powers—as in Cyprus or, until their withdrawal, the Gaza Strip—may help to cool down specific trouble situations. It is not inconceivable that the major powers may jointly guarantee and police the observance of a specific international agreement (e.g., in conjunction with an Israel-Arab peace treaty). But essentially, the prospects—not of guaranteeing peace and security but of avoiding major armed catastrophes—will continue to rest for the foreseeable future on a precarious balance of power between the superpowers, and on the influence which, particularly by the granting or withholding of vital supplies and technical services, they may exercise on the behavior of smaller nations. It is the balance of power policy transferred to a wider and more dangerous scene.

The hard but inescapable conclusion is that the quest for permanent, institutional transfer of the power to use force in international relations from the nation state to an organized international community—a quest pursued by the League of Nations and resumed after the end of the Second World War through the United Nations Charter—has failed. This failure is reflected in the relative impotence of the Security Council, designed to be the primary organ of international security enforcement, and the transformation of the General Assembly into a debating forum, in which a mounting flood of resolutions, the setting up of more and more weak institutions, and the formation of antagonistic regional or political blocs is simply "conflict writ large," transferred from the various capitals to an international debating forum. Perhaps this helps on occasion to defuse the conflict, to lower the temperature; but it is a far cry from organized international security.

Meanwhile, however, issues that even a generation ago appeared to be secondary to the primary quest for collective security from aggression have assumed an overwhelming urgency. They have moved from the realm of ideology to that of necessity—of human survival. The explosive growth of the world population, greatly widening the already enormous gap between the standards of living of a minority of the rich and a majority of the poor nations, the growing pollution of the atmosphere and the oceans, accompanied by the partition of increasing sectors of the seas by coastal nations, the increasingly close connection between the expansion of international transport and communications and the international spread of disease, and above all the increasingly ominous consequences of man's interference with the environment—these and many other matters have become the first priorities in international relations. It would therefore seem timely to reorder our priorities and to pursue progress in international organization—which inevitably means a great expansion and intensification of the international law of cooperation—in the areas in which the sovereignty of the national state may be bypassed rather than overcome by frontal attack. The evidence is indeed overwhelming that a direct attack on the prerogatives of the national state—through the transfer of major decision-making powers from the national to the international level—has not been achieved and will not be achieved within this generation. Not only has the number of national states mushroomed (it is now well over double that of a generation ago) but there has never been a more intensive race for the concentration of military, political, and economic power in the hands of the nation state, big or small. Small as well as big powers seek to increase their armaments technology, to extend their national boundaries, particularly in the seas, and to appropriate to national jurisdiction as much as possible, inevitably at the cost of others. While air space has been considered national territory since 1919, the seas are becoming increasingly nationalized as the technologically advanced maritime nations push their claims to sovereignty over seabed resources further and further outward, while many weaker coastal states compensate by proclaiming 200-mile limits of exclusive national jurisdiction. Canada has recently established a 100-mile Arctic pollution control zone which is likely to expand into full control over all activities.

In the postwar period, the only notable successes in bypassing this destructive expansion of nationalism have been organized attempts in specific areas. On a worldwide level, far and away the most successful specialized international agencies have been the World Bank and the International Monetary Fund. The former, with its more recent affiliate organizations, has effected some redistribution of resources from the rich to the poor. The latter has achieved a modicum of international monetary stability, compared with the chaos of the interwar period. On a regional level, the halting but marked progress of the European Economic Community of six states—likely to be enlarged by Britain and a number of other European states —has been achieved not by federation or other direct forms of transfer of constitutional authority, but by the partial transfer of functions to the community in specialized areas. Hitherto the most significant achievement has been the Customs Union and the establishment of a common pricing policy in agriculture. There has been some progress toward freedom of movement of businesses and labor, an assimilation of social security benefits and the preparation of a common company law. The most recent move is the decision to create gradually a common currency, from which there would inevitably flow the gradual establishment of a common economic policy. Confederation, if it is achieved, will come at the end, not at the beginning.

Following a pioneering pamphlet published by David Mitrany in 1944,[6] this approach may be described as "functionalist." I happen to believe that, at the present time, it offers the only slender hope of saving mankind, not from the always possible sudden disaster of nuclear war, but from the more gradual and also more certain disaster of the gradual destruction of civilized life, through uncontrolled population growth, the proliferation of giant slum cities, the pollution of the oceans, the gradual exhaustion of the mineral as well as the living resources of the earth and the oceans, and the suffocation of mankind through uncontrolled wastage. Since most of these challenges can only be met on an international level, there has never been a more vital task for international law. But the kind of international law that we must develop to meet these challenges is emphatically the international law of cooperation and organization. Never has the traditional law of coexistence been more inadequate to meet the challenges of society. This also means on the international level—as has long been the case on the national level—the end of a laissez-faire approach. Some minimum ordering of the oceans through the establishment of an international seabed authority and internationally enforced standards of exploitation of living and mineral resources, an intensification of the redistribution of resources from the developed to the developing countries, which more and more must be coupled with international cooperation on population growth and on the balance of urban and agricultural growth, and countless other matters require international planning and *positive* regulation. Even the greatest achievement of classical international law, the freedom of the seas— principally of fishing and navigation—can no longer be

[6] *A Working Peace System* (Royal Institute of International Affairs, 1944).

preserved by laissez-faire methods. It must be coordinated with the conservation and development of resources and with the redistribution of international and national competences. Fishing and navigation must become part of a concerted attack upon the closely interrelated problems of communications and resource exploitation. The need to pass from a more-or-less chaotic state of semi-laissez-faire to one of planning is no longer a question of ideology. Controversy will continue on the best method of achieving it, on the proper balance between centralized and decentralized decision-making, but not on the principle itself. For this need is clearly the product of our overcrowded and overexploited society. On the national level, this has recently become plain enough. Conservative governments in the United States and in Great Britain have proposed minimum income plans for all, based on minimum family needs and totally at variance with the earlier capitalist and puritanical philosophy that material success is the reward for hard work ordained by God or by less divine agencies. The U.S. Government has given support to nationally vital enterprises, such as Lockheed Aircraft or the new National Railroad Passenger Corporation, and in 1971 instituted drastic wage and price controls, while the Conservative British Government has had to nationalize the bankrupt but nationally important Rolls Royce Company, thus adding a major manufacturer to the basic industries which were nationalized after the war.

Internationally, we are still far from the realization of even an elementary welfare society. However, it is not sufficient to stress the urgency of international organization of an increasing number of vital international concerns. It is equally important to reassess priorities. For the response to the needs of survival will clearly be propelled not by idealistic visions of human brotherhood, for which there is very little prospect, but by recognition of the urgency of international regulation of vital areas as a matter of self-preservation and national interest.

Generally, the international organization of human needs will proceed in proportion to the extent to which shared interests and common standards will prevail over basic divisions among larger or smaller groups of nations. From this simple assumption some uncomfortable but inevitable conclusions emerge. The two noblest efforts at achieving international minimum standards have been in the fields of social justice and of human rights. The preamble to the oldest of the U. N. specialized agencies, the ILO, established in 1919, speaks of improvement of "conditions of labor . . . involving such injustice, hardship and privation to large numbers of people as to produce unrest so great that the peace and harmony of the world are imperiled. . . ." as paramount for the establishment of international peace. But more than half a century later the legislative achievements of the ILO have remained limited to a few matters and a relatively small number of states. The reason is obvious: standards of labor and social welfare are deeply intertwined with the political, social, and economic structure of the various nations, and they differ correspondingly. It is not surprising that much greater—though still far from complete—progress in this area has been made between the far more homogeneous member states of the EEC.

The goal seems even more distant in the area of human rights. Although in the period of nearly two decades since the Universal Declaration on Human Rights of 1948, two human rights covenants have been passed by resolutions of the General Assembly, there is very little prospect that they will become internationally binding treaties. They are essentially declamations, although of a more specified nature than the 1948 Declaration. The reason for this is perhaps even more obvious than in the area of labor and social security: the position of the individual and the degree of protection afforded to such vital aspects of human rights as freedom of speech, assembly, and worship or property rights varies drastically from nation to nation. In many of the world's contemporary political systems, they are virtually nonexistent. They are heavily circumscribed in many others and effectively implemented in no more than a small minority of the world's 130 nation states. It is in a more limited area, i.e., among the member states of the European Convention on Human Rights (to which one of the major Western states, France, has not subscribed) that some progress has been achieved. The Convention has an institutional structure, with a Commission and a Court to which nationals of the member states may appeal against violations of their rights by their own governments.

The vast majority of the hundreds of applications that come before the screening body, the European Commission, are declared inadmissible, usually because they touch matters of internal judicial process or administrative discretion. But in a small number of cases—declared admissible by the Commission—the European Court of Human Rights has exerted at least a marginal power of international supervision. It has ordered a minor rectification in the bitter Flemish-Walloon linguistic dispute between the two major ethnic groups in Belgium; it may hear a case in which Kenyans accuse the United Kingdom of having violated their rights as citizens.[7] In a few cases the prospect of a judicial hearing has induced a modification in the law of the defendant state.

But what is, even within the context of Western Europe, an essentially symbolic move toward a direct judicial affirmation of individual rights against their own states remains a very distant aspiration on the wider international scene. Quite apart from the constitutional obstacles—which have hitherto made it impossible for the United States to ratify as elementary a document of human rights as the Genocide Convention—the

[7] The European Commission of Human Rights has declared 31 applications admissible, and the case will go to the Committee of Ministers, and from there to the Court, unless it is settled before.

enforcement of covenants of human rights between, for instance, the Soviet Union, Franco's Spain, the Greece of the
colonels, Allende's Chile, and the Western democracies is
clearly not within the realm of realizable possibilities.

It is therefore to fields less affected by basic political and social beliefs that we must turn for some hope that the sheer ur-
gencies of civilized survival will promote the development of
international legal institutions and standards. The three areas
in which the most significant developments have either occurred or may be expected are: first, the area of global communications; second, the area of development and sharing of
scarce resources; third, the preservation of the environment
from global destruction or pollution.

GLOBAL COMMUNICATIONS AND TRANSPORT

The need for some international regulation of communications
and transport is dictated by the simple fact of a shrinking and
increasingly interconnected globe. The skies are filled with
thousands of passenger, military, and cargo planes, while the
airwaves are getting more and more crowded, although this
latter situation is being relieved somewhat by the new communications satellites. Mutual self-interest dictates the avoidance
of chaos. A recent monograph on this subject [8] has shown how
in this field—often without specific legal regulation—the decision-making powers of permanent international organs have
been allowed to develop as a result of sheer necessity. Of the
older U.N. specialized agencies, the Council of the International Civil Aviation Organization is—apart from the World
Health Assembly, which has limited powers to adopt regulations concerning sanitary requirements and the prevention of
disease—the only one that has been equipped with certain
quasi-legislative powers. It can enact international standards,
practices, and procedures of air navigation by a two-thirds ma-

[8] See C. Alexandrowicz, *The Law of Global Communications* (1971).

jority, subject to disapproval within a certain period by a majority of the contracting states. In the exercise of these powers, the Council of ICAO, guided by the work of the Air Navigation Commission, has adopted fifteen sets of international standards and recommended practices as well as "procedures for air navigation services" (PANS), although the latter are, strictly speaking, recommendations rather than regulations. The importance of worldwide adoption of air navigation standards is indicated by the fact that in 1970 the USSR, an increasingly important factor in international commercial air transport, joined the ICAO.

In the field of radio frequencies and telecommunications, the ITU, another specialized agency of the U. N., has, by gradual acquiescence, acquired a regulatory power which by and large avoids international chaos in overlapping frequencies. In the older Universal Postal Union, the permanent secretariat (International Bureau) has long enjoyed a de facto regulatory power. The status of the newer INTELSAT is less satisfactory from the standpoint of international organization, since it still rests on the overwhelming technological, managerial, and financial predominance of its chief contributor and managing agent, the U. S. COMSAT. Moreover, INTELSAT does not include the USSR and the other communist states. It may be predicted, however, that gradually this consortium of states interested in satellite communications will take the shape of a more tightly organized international organization, since the interest in an expanding system of global radio and television channels will become more and more pressing. A similar strengthening of international organization and decision-making powers may be expected in other fields where the essentially technological common interests of the states outweigh political and ideological differences—for example, in the field of weather observation and exchange of meteorological information. It would, of course, be absurd to conclude that international collaboration and organization in the essentially techno-

logical fields will shut out or even substantially diminish the
deeper political and ideological conflicts. However, institutional collaboration in these areas engenders a practice of cooperation based on joint interests, and this will be at least a
moderate factor in promoting habits of cooperation rather
than conflict.

THE SHARING AND DEVELOPMENT
OF RESOURCES

It is in the field of the sharing and development of natural resources that not only the most significant developments in international organization have occurred but also that the inex-
orable pressure of balanced development for the sake of
general survival may lead to further progress in international
organization.

The organization of international economic development
aid, on worldwide, regional, and bilateral levels, has surely
been the most significant single development of international
organization in the postwar world. The main reason for the
relative success of the World Bank, its two more recent affiliates, the International Finance Corporation and the International Development Association, and the International Monetary Fund is their financial autonomy and the consequent
independence enjoyed by the permanent staffs of these organizations, as compared with the essentially political governing
bodies, composed of ministers, of the member states. The
quota subscriptions of the member states are comparable to
the capital subscriptions of shareholders in companies. They
constitute a permanent capital basis, enabling the World Bank
to multiply its lending powers through the issue of bonds on
various international markets and to finance, out of its considerable income from loan interest and commissions, its weaker
affiliate, the International Development Association, which
makes soft long-term loans at nominal rates of interest. Unlike

the World Bank itself, the IDA depends on recurring appropriations and therefore limps from one financial crisis to another. The World Bank is not, of course, free from politics. The Soviet bloc has never joined it. The less developed countries which have joined it and are the main recipients of loans from the Bank and its affiliates have at times complained of the financial and political supremacy exercised by the principal contributor, the United States. However, such political influence—which culminated in the pressure exercised by the U.S. Government on the World Bank to revoke a loan for the Egyptian Aswan Dam—has receded, as the influx of new members has reduced the relative supremacy of the United States, and new leaders, such as the incumbent president of the Bank, have sought to detach the bank from U.S. political and ideological prejudices. There are indications, the extent of which cannot yet be foreseen clearly, that Mr. McNamara may use World Bank loans for the promotion of objectives that are not strictly financial—such as coupling development aid loans with administrative, educational, or technological reforms, or making loans conditional on protection of the environment and minimum standards of urban planning. Here we come to a very delicate area, generally described as "economic intervention."

Recipient states tend to resent the coupling of financial aid with conditions that touch the sensitive nerves of economic sovereignty. Not infrequently, insistence on "sovereignty" is simply a cover for the reluctance of incumbent regimes dominated by landowners and industrialists to effect urgently needed social and economic reforms. But the cry comes equally loudly from left-wing nationalist regimes, which can appeal to widespread popular support in their hostility to "capitalist imperialism." Since the recipient nations are represented in the government and in the executive bodies as well as on the permanent staff of the World Bank, these criticisms will not be as loud as they are in relation to national development agencies. To what extent it may be possible to couple development aid on the global level with economic and social change is certainly one of the crucial questions of our time. But it is by no means certain that necessity and shared interests will prevail over the divisive forces of political and economic nationalism.

Generally, the second level of institutional development aid, that of government-controlled aid-giving by developed to developing countries, is likely to decline from the peak it reached in the early sixties. During the fifties, the major Western powers, led by the United States, had established permanent governmental aid agencies, which accounted for the bulk of development aid. Such aid was given sometimes in the form of grants but principally in the form of low interest loans—although the latter were often, in law or in fact, tied to purchases from the aid-giving country. The goal, more or less accepted some years ago by the aid-giving countries and formulated in various resolutions of UNCTAD, which is dominated by the aid-receiving countries, was a target of 1 percent of the GNP to be devoted to development aid. But this goal has receded in recent years, most notably in the United States. The cause is not only disillusionment with results, reinforced by the obvious fact that voting for foreign aid does not gain votes in national constituencies, but also the increasing political tensions between the principal donor and recipient countries. Left-wing revolutions in various Latin American countries and in some parts of Africa and Asia seem to indicate that bilateral aid from government to government will increasingly decline. Apart from some transfer of resources to the World Bank, the place of bilateral aid may be taken by regional organizations. The most important of these at this time is the Inter-American Development Bank—also principally equipped with U.S. funds and composed of twenty Latin American states as well as the United States. There is an urgent need for strengthening of parallel regional development institutions such as the Asian and African Development Banks. The latter has hitherto been hampered by excessive nationalism and divisions among the African states, which concentrate their limited resources on national development schemes and leave only a meager overspill for the regional organization. In the case of the Asian Development Bank—which has major capital contributions from Japan and the United States—the Indochina War has prevented it from embarking on its major tasks.

An increase in the role of regional development banks of Latin America, Africa, and Asia will be particularly important if progress is to be made in the sharing of the resources of the sea and of the ocean floor. Present developments are greatly disadvantageous to the landlocked states, of which there are a number in all these continents, but notably in Africa. Their poverty increases the handicap of their situation, and it is only through regional organizations that they may hope to participate in the envisaged internationalization of the seabed resources outside national jurisdiction.

Perhaps the most important source of development of international law arising from resource exploitation in developing countries, is the semipublic sphere of development agreements between private foreign investors and the countries owning these resources. For the traditionalist international lawyer, economic development agreements and the increasingly important joint international business ventures, in which equities are shared between the foreign investor and the host country (either a government development corporation or private entrepreneurs), fall outside the realm of international law. But this is clearly an outmoded view. It is this type of bilateral or multilateral transaction that has been the major source of development of an international commercial law, as F. A. Mann and others have outlined it. And it is in this area that it is particularly important to note Philip Jessup's observation that "the use of transnational law would supply a larger storehouse of rules on which to draw, and it would be unnecessary to worry whether public or private law applies in certain cases." [9]

As Myres McDougal observed in his Hague Lectures of 1953,[10] a contemporary international law must include not only the nation state but also international government organizations, private associations, and the individual human being. In short, a contemporary public international law, which must put increasing emphasis on economic and social relations, can only grow through the absorption of private law into public law, the inevitable corollary of the vertical extension of international relations from the sphere of interstate diplomatic relations to economic, social, and other human concerns. But by the same token, the essentially commercial aspects of what were formerly private international transactions, by their transfer to the public or semipublic sphere, will be increasingly mingled with political tensions and confrontations. The Iranian Oil Agreement of 1954 provided a foretaste of the mixture of commercial and diplomatic relations for which, with much assistance from concerned governments, the parties found their temporary solution in the agreement between the Iranian Government on the one part and seven major oil companies on the other part. Since then the oil producing companies have formed a collective bargaining organization, the Organization of Petroleum Exporting Countries (OPEC), which in the 1971 negotiations confronted twenty-two major western oil companies in a tough international collective bargaining process. While one of the parties was composed of governments and the other of private companies (though some of them government controlled), the issues were clearly political as well as commercial. The level of oil prices affects not only the industrial processes of the Western countries, but also the tax revenue and the balance of payments of the governments

[9] Jessup, *Transnational Law* (1956), 15–16.
[10] McDougal, "International Law, Power, and Policy: A Contemporary Conception," 82 Hague *Recueil des Cours* 133 (1953-I).

concerned. But whatever the tensions and conflicts, it is now clear that international economic transactions have become a major concern of international law.

RESOURCES OF THE SEA AND GLOBAL POLLUTION

Recently, an even more urgent challenge has been posed by the growing technological possibilities in the exploitation of oceanbed resources. The increasing exploitation of oil and other mineral resources has not only begun to affect the traditional freedoms of fishing and navigation, it has also intensified the problems of international pollution, a major target in the battle for the preservation of the environment. The opening up of the oceans has been accompanied by an increasingly critical legal battle for ownership and national jurisdiction. There is, indeed, no area in which the choice between an ever-sharpening confrontation of national claims and jurisdictions and the establishment of an international system of sharing and redistribution of resources is more crucial. Since Arvid Pardo's historic speech to the United Nations of August 1967, the principal legal developments and problems have been discussed so widely that it is neither necessary nor possible to retrace them here.[11] The starting point was the Truman Proclamation of 1945, proclaiming the exclusive sovereignty of the United States over the continental shelf, extending out to the 200-meter isobath. Within a few years, all coastal states had adopted this new extension of national jurisdiction, which was confirmed by the Geneva Convention on the Continental Shelf of 1958. But this Convention permitted extension of the continental shelf to a point "where the depth of the superjacent waters admits of the exploitation of the natural resources of the

---

[11] The major developments, writings and debates are summarized in the present writer's *The Future of the Oceans* (1971). For the most recent developments, see "Selden Redivivus—Towards the Partition of the Oceans," 5 *Am. J. Int'l L.* 757 (1971).

seabed and subsoil." This provided an excuse for a continuous outward and downward expansion of national claims, in the course of which the very concept of "continental shelf" is being increasingly displaced by the concept of "continental margin," which would extend national jurisdictions to roughly a quarter of the ocean bed, up to the edge of the abyssal depth. This would include the overwhelming majority of exploitable mineral resources. Inevitably, the machinery and operations necessary for such exploitation will increasingly affect the biological resources of the sea as well as navigation. The principal counter to this disastrous extension of national frontiers to the bottom of the oceans has been the U.S. Draft Convention of 1970, which proposes a redefinition of the continental shelf in terms of the original Truman Proclamation and an "intermediate zone" reaching to the edge of the continental margin, to be administered by coastal states as trustees for the international community, with responsibility for safety, pollution and technological standards, and an obligation to hand over at least 50 percent of the license and royalty revenue to an international seabed authority. The latter would have exclusive jurisdiction over the remainder of the open seas, and it would include landlocked as well as coastal states. The United Nations by General Assembly Resolution 2749(XXV) of December 17, 1970 accepted the principle of an international seabed authority but left the "limits of national jurisdiction," and therefore the crucial question of the extent of international authority, open for further debate. The prospects for an early solution are dim, since oil and other industrial interests in technologically advanced countries press for maximum extension of national jurisdiction, while almost all the Latin American states now proclaim sovereignty over the seas 200 miles from their coasts, mainly to protect their fisheries from foreign exploitation. Meanwhile, even traditionally internationally minded states like Canada have proclaimed extended national jurisdiction (an Arctic control zone of one hundred miles, for the prevention of pollution as well as extended control zones over fishing and navigation); at the same time, a major power like the USSR, whose own coastal resources are limited but whose fishing fleets are worldwide and immense, is naturally opposed to any extension of fishing boundaries but at the same time strongly opposes an effective international seabed authority.

OUTLOOK FOR THE FUTURE

The next few years—and particularly the forthcoming Sea Law Conference of 1973 and the Stockholm Conference on Pollution in 1972—will show whether and to what extent mankind will make the hard but necessary choice: whether it will see that continuing conflicting expansions of national jurisdictions, now extended from the land and the air to the seas, can only lead to an ultimate confrontation in which the major powers by virtue of their financial, military, and technological strength will be the ultimate winners and probably will then confront each other in an ultimate struggle for power. Will the overcrowding of the earth, accompanied by an uncontrolled overexploitation of its resources and the pollution of the environment, induce nations to establish effective international institutions in the common interest? The issue is open, and no one who has observed the international developments of the last few decades can be overoptimistic as to the result.

But what does stand out clearly is that the establishment of international organizations, and the corresponding extension of international legal rules, in the areas that most immediately touch the interests of the nations, i.e., in the areas of communications, resources, and environment, offer the only realistic chance for the consolidation and expansion of international law.[12] Evidently, these various areas are interconnected.

---

[12] The establishment of an International Environmental Authority has been suggested by George Kennan, 48 *Foreign Affairs* 401 (1970) and Richard Baxter, Proceedings, Columbia University Conference on International and Interstate Regulation of Water Pollution, March 970, 3, 76.

Growing subsonic and supersonic air transport increasingly pollutes the atmosphere; mineral exploitation of the seabed threatens pollution of the oceans and its living resources; the discharges from nuclear power stations affect the temperature of the sea and may change the balance of marine life—as may also the interchange of Atlantic and Pacific fish in a new canal joining the two oceans. Increasingly closer cooperation between the various functional agencies will be needed. Eventually, they may have to be merged in a small number of multipurpose authorities. A constitutional and military super-structure—which might eventually topple the nation state from its present paramount position—will come at the end, not at the beginning of such an evolution.

III

THE CHANGING LAW

FRANCIS DEÁK

Neutrality Revisited

UNTIL THE end of World War I, neutrality was a generally recognized status in public international law. The framework of neutral rights and duties was codified in two of the several Hague Conventions of 1907.[1] In essence, these conventions, which reflected customary law developed during the nineteenth century, imposed on neutral states the duties of nonparticipation in a war between other states, of an attitude of impartiality toward the belligerents, and of protecting their neutrality against any attempts by belligerents to use neutral territory in aid of war operations. The corresponding duties of belligerents were the duty to respect the territorial integrity of the neutral states, to refrain from acts which would impair the sovereignty of neutral states, and to permit continued innocent trade by the neutrals with both the opposing belligerents, subject to limitations of contraband, blockade, and unneutral services. World War I put severe strains on the application of

THE LATE FRANCIS DEÁK was Visiting Professor of International Law, Rutgers University School of Law (Camden).

[1] Convention No. V respecting the Rights and Duties of Neutral Powers and Persons in case of War on Land, 36 Stat. 2310, T.S. 540, 1 Bevans 654; *Nouveau Recrueil Général de Traités* [*Martens*] (3rd Series, No. 3 at 504); and Convention No. XIII concerning the Rights and Duties of Neutral Powers in Naval War, 36 Stat 2415, T.S. 545, 1 Bevans 723; *Martens (3d Series, No. 3, at 713).*

these rules. Such strains resulted from the geographic extent of
the war on the one hand, and on the other hand the changing
character of the conduct of the war, including resort to economic warfare in a vastly more sophisticated form than was
practiced during the Napoleonic wars. Nevertheless, belligerents did observe—or at least gave lip-service to—neutrality
rules. Attempts were made to justify departures therefrom
through a variety of arguments, as shown by diplomatic correspondence of the period.

The situation changed after 1919 with the establishment of
the League of Nations. International lawyers began debating
whether neutrality was compatible with League membership.
Some authorities took the position that neutrality, as defined
in the Hague Conventions, was incompatible with the obligations accepted by League members vis-à-vis a member state
which resorted to war in breach of the Covenant (particularly
Article 16), however limited these obligations were. Others
argued that because of the "gaps" in the Covenant, it was possible that no collective League action would be taken against a
Covenant breaker. In that case members would be free to
adopt a neutral stance toward the belligerents. Also, they
pointed out that League membership was not universal; that
even the feeble limitations on the theretofore unlimited sovereign right to resort to war were not binding on states which
remained outside the League. Those nonmember states remained free to stay neutral even in the face of collective
League actions against a Covenant breaker.

The next development which intensified the debate over
neutrality was the conclusion in 1928 of the Pact for the Re-
nunciation of War (the so-called Kellogg-Briand Pact).[2] It is
fair to say that, despite its vagueness, the Kellogg-Briand Pact
did to some extent fill the gaps in the Covenant. It expressly
"outlawed" war "as an instrument of national policy," however
difficult it may be to determine when a state resorts to war in

[2] 46 Stat. 2343; 94 L.N.T.S. 57.

pursuance of national policy. Such proof as the invasion of Ethiopia by Italy, the Pearl Harbor attack, or the overwhelming evidence showing that Nazi Germany did prepare for war as a matter of policy will seldom be available. Nevertheless, the Kellogg-Briand Pact did impose further limitations on the sovereign right of states under pre-League international law to resort to war for whatever reasons, but it provided no mechanism to enforce the prohibition by collective action of the signatories. Hence, the Pact supplied additional argument to those who believed in the incompatibility of neutrality for League members and/or signatories of the Kellogg-Briand Pact.[3]

Writing in late 1935, Professor Jessup posed the question whether, in view of the impact of the League Covenant and the Kellogg-Briand Pact, neutrality was dead.[4] After analyzing the relevant provisions of the Covenant and the Pact, he concluded that the traditional status of neutrality, with the reciprocal rights and duties of belligerent and neutral states, still had a place in international law. In reaching this conclusion Professor Jessup recognized that the classic concept of neutrality had been inevitably affected by the changing concept of war, namely that it was no longer deemed to be the unrestricted exercise of sovereignty—at least as far as League members and signatories of the Kellogg-Briand Pact were concerned. But his conclusion that a place for neutrality remained proved to be correct soon after he posed the question. First, the half-hearted sanctions imposed by the League in response to Italy's aggression against Ethiopia were ineffective; second, several League members (Switzerland and the Scandinavian countries) could and did decline participation in these sanctions.

[3] In a memorandum to Parliament dated December 13, 1929, the British Foreign Secretary, Sir Arthur Henderson, wrote: ". . . as between Members of the League there can be no neutral rights, because there can be no neutrals. . . ." Hackworth, *Digest of International Law* 670, quoting from Brit. Parl. Papers, Misc. No. 12, 1929; Cmd. No. 3452.

[4] P. Jessup, *Neutrality: Today and Tomorrow*, 86 ff. (1936).

Three years later, upon the outbreak of World War II, a
number of countries, including the United States, issued neutrality proclamations,[5] hoping to stay out of the war. Some of
these countries were League members and/or signatories of
the Kellogg-Briand Pact. We may take notice of the fact that
few of these countries succeeded in maintaining their neutrality, however scrupulously they sought to observe the basic
neutral duties of impartiality and nonparticipation. In some
cases, belligerents simply ignored the reciprocal obligation to
respect the territorial integrity of neutral states (vide the German invasion and occupation of Denmark, Norway, Belgium,
Luxembourg, the Netherlands, Yugoslavia, and Greece, and Soviet Russia's unprovoked attack on Finland). In other cases,
neutral countries gradually got involved as the war expanded.
In fact, only five European countries succeeded in maintaining
their neutrality intact throughout World War II: Portugal, Ire-
land, Sweden, Switzerland, and Spain. Among these countries
Spain's conduct was, until the concluding phases of war, more
in the nature of partiality for the Axis powers than true neutrality. Sweden had to pay a price by permitting the transit
through its territory of raw material for German industry and
the transit of German troops.[6] Switzerland was perhaps the
strongest neutral, thanks to her geography, which would have
made any attack on her too costly for Germany to undertake.

So much for past history.

Let us now consider the contemporary international scene
within the United Nations framework. Obviously, the shape of
the international community today is very different than it was
between the two world wars. The United Nations is a far more
universal organization than the League of Nations was. Even
though one of the potentially great powers, the People's Re-

[5] It should be noted that the so-called American Neutrality Laws of 1935–
1939 hardly reflected the traditional concept of neutrality.

[6] For explanation of the circumstances which forced Sweden to depart from
strict neutrality see G. Hägglöff, "A Test of Neutrality: Sweden in the Second
World War," 36 International Affairs 153 (1960).

public of China, was excluded from the U.N. until just recently and the cold war has hitherto prevented admission of a
divided Germany, the overwhelming majority of independent
states, with the great majority of the world's population, are
United Nations members. The changes in the international
community have, of course, significantly affected the scope
and content of international law,[7] including the laws of war
and neutrality.

What is important for our purposes is that the Charter prohibition of war—or, to be exact, the prohibition of the use or
threat of force in Article 2(4)—taken literally is broader, more
emphatic, and more comprehensive than the corresponding
provisions in the League Covenant. The only permissible use
or threat of force is the "inherent" right of self defense in case
of armed attack under Article 51 and actions taken by member
states pursuant to Security Council decisions under Chapter
VII of the Charter. These Charter provisions were designed to
achieve one of the main purposes—if not *the* main purpose—of
the United Nations, namely, to eliminate war, or at least to reduce the likelihood of armed conflict to the irreducible minimum, more effectively than was demonstrated within the
League of Nations system.

It is not surprising, therefore, that international lawyers
began to debate the question whether, in case of armed conflict, neutrality in its traditional terms is compatible with obligations of member states under the Charter. To put it differently: has the Charter filled the "gaps" found in the Covenant?
The debate is still going on, with scholars taking opposing
positions.[8] Some assert that the institution of neutrality disap-

---

[7] See W. Friedmann, *The Changing Structure of International Law* (1964);
O. Lissitzyn, *International Law Today and Tomorrow* (1965).

[8] The literature on the subject is rather extensive. Some scholars deal with the
problems of neutrality in connection with appraisals of contemporary international law. See, e.g., J. Kunz, "La Crise et les Transformations du Droit des
Gens," 88 Hague *Recueil des Cours* 1 (1955-II), especially "Le Droit de
Neutralité," 79–81; J. Stone, *Legal Controls of International Conflicts*, (2d ed.
1959); M. McDougal and F. Feliciano, *Law and Minimum World Public Order*

peared for U.N. members; others argue that the Charter still
has loopholes permitting member states to remain neutral in
armed conflict.

The answer to the question about "gaps" in the Charter requires careful analysis of its provisions, on the one hand, and
the practical application of these provisions in the practice of
the United Nations and its members on the other hand.

As far as the Charter provisions are concerned, here are
some specific questions which may be posed. Is the use or
threat of force against a member state proscribed by Article
2(4) if such use or threat is not directed against its territorial
integrity or political independence? Or is the proscription
broader, covering *any* use or threat of force "in any other manner inconsistent with the Purposes of the United Nations"? Is
the use or threat of force proscribed against nonmembers? Or
does Article 2(6) imply that while nonmembers are not bound
by the Charter, they are obliged to act "in accordance" with
the Charter principles "so far as may be necessary for the
maintenance of international peace and security"?

Under Article 48, actions required to carry out Security
Council decisions for the maintenance of international peace
and security shall be taken by *all* members, "or by *some* of
them, as the Security Council may determine." (Emphasis
added.) Thus, it is conceivable that the Security Council
would entrust only some member states with carrying out the
required action; could the other members remain neutral? Or

(1961), especially "Participation and Nonparticipation in Coercion: Neutrality
in Context," 384–519. *Manual of Public International Law,* (Sorensen, ed.)
840–43 (1968). See also Henkin, "Force, Intervention and Neutrality in Contemporary International Law," *Am. Soc. Int'l L. Proceedings* 197 (1963). Others
confine themselves to analyzing neutrality within the framework of the United
Nations; see, e.g., H. Kelsen, "La Charte des Nations Unies et le Droit de la
Neutralité," in his "Théorie du droit international public," 84 Hague *Recueil
des Cours* 57–61 (1953-III); T. Komarnicki, "Problems of Neutrality under
the UN Charter," 38 *Transactions of the Grotius Society* 77 (1953); C. Chaumont,
"Nations Unies et Neutralité," 89 Hague *Recueil des Cours* 191 (1956-I);
D. Schindler, "Aspects contemporains de la Neutralité," 121 Hague *Recueil des
Cours* 225 (1961-II).

would such neutrality in the classic sense (that is impartiality and nonparticipation) violate their obligation under Article 2(5) to render the United Nations every assistance in any action it takes in accordance with the Charter, and to "refrain from giving assistance to any state against which the United Nations is taking preventive or enforcement action"? [9]

Without dealing in detail with these hypothetical problems, it seems clear that the question posed in 1936 by Professor Jessup in the context of the League Covenant and the Kellogg-Briand Pact should be answered negatively today within the United Nations framework. It is, of course, equally clear that the *raison d'être* of the institution of neutrality as developed and practiced during the nineteenth and early twentieth centuries has disappeared. But the establishment of the United Nations and changes in the contemporary international society and international law have by no means rendered neutrality (perhaps in a modified form) obsolete. This position is supported by positive rules of contemporary international law.

In the first place, two of the several Hague Conventions of 1907 which codified the laws of neutrality [10] survived both the League Covenant and the United Nations Charter and are in force today for most of the major powers (i.e., France, Japan, the United Kingdom, the United States, and the Soviet Union). True, only two newly independent states have adhered to these conventions—namely Laos and the Philippines; but it is also true that 42 states, all U.N. members except Germany, are bound by them. It may be argued that the obligations of these Hague Conventions conflict with member states' obligations under the Charter and, therefore, pursuant to Article 103, the Charter obligations prevail. Consequently, member states could not avail themselves of the rights and are not re-

[9] Interestingly this seems to be the Soviet position, which denies the incompatibility of neutrality with Charter obligations. See *International Law* (Moscow: Foreign Languages Publishing House, n.d. but perhaps 1961) 442–43.

[10] See footnote 1, *supra*.

quired to observe the obligations of neutral powers set forth in the Hague Conventions whenever the Security Council decided on measures to be taken to maintain or restore international peace and security. (Article 39 of the Charter.) This argument may be supported, as already suggested, by reference to Article 2(5) of the Charter.

This indeed sounds like a persuasive argument supporting the thesis that classic neutrality, with its duty of impartiality and nonparticipation, is incompatible with Charter obligations. But this argument can be rebutted by referring to the four Geneva Conventions of August 12, 1949, which make frequent references to and assign important roles to "neutral" powers.[11] Since the overwhelming majority of the signatories of these conventions, negotiated and concluded when the U. N. was a going concern, are U.N. members, it is safe to assume that they envisaged the possibility (if not, indeed, the necessity) of neutrality or, at least, nonbelligerency as being compatible with the Charter obligations of members.

The conclusion that neutrality is not yet dead even under the Charter can be further supported by pointing to the continued existence of permanently neutral states. There is, of course, a difference between the classic concept of neutrality, which becomes operative only in time of war by the unilateral

---

[11] These four conventions, with annexes, are published in 75 U.N.T.S. They deal respectively with the Amelioration of the Condition of the Wounded and Sick in Armed Forces in the Field, 6 U.S.T. 3114, T.I.A.S. 3362 (Art. 4 provides that *neutral* powers shall apply the provision of the Convention; Art. 27 speaks of *neutral* countries and governments; Art. 43 refers to medical units belonging to *neutral countries*); the Amelioration of the Condition of the Wounded, Sick and Shipwrecked Members of Armed Forces at Sea, 6 U.S.T. 3217, T.I.A.S. 3363 (Art. 10 speaks of "any *neutral* Power"; Art. 32 decrees that hospital ships are not classed as warships as regards their stay in *neutral* ports); the Treatment of Prisoners of War, 6 U.S.T. 3316, T.I.A.S. 3364; (Art. 4(B)(2) and Art. 122 speak of "*neutral* or non-belligerent powers", and A. IV, sect. I bears the title Direct Repatriation and Accommodation in *Neutral* Countries); and Protection of Civil Persons in Time of War, 6 U.S.T. 3516, T.I.A.S. 3365 (Art. 4 refers to nationals of a *neutral* state, Articles 61 and 132 refer to *neutral* powers.)

decision of the state concerned, and the permanent, internationally recognized neutrality of countries like Switzerland and, until World War I, Belgium and Luxembourg. Despite this difference, there are basic common ingredients in *ad hoc* and permanent neutrality: both give precise rights and impose precise obligations on belligerents and neutrals.

The oldest of the permanently neutral countries is Switzerland. Her neutrality was internationally recognized by the Congress of Vienna in 1815; it was reaffirmed a century later in the peace treaties at the end of World War I.[12] In becoming a member of the League of Nations, Switzerland sought to safeguard her status of permanent neutrality by seeking and obtaining relief from participating in military sanctions which could be imposed by the League.[13] But following the Italo-Ethiopian war, Switzerland returned to complete neutrality by declaring that she would not participate even in economic or other sanctions, a declaration duly noted by the League Council on May 14, 1938.[14]

Based apparently on her experience with the League of Nations, Switzerland decided not to seek membership in the United Nations. The official postwar Swiss attitude on neutrality was set forth in a statement issued by the Federal Political Department on November 26, 1954.[15] This recent official exposé of the Swiss concept of neutrality is interesting because it reflects the institution's classic characteristics. It differentiates between *ad hoc* and permanent neutrality; while the former comes into being only in case of war, the latter creates rights and imposes duties in peacetime as well. To discharge the

[12] See Art. 435 of the Treaty of Versailles, and the corresponding provisions in the treaties of St. Germain, Trianon, and Neuilly.

[13] See resolution of the Council of the League, February 13, 1920, [1920] *League of Nations Official Journal*, p. 57.

[14] 19 *League of Nations Off. J.* 369, 375, 385 (1938).

[15] Text in *Jurisprudence des autorités administratives de la Confédération*, 1954, Fac. 24, No. 1; also in 14 *Schweizerisches Jahrbuch fuer Internationales Recht* 195 (1957).

duty of nonparticipation in wars, the permanently neutral state must avoid any commitments which may lead to war, as, for example, joining any alliances, treaties of guarantees, or collective security arrangements (hence Switzerland's absence from the U.N.). According to the statement, once war occurs, the rights and duties of the permanently neutral states are identical with those of *ad hoc* neutral states as embodied in the Hague Convention of 1907, referring especially to Conventions No. V and No. XIII,[16] as well as to Convention No. I for the Pacific Settlement of International Disputes.[17] The statement makes it clear that Switzerland as a permanently neutral state considers herself bound by the classic rules of neutrality, irrespective of any changes in these rules as they affect United Nations members due to the collective security provisions of the Charter.

More significant than the continued recognition of the century-and-a-half-old neutrality of Switzerland is the creation of two permanently neutral states since the establishment of the United Nations.

Chronologically, the first of these states was Austria. Her permanent neutrality was initiated by a unilateral declaration of her government during the Berlin conference of 1954. Subsequently, during a meeting between the Austrian and Soviet governments held in Moscow in April 1955 regarding the peace treaty, the Austrian representative reaffirmed his government's intention to undertake the international obligation to practice in perpetuity a neutrality of the type maintained by Switzerland.[18] The Austrian State Treaty of May 14, 1955 [19]

[16] See footnote 1, *supra*.

[17] 36 Stat. 2199. On Swiss neutrality see D. Robert, *Etude sur la Neutralité Suisse*, (Zurich, 1950); and E. Bonjour, *Geschichte der schweizerischen Neutralität*, (2d. ed. Basel, 1965–1967).

[18] See English text of the Memorandum concerning the Results of Conversations between the Austrian and Soviet Delegations in Moscow, April 12–15, 1955, in 49 *Am. J. Int'l L., Official Documents*, 191 (1955).

[19] 6 U.S.T. 2369; T.I.A.S. 3298; 217 U.N.T.S. 223.

does not directly refer to Austria's neutrality; but the memorandum referred to above was annexed to that treaty. Therefore, the treaty itself does not constitute international recognition of Austria's neutrality unless it be argued that Austria's unilaterally declared intention for permanent neutrality was thus "incorporated" in the State Treaty—a rather far-fetched argument. Neither did the Austrian federal statute enacted on October 26, 1955 [20] change the unilateral status of Austria's neutrality. It became internationally effective only when, responding to the request addressed by the Austrian government to all governments with which it maintained diplomatic relations, the majority of those states, including the permanent members of the Security Council, gave recognition to Austria's permanent neutrality. It should be noted that Austria was subsequently admitted to membership in the United Nations. Hence, neither the appropriate United Nations organs deciding on membership nor any member deemed permanent neutrality incompatible with obligations to participate in collective security measures.[21]

Laos, already a U.N. member, declared in 1962, during the Geneva Conference on Settlement of the Laotian Question, that it had resolved "to follow the path of peace and neutrality." As in the case of Austria, this was a unilateral declaration of neutrality which was in no way binding on other states. Responding to the appeal contained in the Laotian declaration to all states, but primarily to the participants in the Geneva conference, "to recognize the sovereignty, independence, *neutrality*, unity and territorial integrity of Laos," the participating

[20] English text of the statute in 50 *Am. J. Int'l L.* 420 (1956).

[21] For a thoughtful study of permanent neutrality in general and Austria's neutrality in particular see S. Verosta, *Die dauernde Neutralität* (Vienna, 1967). On Austria's neutrality see also Chaumont, "La Neutralité de l'Autriche et les Nations Unies," 1 *Annuaire français de droit international* 151 (1955); Verdross, "Austria's Permanent Neutrality and the United Nations Organization," 50 *Am. J. Int'l L.* 61 (1956); Kunz, "Austria's Permanent Neutrality," 50 *Am. J. Int'l L.* 418 (1956).

governments, in their Declaration on the Neutrality of Laos, signed July 23, 1962, solemnly declared, "in accordance with the will of the Government and of the Kingdom of Laos . . . that they recognize and will respect in every way the sovereignty, independence, *neutrality*, unity and territorial integrity of the Kingdom of Laos." (Emphasis added.) [22] This is an unequivocal recognition of the continued viability of at least permanent neutrality and its compatibility with U.N. membership obligations. The fact that the solemn commitment made by some of the signatories of the Geneva Declaration was broken before the ink dried on it and that the neutrality of Laos was not respected as promised does not affect this conclusion.[23]

What about the practice of the United Nations and of the member states?

It should be noted that none of the great number of armed conflicts that have occurred since 1945 have been preceded by formal declarations of war. Only in two instances has a state of war been formally recognized: in the Arab-Israeli conflict and in the Indo-Pakistani war of 1965.[24] Attention may be called in this connection to another instance where neutrality seems to have survived the Charter. In the Middle East conflict the United Arab Republic, a United Nations member, operated a

[22] For the text of this Declaration see 14 U.S.T. 1104; T.I.A.S. No. 5410; 456 U.N.T.S. 301. It was signed by Burma, Cambodia, Canada, the People's Republic of China, France, India, Poland, Thailand, the Soviet Union, the United Kingdom, the United States, the Republic of Vietnam (South Vietnam), and the Democratic Republic of Vietnam (North Vietnam). Except the People's Republic of China, North and South Vietnam, all signatories were U.N. members.

[23] The U.S. view was clearly expressed in President Kennedy's statement issued on the day the Declaration was signed: "The agreement represents a solemn commitment not only by the United States but by all the other signatories to ensure a free, independent and *neutral* Laos. This can be accomplished only by full and continued observance of the agreement by all the signatories." (Emphasis added.) 47 *Dep't State Bulletin* 259 (1962).

[24] See Urs Schwarz, *Confrontation and Intervention in the Modern World* 4–5, (1970).

Prize Court, which, in its numerous decisions affecting "neutral" ships and cargo, applied the Hague Convention of 1907. The Court repeatedly asserted that its decisions conformed to international law set forth in that Convention as interpreted during World War II.[25]

The great majority of the armed conflicts in the last twenty-five years were civil wars within one nation—as, for example the Congo, the Nigerian civil war—where United Nations action under Chapter VII of the Charter was not applicable. This raises the question of how far rules of neutrality, whether in its classic sense or, possibly, with modifications, can apply in undeclared wars, or more particularly, in civil wars. Clearly, this is a practical problem to be explored by international lawyers in their endeavors to adjust neutrality laws to the realities of contemporary international society.

In considering armed conflicts across international boundaries which came before the United Nations, the records show that in no case did the Security Council render a decision that would have obligated member states (or at least some of them) to render assistance to one belligerent and to refrain from giving assistance to the other. Even in the Korean conflict, the only instance where the Security Council did unequivocally determine that an act of aggression and a breach of peace had occurred and did decree enforcement action (a decision made possible by the absence of the Soviet representative), only some and not all United Nations members participated in that action. None of the nonparticipating members—those who remained "neutral"—were charged with having violated their Charter obligations. Indeed, the Korean Armistice Agreement of July 27, 1953 provided for the establishment of a "Neutral Nations Supervisory Commission" (composed of representa-

[25] J. Trappe, "On the Jurisdiction of the Egyptian Prize Court, 1948–1960," 16 *Revue égyptienne de droit international* 60 (1960); T. D. Brown, Jr., "World War Prize Law Applied in a Limited War Situation: Egyptian Restrictions on Neutral Shipping with Israel," 50 *Minnesota L. Rev.* 849 (1966).

tives of Sweden, Switzerland, Poland, and Czechoslovakia);
"neutral nations" in this context were defined as those nations
whose combat forces had not participated in the hostilities in
Korea.[26] It may be concluded that the practice of the United
Nations and of its members does not give a conclusive answer
to the question of the compatibility of neutrality with the
Charter.

The history of U.N. endeavors to maintain or to restore
peace cannot be said to measure up to the hopes and expectations generated by the establishment of the organization
twenty-five years ago. For a variety of reasons, the Security
Council, which under the Charter is the guardian of international peace and the only United Nations organ invested with
the power of rendering binding decisions, has proved to be in
most instances ineffective and impotent. This lack of effectiveness was largely, if not exclusively, the result of the cold war
and constant disagreements among the permanent members of
the Security Council. Disregarding modern techniques used to
undermine the political independence and territorial integrity
of states by subversion and clandestine infiltration, open resort
to force across national boundaries produced at best resolutions of disapproval, censure, and exhortation (e.g., the sup-
pression of the Hungarian Revolution in 1956, the occupation
of Czechoslovakia in 1968 by the Soviet army, India's action
against Portuguese Goa, Indonesia's "confrontation" with Ma-
laysia, and United States action in the Dominican Republic).
In none of these incidents did the Security Council decree enforcement action to be obeyed by member states. And while
the "Uniting for Peace" resolution gave the General Assembly
a greater role in the preservation or restoration of peace, the
Assembly's powers, limited to recommendations, have not
been enlarged.

[26] See 29 *Dep't State Bulletin* 132 (1953). The Agreement also established a
"Neutral Nations Repatriation Commission" to supervise and assist the repatriation of prisoners of war.

In assessing the record of the United Nations in its role of maintaining and restoring peace, its successes in peace-keeping operations should be recognized. Reference is made in this connection to the Congo and Cyprus operations and to the peace-keeping force in the Middle East, which was quite effective until its withdrawal at the request of the United Arab Republic. It should also be recognized that in many areas, such as cooperation with respect to economic development, health, social and cultural matters, the United Nations and its specialized agencies have accomplished a great deal—much more than the League of Nations did. But it must be admitted that in using collective action to prevent the use or threat of force or acts of aggression and to restore peace, the record of the United Nations is thus far a meager one.

The question of whether a member state can remain neutral in case of armed conflict across international boundaries remains unresolved. In seeking to resolve it, international lawyers must take into account important changes in the scope and structure of international law.

In the first place, it must be recognized that—as already indicated—the classic concept of neutrality has been significantly affected by restrictions on the resort to force and by the slowly developing institution of collective security. The nature of the change is difficult to assess as long as United Nations members espouse conflicting views as to when resort to force constitutes a breach of the Charter. Specifically, the assertion that "wars of national liberation"—whether wars across international borders or civil wars—are not prohibited by Article 2(4) of the Charter renders the definition of war or the use or threat of force difficult, if not impossible. The same difficulty is encountered in the failure thus far to establish workable tests for determining when states resort to force in exercise of the "inherent right of self-defense." Moreover, the demonstrated weakness of collective security as envisaged in the Charter, coupled with often exaggerated insistence on sovereignty, leaves member states wide discretion in determining their obligations under the Charter. The conclusion is inevitable that until the international community is better structured and states become more aware than at present of the need to balance national interests with the interests of the community of nations, there remains a place as well as a need [27] for the institution of neutrality—admittedly with some modifications of the classic rules.

In searching for adjustment of the rules of classic neutrality to fit the contemporary stage, international lawyers must also take account of another development which has gradually occurred in this century. Even before World War II, Professor Wolfgang Friedmann called attention to the ever-growing intrusion of the state into areas and fields of activities theretofore deemed to be outside of government concern and reserved almost completely to private enterprise.[28] The assumption of state control over and often state operation of activities theretofore conducted by private individuals or corporations had a profound impact on the content of the classic rules of neutral rights and duties as laid down in the Hague Conventions of 1907. This is particularly true with respect to the provisions of Article 7 of both Hague Conventions V and XIII, which impose no duty on neutral states to prevent trade in arms and munitions of war by private enterprise. When these provisions were adopted, few governments controlled trade in war materials; perhaps none was engaged in their manufacture or trade. That situation has changed completely. In a number of countries, the manufacture of war materials

[27] Such need has been demonstrated in the establishment of the "Neutral Nations Supervisory Commission on Korea" already adverted to and by the composition of United Nations peace-keeping forces recruited almost exclusively from "neutral" (or "nonaligned") nations; and by control commissions supervising cease-fire and armistice agreements which have been manned by representatives of "neutral" governments.

[28] See Friedmann, "The Growth of State Control over the Individual and its Effect upon the Rules of International State Responsibility," 19 *British Yearbook of International Law* 118 (1938), especially 130–41.

has been taken over by the state; and in most countries the government exercises more or less strict control over the export of arms and ammunition, even if their manufacture has been left in the hands of private enterprise. Obviously, the relief of a neutral state from the duty of preventing trade in war materials by private individuals—whether nationals or alien residents in that country—no longer has justification.

Finally, international lawyers ought to consider the lessons of the last twenty-five years. None of the numerous armed conflicts during this period arose between the major powers—that is, the powers with nuclear capability. It may be assumed that while the "delicate balance of terror" is maintained, the so-called superpowers are likely to avoid direct participation in conflicts between minor or small states. They may intervene in other ways, but they are likely to refrain from using force which may lead to confrontation with another superpower. Hence, they may adopt a status somewhat akin to neutrality.

In the search for new rules of neutrality, account should be taken of Professor Jessup's suggestion some years ago that it may be desirable to recognize an intermediate status between belligerents and states that—without being neutral in the classic sense—wish to remain outside such conflict.[29] A version of his suggestion has been repeatedly advanced, particularly by spokesmen of the so-called Third World, under definitions of "nonbelligerency," "nonalignment," and "neutralism" as a new, modern form of neutrality.[30] However, what these spokesmen advocate is not a legal institution but a policy. Unlike classic neutrality, nonbelligerence, nonalignment, and neutralism do not call for reciprocity between belligerent and neutrals. The proposed policy contains no requirement for equal treatment

[29] Jessup, "Should International Law Recognize an International Status between Peace and War?" 48 *Am. J. Int'l L.* 98 (1954). See also McDougal and Feliciano, *supra* footnote 8.

[30] See, e.g., B. Jankovic, "De la neutralité classique à la conception moderne des pays non-alignés," 21 *Revue égyptienne de droit international* 809 (1965).

of both parties to the armed conflict by the nonbelligerent states, although it does imply nonparticipation.

As this brief survey shows, reformulation of the laws of war and neutrality to fit the changed and changing structure of international law is a difficult and complex task. Yet, it needs to be undertaken in order to create greater certainty and stability in the relations among nations and thereby point the road to a more peaceful world and, perhaps, induce nations to seek resolution of international conflicts by peaceful processes rather than by force. We can only hope that international lawyers everywhere will be equal to this task.

LOUIS HENKIN

The Once and the Future

Law of the Sea

PHILIP JESSUP'S doctoral dissertation [1] was devoted to confirming the effective sovereignty of coastal states in their territorial sea and their special rights in a contiguous zone beyond. He was concerned with dissipating the unrealism of those who resisted recognizing qualifications of any kind, anywhere, to "the honored concept of the freedom of the seas," "deeply rooted in international law." [2] Less than fifty years later the freedom of the seas is dishonored, uprooted, surely redefined; the claims of coastal states cry to be limited rather than confirmed; the law of the sea generally, once apparently firm and immutable, is in disarray. The principal latinisms of traditional law of the sea are not only out of contemporary international fashion; the issues they embodied have been overtaken by new interests in the seas and overwhelmed by new configurations of political forces asserting new-fashioned claims.

The changing law responds, of course, to the changing seas

LOUIS HENKIN is Hamilton Fish Professor of International Law and Diplomacy, Columbia University.
[1] *The Law of Territorial Waters and Maritime Jurisdiction* (1927).
[2] *Id.* at xxxv, 75.

of a changing world. Ever since Grotius prevailed over Selden, the traditional law has meant principally national autonomy and freedom of enterprise: the sea was a public highway for friendly transport and commerce in peace and for hostile transport, for battle, and for related purposes in war; it was a limitless source of fish and a limitless receptacle for waste. Today transport remains an important use of the sea, and freedom of navigation, subject to rules of the road, remains important law. Although the United Nations Charter has largely outlawed war, the sea retains substantial traditional military significance; it retains importance as a source of fish, though they have proven far from limitless; it accommodates more and more-varied waste. Now, however, the sea has also become a vital airway for commercial and military aviation, and the sea itself a vital base for submarine engines of war of global strategic import; now the sea provides new forms of food, and the seawater itself is becoming available for human consumption; mineral resources of the seabed are increasingly accessible to exploitation, and the waters themselves contain interesting mineral possibilities for the more distant future; there are promises of new forms of transportation and other human sojourn and activity on the seabed, on and in the sea, or on platforms rising above the sea; and the seas will be prominent in efforts to control weather and climate. Increasingly, the new uses of the sea compete with and complicate old uses; increasingly, the seas cease to appear discrete and self-contained and are recognized as part of an integrated human environment. Fishing and transportation are hampered by nuclear testing or by mineral exploitation; the disposal of nuclear and other waste threatens fish and hampers recreation and other uses of coastal sea and land, disturbs the marine ecology generally, impinges on life on land.

The new sea will bring new law, and one would be hardy to guess what students of international law will confirm as the law of the sea even a few years from now; one can only discern the trends, and crudely appraise the forces that will struggle to produce the emerging law. In the world of which the seas and its law are a part, revolutionary technology, the inescapable military and technological dominance of super-powers (whether in competition or cooperation), and the "radical" politics of new nations that yearn for modernization and dominate international institutions have modified the "sources" of international law and the forces that shape and make it. That the sea is *res communis* everywhere for all purposes is effectively rejected as, daily, coastal states reach farther and deeper into the sea for more and more purposes. That in the seas at large *res communis* implies "freedom of the seas" is increasingly challenged; in wide border-seas where the claims of coastal states are disputed, and beyond, where none would dare assert national jurisdiction, the struggle is on between competing national interests, between state and community, between freedom and responsibility, between laissez-faire and regulation, between competitive enterprise and cooperation for welfare.

I.

A principal though variable modifier of the law of the sea is and will be the reach of the coastal state. Coastal states claim exclusive rights to resources in coastal zones; they assert jurisdiction to regulate various uses by others; they pretend to both monopoly and jurisdiction, and more, when they assert full territorial sovereignty (subject only to "innocent" navigation).

How the law of the coastal sea arrived where it is, pointed toward where it is going, is neither mysterious nor surprising. Coastal states began long ago to nibble at the "commonage" of the seas and its freedom for common uses—from fear of who might come against their shores by sea, from concern to keep the wars of others at some distance, from desire to retain for their own the most accessible fish, from interest in preventing violation of their territorial sovereignty through the smuggling of things and people across their sea frontiers. In time, wishes became claims to jurisdiction, and jurisdictions hardened and expanded into sovereignty. A band of sea became "territorial," and the width of that band slowly expanded. The now-enlarged territory, in turn, required special jurisdictions in contiguous areas for its protection; these contiguous zones, too, grew in size, and the purposes for which coastal states claimed jurisdiction there proliferated.

In our day coastal state jurisdiction crept—or galloped—into the seas in other ways and for other reasons. As technology made possible new uses, and old uses farther from shore, coastal states were in the best position to exploit them and asserted legal rights to do so, while others perceived no immediate interest or did not succeed in challenging the claims of the coastal states. In the most famous and seminal instance, President Truman's claims to the resources of the continental shelf launched "instant customary law," even before the International Law Commission proposed it for codification and the Geneva Conference of 1958 legislated it in the Convention on the Continental Shelf. Carelessly, that Convention fostered additional expansions: the coastal state was given also exclusive rights to sedentary living resources; it was effectively given control of scientific research on the shelf and authority in regard to navigation above the shelf; and the rights of coastal states under the Convention were extended to all "islands," indiscriminately.

What the law gave to coastal states inspired them to claim more. The Convention recognized sovereign rights in the seabed for the purposes of extracting its natural resources; some soon asserted full sovereign rights in that seabed for all purposes. As technology promised access to resources beyond the geological continental shelf, some exploited (and, I believe, distorted) ambiguity in the 1958 Convention to claim rights not only in the geological shelf, not only in seabed "adjacent," near to the coast, but in the entire continental margin (regardless of extent) out to the deep ocean basin. Of course, coastal states insisted on the need to take measures on and above the shelf to protect their mining activities; it was only a step to claim the right to establish defense installations generally. Coastal states were entitled to exclude mining activities of other states; but some resisted all "intrusion" by other states, even inspection in support of international agreement to disarm the seabed. States had to apply their laws to govern the exploration and exploitation of resources; it was natural to extend the jurisdiction of their laws generally.

Other coastal states, not blessed with continental extensions rich in minerals, had no direct interest in a wide legal continental shelf or in comprehensive authority over it, but they learned from those who did, and bettered their instruction. They could not see why the seabed and its resources should be governed differently from the superjacent water and its resources, why their needs (as they saw them) did not entitle them to analogous rights: for example, wide, exclusive fishing zones and even wider fish-conservation areas, air-defense identification zones, antipollution zones, even extravagant zones for all purposes, i.e., extravagant territorial sea. (While the boldest claims will probably not survive, the 12-mile contiguous zone established in 1958 is being effectively translated into a 12-mile territorial sea, partly in the hope of keeping it from growing still larger.)

The press of coastal state jurisdiction has been ineluctable. Increasingly, in coastal areas the claims of freedom and of "commonage" have few voices, and traditional legal doctrine is given little heed or hearing. Today, the beginnings and impulses of coastal state expansionism are forgotten, and its presumptions, one might say, are reversed. The rights of coastal states are ceasing to be exceptions carved from the public domain to be jealously resisted and confined; rather, for some

and growing distance from shore, the seas are not free, and
common interests survive, if at all, by grace of the coastal
state. Indeed, the expansionist claims of coastal states have
begun to acquire jurisprudential underpinnings. Proponents of
coastal state expansion on the seabed, for example, have taken
to quoting the opinion of the International Court of Justice in
the *North Sea Continental Shelf Cases*. The Court said:

. . . what the Court entertains no doubt is the most fundamental of
all the rules of law relating to the continental shelf, enshrined in
Article 2 of the 1958 Geneva Convention, though quite independent of it—namely that the rights of the coastal State in respect to
the area of the continental shelf that constitutes a natural prolongation of its land territory into and under the sea exist *ipso
facto* and *ab initio*, by virtue of its sovereignty over the land, and
as an extension of it in an exercise of sovereign rights for the purpose of exploring the sea-bed and exploiting its natural resources.
In short, there is here an inherent right.

and later:

What confers the *ipso jure* title which international law attributes
to the coastal State in respect of its continental shelf, is the fact
that the submarine areas concerned may be deemed to be actually
part of the territory over which the coastal State already has
dominion—in the sense that, although covered with water, they
are a prolongation or continuation of that territory, an extension of
it under the sea.[3]

This, some argue, supports the right of the coastal state to all
the "natural prolongation" of its territory—not merely the geological shelf, not merely as much of it as is "adjacent," near the
coast, but the entire submerged continental landmass, regardless of its extent. In time, one may expect, this opinion will be
said to support exclusive rights for purposes other than mining, perhaps to complete territorial sovereignty over that
seabed.

The argument, I am satisfied, is a distortion. Surely the

[3] [1969] *ICJ Reports* 1, at 22, 31.

Court was not suggesting a general principle that the "natural prolongation" of a state's territory *ipso facto* belongs to it without acquisition by one of the methods recognized in law. Neither was it suggesting such a principle for "natural prolongation" under the sea. That the submerged land mass was a "natural prolongation" of the continents was, of course, known to the ancients, but until 1945 few suggested that the coastal state had any more rights in it than anyone else; the Truman Proclamation which launched the modern customary law of the continental shelf gave the coastal state only limited rights and only in the geological shelf; in the deliberations of the International Law Commission and in the Convention as drafted and as later adopted, the coastal state was given rights only as regards resources, only in "submarine areas adjacent [i.e., near] the coast."

The Court's dictum purported only to restate the law of the continental shelf and intended only what is provided in Article 2(3) of the 1958 Convention: "The rights of the coastal state over the continental shelf do not depend on occupation, effective or notional, or on any express proclamation." It expressed one of the reasons for the contemporary doctrine giving the coastal state special rights in the coastal seabed; it said nothing about how far they reach. Natural prolongation is a basis for rights only to the extent and for the purposes given by the modern customary law of the continental shelf and by the 1958 Convention. Perhaps, indeed, the Court considered that only the continental shelf (not the whole of the submerged land mass) was a "natural prolongation"; in any event its statement was expressly limited to "the area of the continental shelf," and other statements by the Court suggest that the coastal state's rights are limited to seabed that is "adjacent," near, as narrowly conceived.

If extravagant claims to the seabed by coastal states have flimsy legal legs, their instruction, too, has been bettered by coastal states with other, broader interests. Without distinguishing between mineral resources and other resources, between right to resources and general sovereign authority to govern, between seabed and sea, Latin American governments have declared, again at Lima in August 1970, "as common principles of the law of the Sea":

1. The inherent right of the coastal State to explore, conserve and exploit the natural resources of the sea adjacent to its coast and the soil and subsoil thereof, likewise of the Continental Shelf and its subsoil, in order to promote the maximum development of its economy and to raise the level of living of its people;
2. The right of the coastal State to establish the limits of its maritime sovereignty or jurisdiction in accordance with reasonable criteria, having regard to its geographical, geological and biological characteristics, and the need to make rational use of its resources;
3. The right of the coastal State to take regulatory measures for the aforementioned purposes, applicable in the areas of its maritime sovereignty or jurisdiction. . . .[4]

We have then, apparently, the startling assertion that the law permits a coastal state to reach into the sea as far as it likes for any national purpose, subject only, at best, to the requirement that its criteria be "reasonable."

How such jurisprudence and the claims built on it will fare remains to be seen. Some law will result from the actions and inactions of governments, and some will be made by agreement. Although the "unanimity principle" is hardly dead and international law is not made by majority vote, numbers will weigh heavily, and the emerging law will be a vector of the complex interplay of national forces and international alignments and configurations in which different sea-interests will be at stake and in which the law and politics of the sea will be accommodated to other law and other political interests. *Inter multa alia* it will reflect the balance of advantage as seen by

[4] 10 *Int'l Legal Materials* 207, 208 (Jan. 1971).

important states (or groups of states), their influence in the sea, in the international legal system, and in the international system generally; it will reflect too, one may hope, some national self-restraint and the restraints of established law.

The coastal states will surely have a substantial say as regards the law governing the substantial portions of the sea that are plausibly within reach of some coast of a continent or island. Many coastal states sit along or astride strategic straits and airlanes or rich resource fields; even small states so happily situated have effective "possession" and can spread the sacred mantle of "territorial sovereignty" far from shore, and even the powerful are substantially at their mercy. (The use of force, even to assert the freedom of the seas, is no longer legally or politically acceptable, though some states might be tempted to resort to various forms of intervention to help assure that key coastal states have friendly governments.) But coastal states *qua* coastal states will not have it all their own way in making and remaking the law of the sea, even as regards areas that are admittedly or plausibly "coastal." Although most of the world's states have some seacoast, contiguity to the sea, for many of them, is not a primary or dominant focus of interest, and other "qualities" throw up other interests and domestic political forces tugging toward a different law. In the end, for a notable example, powerful states with extensive coasts (in different ways and degrees, the United States, Russia, China, Japan) might well see their dominant interests in maximum freedom in a maximum of sea, for military uses, for navigation, for fishing, eventually even for mining, and might forego extensive claims as coastal states in order to deny such claims to others.

Even so, were the issue only between maximum monopoly or regulatory authority for coastal states and maximum freedom for other powers, the "sovereign" claims of a few, insistent coastal states might largely prevail. But there is a growing recognition of a common interest in the resources and in the uses of the international sea, and if some coastal states will nonetheless prefer to aggrandize their particular claims in coastal zones at the expense of the common sea (and of their share in it), others—including many coastal states—will prefer the common interest and resist coastal states that would invade it.

What the law will become I do not know. I venture one safe guess, and one more daring guess, or hope. There will be some disposition to fix a single boundary between national jurisdiction and the "international sea" for all levels—seabed, sea, air —and all purposes. But the single line would tend to be the highest denominator common to coastal state claims for different purposes, and would render as much as a quarter or more of the seas (plus large, additional regions adjacent to islands) the private domain of particular states. This, I expect, will be unacceptable and the emerging law will retain, in addition to a somewhat enlarged territorial sea, varied zones giving coastal states different rights in areas of different size for different purposes.

Other distinctions in the law, however, might disappear or be modified. There might emerge, for example, no distinction —or less distinction—in principle between national rights in seabed and national rights in the sea and sea air: both seabed and sea will be subject to national sovereignty or authority up to some point (or points) but neither will be beyond. And a coastal state's right to resources will not turn on whether they are resources of the seabed or of the sea: despite historical, economic, and technical differences relevant to law and to politics, coastal states might achieve a monopoly in fish as well as minerals. On the other hand, there will perhaps emerge a clearer, sharper distinction between a coastal state's reach for purposes of claiming a monopoly of resources and its reach for regulating other uses of the sea by other users. The two kinds of coastal state authority are different in origin, in principle, and in conception; and there is no reason why they must be congruent in extent. The area of a coastal states' monopoly in resources is developing law, reflecting largely economic considerations and the politics they promote. Regulation of another's uses which threaten some recognized coastal interest corresponds to traditional notions that a state may protect itself against acts that have effect on its territory, even if they originate in the territory of another; and surely the "freedom" of the offending state on the seas is not greater than in its own territory. If as regards injury originating on another's territory, the victim state generally has been limited to compensation by the tortfeasor, at sea it may also take some preventive measures: that is the concept of the contiguous zone. The question has been how far out it may reach and in what ways. Canada's claim in 1970 to a 100-mile antipollution zone in the Arctic, for example, was questionable only as regards the large area of high seas in which it claimed to regulate and the stringency and intrusiveness of the measures it proposed. (If a coastal state can unilaterally determine the specifications for tankers which may ply its contiguous zone, it can effectively determine tanker-construction specifications for the world, and inconsistent specifications by different states could cripple an industry.) But unless the community of states effectively regulates offending uses to protect coastal states as well as the commonage of the seas, the coastal state will acquire extensive, intensive rights to regulate them.

II.

Beyond the reach of coastal states, the sea has been and remains free and common. This is as true of the seabed as of the sea and the sea air: although some suggested long ago that in principle the seabed was subject to national appropriation, and some would have interpreted the 1958 Convention on the Continental Shelf as dividing up all of the bed of all of the seas among the coastal states that border them, the states of the world, in the U.N. General Assembly, have affirmed that there is an area of seabed beyond national jurisdiction. This implies that coastal-state rights depend on some criterion, presumably "adjacency" (however defined). At some depth of water, then, some point of geographic change, some distance from coasts of continents and islands, no coastal state is relevant, and the vast bed, the large seas, and their air retain their commonage.

In the past, the law of the sea-beyond-national-jurisdiction was free in both respects I have distinguished: its resources— fish—were free for the taking (subject to historic rights and special agreements); and activities there were regulated only by the rules of international law that applied generally (the laws of status, nationality, tort, property, contract, war), by their special maritime applications, and by accepted rules of the road and other accommodations to navigation. (There were also, of course, the interferences with freedom that inhere in competitive or conflicting uses, and occasionally a state claimed the right to launch a special use which interfered substantially though temporarily with the rights of others, e.g., nuclear testing.)

In future, no doubt, the seas will remain *res communis,* but the import of that concept is already changing. That the sea is common property will probably no longer mean that all of its resources are free to the first taker; *res communis* also will no longer mean laissez-faire but will begin to require meaningful regulation of some uses to protect other users and other uses, of activities at sea to protect interests on land. New international institutions of a new kind are coming. As the sea is better integrated into the human environment, the law of the sea will be better integrated into a total international law.

As regards the surely international sea, however, the forces for change are less strong and less sure than for the coastal sea. The freedom of the coastal sea has been pressed hard by particular coastal states with particular interests adverse to a law of free-for-all, and other states have been unwilling or unable to resist. The freedom of the international sea, on the other hand, does not adversely affect particular interests of states able to help themselves. Many states have yet to achieve a common perception that free enterprise permits a few to take resources that should belong to all, that laissez-faire permits some to use the seas in ways that interfere unduly with uses by others. Such a perception, perhaps easy to achieve, will be difficult to maintain effectively among the complex forces of the international system, against the traditional law and traditional attitudes toward the law and toward the sea; it will be less difficult for a few to resist it.

Still, the change is coming. It will begin on the seabed and with its resources. With little dissent, the nations of the world in the U.N. General Assembly have declared the seabed beyond national jurisdiction to be "the common heritage of mankind." The import of that phrase is far from agreed upon and is yet to be hammered out at diplomatic tables in hard bargaining involving other sea issues in a large international context; it will not, I believe, remain mere rhetoric. It will mean at least that some revenue from the resources of the seabed will go to common institutions and inure to the benefit of many nations, including those themselves incapable of exploiting the resources and even those that do not have access to the sea. It will perhaps mean also some voice for nations generally, through international institutions, in governing the exploitation and disposition of these resources. New laws and institutions will limit the enterprise of those with technology and capital, regulate mineral exploitation, perhaps control its impact on world markets in competing minerals.

The future law of the international seabed will hang on the delimitation of coastal state authority. For the willingness of some developed states to limit their freedom to appropriate the resources of the "international" seabed, and to accept international authority and institutions there, might have to be bought with assurances of freedom for other uses everywhere, outside narrow coastal zones. And the willingness of many coastal states to forego monopoly in large coastal areas will be determined by what lies for them in the international seabed beyond. For the resources of the seabed, in particular, the issue is no longer between monopoly for coastal states and the right of a few states with capital and competence to grab the resources in free competitive enterprise. The promise of great wealth from the seabed, immediately realizable only in coastal areas, pits coastal states against "less-developed states" generally (including the landlocked) that seek revenue and political authority in the only environment which plausibly offers them. Developing states, even if they are coastal, will have to see whether they might not fare better with a share in the common pot than with exclusive rights off their own coasts only; and many might decide to align behind that law which limits coastal states, so as to leave the largest possible common pot under meaningful common authority and institutions. (The division of the national pot from the common pot and national from international authority might be bridged by some small, hybrid, shared intermediate zone.)

It is not only the resources of the seabed but also the seabed itself that has been declared the common heritage of mankind, and, in time, some will be disposed to subject other uses of the seabed to international authority. But, resources apart, there is little incentive for most nations to battle for authority in the seabed, and the few Big Powers which have the capacity and interest to use the seabed will long resist interference with their freedom of action there. The United States and the Soviet Union have adhered to the Treaty on Prohibiting the Emplacement of Nuclear Weapons on the Sea-bed and Ocean Floor and have undertaken to negotiate toward additional agreements "for the prevention of an arms race" on the ocean floor, but they will surely resist restrictions on military uses of the sea floor which they deem important to their strategic competition. As elsewhere, the Soviet Union will resist meaningful international institutions and authority.

Only the seabed has been declared the "common heritage of mankind," but that formula is only a variant, contemporary vulgate for *res communis,* and there is no apparent reason why the seas (and their air) are or should be less of a common heritage. International authority and institutions for the resources of the seabed will, in time, suggest them for those of the seas as well. The principal resource—fish—indeed cries for cooperative attention: there is critical need for conservation measures, for cooperation in research, for agreements and machinery to improve efficiency and eliminate duplication of effort and capital, to prevent conflict and collision. But, perhaps because it has always been otherwise, fish are not early candidates for "internationalization," for global rules, programs, and institutions, and the years ahead promise only more of the existing network of national regulation by coastal states and by selective bilateral or regional arrangements.

If the traditions of "free enterprise" are likely to continue as regards exploitation of the resources of the common sea, those of laissez-faire will resist authoritative regulation of some other uses. The major military uses, surely, will remain uncontrolled. Even in a millennial "general and complete disarmament," the weapons and military vehicles of the seas will be last to go; in our day, the strategic balance hangs on submarine weapons, and neither the U.S. nor the USSR will think of limiting them. Other uses, however, will probably not remain forever free. There is a reasonable prospect for new law to protect the sea environment and the sea-land-air environment generally. Contemporary efforts have been small and primitive, in part because conferences and institutions have been dominated by shipping states which have not been eager to increase costs and assume other burdens for the benefit of coastal states or of the common interest in the sea. Canada has responded by unilateral regulation in a wide coastal zone and other coastal states may be moved to use their control over "throats" of navigational highways to compel shippers to greater responsibility. States whose fishing at sea suffers from pollution by shippers or other depositors of waste will also begin to demand regulation and might even assert legal claims against identified polluters. Might *res communis* give to any and every state a claim against a polluter on behalf of the common interest in the sea? Effectively, then, the choice will be not between regulation by coastal states and the right of others to carry on at will, but between unilateral regulation by coastal states and common regulation that would accommodate the interests of different users as well as those of coastal states.

The future seas will remain "common," but the common sea will be reduced by coastal state appropriations and its uses limited by proliferating coastal state regulations in an enlarged "contiguous zone." Beyond the reach of coastal states the commonness of the sea will be not one of full freedom for preemptive enterprise, or for other national autonomy, but one of increasing regulation. Control, of course, does not promise (or threaten) supranational institutions, and surely none governed by majorities. And control will not come easily. Neither the reach of coastal states in the near seas nor that of the rich and powerful in distant seas will give way early or easily. The conference on the law of the sea tentatively scheduled for 1973, if it takes place and if it achieves agreement, is not likely to harness powerful and divergent forces. There or elsewhere, we are likely to get some rules and even some institutions governing the resources of the seabed. That will be a beginning. Like the law of particular nations, like the law of nations generally, the future law of the sea will have less particular monopoly, less national autonomy, less conflict and ad-hoc accommodation, and more regulation, more cooperation, and more concern for the general welfare.

EDUARDO JIMÉNEZ DE ARÉCHAGA

International Responsibility of States for Acts of the Judiciary

IN THE *Barcelona Traction* [1] case before the International Court of Justice, both the applicant and the respondent states submitted extensive written and oral pleadings dealing with the various factual and legal issues directly or indirectly related to the merits of the case. The question in issue concerned, as is well known, the alleged responsibility of Spain toward Belgium, mainly on account of various acts and omissions of Spain's judicial organs.

The International Court of Justice did not enter into the merits of the dispute, disposing of the case on the basis of a preliminary objection joined to the merits. However, the written and oral pleadings in that case, among many issues of perhaps secondary or ephemeral interest, contain a substantial discussion on the fundamental principles governing the international responsibility of states on account of acts of their judicial organs.

EDUARDO JIMÉNEZ DE ARÉCHAGA is a Judge on the International Court of Justice.

[1] Case Concerning the Barcelona Traction, Light and Power Company, Limited (New Application: 1962) (Belgium v. Spain) Second Phase, [1970] *ICJ Reports* 1, IX *Int'l Legal Materials* 227 (March 1970).

A summary of that discussion may be of interest for international law, in view of the number and variety of acts and omissions of the Spanish judiciary about which Belgium complained and the intensity of a debate which was pursued by distinguished international lawyers in four successive written pleadings and in two rounds of oral presentations. All this afforded the occasion for an analysis in depth of the various grounds upon which state responsibility for acts of its judiciary may arise, as well as of the different conditions governing the establishment of such a responsibility.

It may even be possible to discern, as one of the most interesting features of the pleadings and oral proceedings before the International Court, that in the final stages of the proceedings, the contending parties, while remaining in complete opposition as to the facts and their respective interpretations of them, gradually but to an increasing extent reached common ground on the legal plane as to the correct definition of the various categories of grounds determining such responsibility and as to the legal principles and conditions applicable to each of those grounds.

Professor H. Rolin, the distinguished international lawyer who was leading Counsel for Belgium, gave cogent expression to this aspect of what would otherwise appear as a fruitless discussion, when he stated in his oral reply: ". . . in my opinion, the whole point of a case such as this is to show up the gaps and shortcomings of certain approaches and to induce theorists to adapt their writings better to the very diverse realities which only practice brings to light." [2]

[2] C.R. [Verbatim Record] of the hearing of June 26, 1969, English translation (1), p. 15. The case was conducted almost entirely in French: the translation used in this and subsequent quotations is the unofficial translation prepared by the Registry for the use of the Court, which is not published in the Court's *Pleadings* series.

THE NOTION OF DENIAL OF JUSTICE
IN THE BELGIAN MEMORIAL

In the Belgian Memorial, as in the diplomatic correspondence preceding the submission to the Court, all acts of the Spanish authorities complained of by Belgium were lumped together under the broad description of "denial of justice," or rather, a "series of denials of justice." This included not only acts or omissions of judicial organs but even those attributed to Spanish governmental and administrative authorities; one of the sections of the Belgian Reply bore the somewhat surprising title of "the deliberate denials of justice committed by the administrative authorities." [3]

The Belgian Memorial classified "the various forms which the denial of justice took in particular instances" in three categories: first, the "usurpation of jurisdiction" resulting from the adjudication in bankruptcy of a Canadian company in Spain; second, the "formal denial of justice"; and third, "the substantive denial of justice." [4]

A formal denial of justice exists, according to the Memorial, "whenever a litigant is refused access to the courts, whether a decision concerning him has been taken without his having been able to secure a hearing, or if he is unable to bring his complaints in respect of a measure by which he is prejudiced before any court, or if when a remedy has been sought in a competent court investigation of the matter is indefinitely postponed by the court." [5]

The substantive denial of justice is defined as existing "whenever a litigant is the subject of discriminatory or arbitrary acts on the part of the judicial authorities of a foreign State, in such a way that the judgment or judgments delivered against him are of a manifestly unjust nature." [6]

[3] Section VIII, Subsection (1) and Memorial para. 332.
[4] Memorial, para. 332.   [5] Memorial, para. 343.
[6] Memorial, para. 353.

It is understandable that the claimant state in a case involving international responsibility would wish to give as wide a meaning as possible to the expression "denial of justice." After all, this is one of those "magic formulas" that like "natural law," have always added strength and prestige to any claim. It was said in Mexico, at a time when claims of international responsibility were frequent, that a denial of justice is for the United States whatever we do in Mexico which is not to the liking of the Department of State.

The distinction introduced in the Belgian Memorial between formal and substantive denial of justice also constitutes an ingenious means of enlarging that notion, so as to bring under a banner which enjoys considerable traditional prestige any acts of a foreign judicial organ which have given rise to complaint.

THE NOTION OF DENIAL OF JUSTICE
IN THE SPANISH COUNTER-MEMORIAL

The Spanish Counter-Memorial did not accept the broad notion of denial of justice advocated in the Belgian Memorial, and suggested that the use of the term should be confined to "a specific breach of the obligation imposed upon a State by general international law to give foreigners access to its courts and not to subject them to absolutely unwarrantable delays." [7]

The Spanish Counter-Memorial contended that this was the proper meaning of the term as defined by mediaeval writers and taken up by Grotius, Vattel, and Anzilotti: a denial of justice only exists if a foreigner has not obtained free access to the courts for the defense of his rights or when undue and inexcusable delays occur in rendering judgment.[8]

---

[7] Counter-Memorial, chap. IV, para. 1.

[8] Counter-Memorial, chap. IV, paras. 2 and 95. For a more detailed explanation of the origin and scope of this notion see *Manual of International Law*, chap. 9, para. 12, 553–54 (Soerensen ed. 1968) and bibliography cited therein.

The Spanish Counter-Memorial also observed that the Belgian Memorial sought to classify under the head "formal denial of justice" certain complaints to which even the concept of denial of justice, properly so called, could not be applied. What the Belgian Government claimed under this ground was not that Barcelona Traction or its subsidiaries were denied access to the Spanish courts, nor that there were delays in giving decisions on their applications and appeals. The Belgian Memorial complained under this head of the content of the decisions, of the rejection of certain appeals and applications on the basis of lack of the particular applicant's *jus standi* in bankruptcy proceedings, and of alleged discriminatory measures. But, as Spain observed, there can be no denial of justice when the courts have taken a decision on a foreigner's claim, even if they declare the claim to be inadmissible on grounds of lack of a right of action.[9] In those instances there could be *injustice rendue* but not *ex hypothesi, justice déniée*.

It was further observed in the Counter-Memorial that such an expansion of the concept of denial of justice as to render it synonymous with the notion of "due process of law," advocated by certain United States writers, had been discarded in authoritative arbitral awards and was deliberately rejected by the states present at the Conference for the Codification of International Law held at The Hague in 1930.[10]

The position assumed by the Spanish Counter-Memorial did not signify the adoption of what is currently described as the "Latin American" doctrine, propounded, for instance, by Guerrero, which rejects all international responsibility for judicial acts except in case of denial of justice properly so called. The Spanish Counter-Memorial did not consider that state responsibility for judicial acts was wholly confined within the strict

[9] Counter-Memorial, chap. IV, paras. 2 and 87.

[10] Counter-Memorial, chap. IV, para. 88. For a more detailed examination of these authorities see again *Manual of International Law*, chap. 9, para. 12, 555–57.

notion of denial of justice. On the contrary, it admitted that it could also arise on other grounds, but contended that these had to be carefully defined.

THE THREE GROUNDS OF STATE RESPONSIBILITY ON ACCOUNT OF JUDICIAL ACTS PROPOSED BY SPAIN AND BELGIUM'S REACTION TO THEM

The Spanish written pleadings proposed a tripartite classification of the grounds upon which state responsibility may be incurred by reason of acts of the judicial authorities:
   (1) a decision of a municipal court clearly incompatible with a rule of international law;
   (2) a denial of justice properly so called;
   (3) in exceptional circumstances, an erroneous decision of a municpal court (*mal jugé*).
We will examine these three grounds and the Belgian reaction to each one of them in its further pleadings and oral presentations before the Court.

A DECISION CLEARLY INCOMPATIBLE WITH A RULE OF INTERNATIONAL LAW. The first category is designed to take account of municipal judicial decisions which clearly and directly contravene rules of international law, such as a judicial decision violating the immunities and privileges of a diplomat or of a foreign state. It is obvious that in these cases state responsibility arises *ipso facto,* regardless of the subjective attitude of the judges.

According to the Counter-Memorial, the first accusation of the Belgian Memorial, that concerning an alleged usurpation of jurisdiction, while unfounded as to the facts and the law, belonged in this first category.[11]

The Belgian Reply accepted explicitly that the alleged "usurpation of jurisdiction" fell into this first category and

---

[11] Counter-Memorial, Chap. IV, para. 5.

therefore had to be excluded from its original notion of "denial of justice." The Reply, in this retreat from its previous position, recalled statements made at the 1930 Codification Conference by President Basdevant and Sir Eric Beckett to the effect that it was necessary to exclude from the concept of denial of justice cases where a judge exceeds his authority according to international law (as in the *Costa Rica Packet* case) [12] or commits any direct breach of a rule of international law.[13]

THE DENIAL OF JUSTICE PROPERLY SO CALLED AND ITS NONAPPLICATION TO ADMINISTRATIVE AUTHORITIES. A second change in the Belgian attitude, which represented a further convergence in the points of view presented by the parties on the purely theoretical plane, was the exclusion from the notion of denial of justice of any acts of the Spanish administrative or governmental authorities.

This was announced in the oral hearings by Professor Rolin, who admitted that the expression "the deliberate denials of justice committed by the administrative authorities" employed in the Reply.

. . . is not very satisfactory for various reasons, on the one hand because it appears preferable not to use the term "denials of justice" in this connection but to reserve it for failures to observe the rules relating to the administration of justice with regard to foreigners.[14]

Professor Rolin maintained the Belgian complaints against the Spanish administrative authorites but based them on the concepts of "abuse of rights" and "misuse of powers," leaving aside in this respect the notion of "denial of justice." So, while the accusations and counter-accusations remained unchanged,

[12] Paper relating to the arbitration in the case of the "Costa Rica Packet." Great Britain Foreign Office, May 1897, Command No. 8428. See also H. A. v. Karnabeek, *De "Costa Rica packet" arbitrage* (Utrecht 1900).

[13] Reply, paras. 444 and 446.

[14] C.R., hearing of April 16, 1969, English translation, 3.

a further consensus was reached in the field of legal theory and terminology.

EXCEPTIONAL CHARACTER OF THE INTERNATIONAL RESPONSIBIL-ITY WHICH MAY RESULT FROM AN ERRONEOUS JUDICIAL DECISION *(Mal Jugé)*. As indicated above, the Spanish written pleadings admitted that in exceptional circumstances international responsibility may arise from an erroneous municipal judgment *(mal jugé)*.

The Spanish Counter-Memorial observed that this third category must by its nature have a very exceptional character because as a rule a state does not incur responsibility toward foreigners for judgments of its courts which are merely erroneous, since no state can guarantee for the benefit of private individuals, be they foreigners or its own nationals, that its courts are infallible.

The Spanish Counter-Memorial stated in this respect:

There is no international obligation requiring a State to guarantee that foreigners will not be victims of decisions by its judicial organs which are merely erroneous from the standpoint of municipal law. At the Conference for the Codification of International Law at The Hague in 1930, Professor Basdevant stated, without being contradicted: "Everybody agrees that an error on the part of a judge is not enough to involve a State's responsibility. That view is in harmony with practice and with the decisions of international courts." [15]

These fundamental considerations were expressly agreed to by Belgian Counsel in the oral proceedings. Professor Rolin stated to this effect:

Underlying the distinction proposed by the Spanish Government there is undoubtedly an idea which is correct. It is true that errors committed by national courts in the verification of the facts submitted to them or in the application of municipal law do not in

---

[15] Counter-Memorial, chap. IV, para 3.

general involve international responsibility and that it is not the business of international courts to revise the judicial decisions of municipal courts and tribunals.[16]

CONDITIONS REQUIRED FOR A STATE
TO BE RESPONSIBLE FOR ERRONEOUS
JUDICIAL DECISIONS (*Mal Jugé*)

The Spanish Counter-Memorial admitted that there have been cases in which a state was held to be internationally responsible as a result of a judicial decision in breach of municipal law; but such exceptional findings have been justified on the basis of the fact that in these particular cases there was not a simple error (*mal jugé*) but a gross, inexcusable, deliberate, and malicious error. He added that the decisions to this effect have stressed that a state is only responsible if the decisions complained of have been given or confirmed by the highest court which could have been seized.[17]

The Counter-Memorial thus indicated, from the standpoint of the teachings of writers and of judicial precedents, the cumulative requirements which must be satisfied for a state to be responsible on this account. These requirements are as follows:

(1) the decision complained of must constitute a flagrant and inexcusable violation of municpal law;

(2) the decision must be one of a court of last resort, all remedies available under municipal law having been exhausted;

(3) a subjective factor of bad faith and discriminatory intention on the part of the courts must have been present.[18]

The initial reaction of the Belgian Reply to the Spanish point of view was to consider it as "a mere quibble" and ex-

[16] C.R., hearing of April 16, 1969, C.R. 69/2, English translation, 20.
[17] Counter-Memorial, chap. IV, para.
[18] Counter-Memorial, chap. IV, para. 106.

amine it under the title of "questions of terminology." The Reply stated:

For once it is admitted that there exist international obligations affecting the actions of the judiciary other than those implicit in what the Spanish Government styles denial of justice proper—and their existence is explicitly admitted in the Counter-Memorial—it is irrelevant whether the greach of them is or is not called substantive or material denial of justice.[19]

However, this is not merely a terminological question. From a practical point of view, describing a complaint against a judicial authority as a "denial of justice" (either formal or substantive) is a very different matter from presenting it as an erroneous decision which, in order to give rise to international responsibility, must fulfil the three requirements above indicated. According to the latter view, the claimant must show that there has been, beyond any doubt, a violation of municipal law, that local remedies have been exhausted, and that the judicial authorities were motivated by ill-will or malicious intent toward the foreigner.

On the contrary, if the qualification of "denial of justice" is applied and accepted, that would imply an *ipso facto* liability, regardless of the question of intent and of the exhaustion of local remedies. When a denial of justice properly so called has been incurred, there is no sense in asking for further proof of the intent of the agent, which is taken for granted in so serious a violation; and normally, the foreigner is not expected to exhaust the local remedies offered by the very jurisdiction which has committed the denial or delay of justice.

What was of importance, therefore, in the Belgian Reply was, on the pretext that this was a mere quibble, the abandonment to its fate of the suggested distinction between formal and substantive denial of justice.

The Reply explains, rather apologetically, that:

19 Reply, para. 448.

This terminology is, as it happens, borrowed from a recent treatise on international law and appears to render fairly well the characteristics of the two kinds of breach. Even so, it need hardly be said that the Belgian Government attaches no importance to its adoption by the Court.[20]

In the oral proceedings it is possible to find in the statements of Belgian Counsel remarks which reveal or imply a certain degree of acceptance of the theoretical basis proposed in the Spanish written pleadings.

Thus, after recalling that "errors committed by national courts . . . do not in general involve international responsibility," Professor Rolin went on to say:

The only time when this is not so is when there has been a gross and manifest error which has given rise to grave injustice, and that condition certainly deserves to be considered as one much stricter than those which come into play in the case of *denials of justice in the proper meaning of the term*. [Italics added.] [21]

Professor Rolin further stated:

. . . one may adopt, of the Spanish observations, their correct starting-point making a distinction between the Belgian complaints which the Court is entirely free to examine and those the examination of which is subject to strict conditions.[22]

The latter category would comprise, in Professor Rolin's view, "gross and manifest errors in the application of municipal law." [23]

INDIVIDUAL ANALYSIS OF THE THREE CONDITIONS FOR STATE RESPONSIBILITY ON ACCOUNT OF ERRONEOUS JUDGMENTS

What is even more revealing is Belgium's tacit acceptance of the contentions advanced by the Spanish Government, re-

[20] Reply, para. 448.   [21] C.R. 69/2, April 16, 1969, p. 20.
[22] *Id.*, at p. 21.   [23] *Id.*

sulting from detailed discussion of each of the three requirements indicated as necessary for the establishment of an
international responsibility.

FLAGRANT AND INEXCUSABLE VIOLATION OF MUNICIPAL LAW.
The first condition—the necessary existence of a flagrant and
inexcusable breach of municipal law—was not really disputed
by the Belgian Government. It confined itself to saying that
it is hard to see why, if a breach of municipal law is deliberate
or is committed in bad faith, it must also be flagrant and inexcusable.[24] And yet the reason is plain. For it is unanimously
agreed that in this subject there is one important presumption:
that municipal judicial decisions are in conformity with both
municipal and international law. The result of this presumption is that the onus of proof is on the claimant state to
demonstrate that the acts of judicial organs are in violation
of municipal or international law. The presumption also implies that in case of doubt, or in the absence of satisfactory
proof, contested decisions must be considered to be in conformity with law. As Vattel rightly said, "in all cases open to
doubt a sovereign should not entertain the complaints of his
subjects against a foreign tribunal." [25]

And in order to determine whether the judicial decision
complained of did or did not commit a breach of municipal
law, the Spanish Government contended that an international tribunal may take into account other elements of
law which were not utilized in the contested decision and
which also justify the result at which those courts arrived, as
for instance, considerations emanating from comparative
law.[26] This was admitted in the Belgian Reply.[27]

[24] Reply, para. 460.
[25] Spanish Counter-Memorial, chap. IV, para. 126 and Rejoinder, Part II,
chap. I, para. 53 and footnote.
[26] Rejoinder, Part II, chap. I, paras. 48 ff., Counter-Memorial, chap. I, Section IV, and Professor Guggenheim's oral statement in C.R. 69/25, 16–17.
[27] Part I, para. 73.

DECISION OF LAST RESORT. The second of the conditions necessary for a state to be responsible for an erroneous judicial decision is that the decision or series of decisions on which the complaint is based should have been given by the highest court possible, after the decisions of the lower courts had been challenged by means of the remedies provided by the municipal legal system.

The basis for this requirement is the fact that in its judicial organization every state makes available remedies of challenge and appeal which are designed to correct the natural human fallibility of its judges. Such fallibility may be remedied either in higher courts or, sometimes, in the same court. If the person who considers himself aggrieved does not use the remedies provided by law for the correction of errors, the state cannot be held responsible for those errors.[28]

A consequence of this requirement is that a state cannot base the charges made before an international tribunal against the decisions of the courts of another state on new objections which have not been raised at the appropriate time before the municipal courts by the private persons concerned. Those contentions or arguments which were not invoked in the domestic proceedings cannot be put forward as grounds of complaint before an international tribunal, since the municipal courts were never given the opportunity to adjudicate the merits of those contentions and to do justice in their own, ordinary way.[29]

THE SUBJECTIVE ELEMENT AND THE QUESTION OF EVIDENCE. The divergence of views between the parties, until the final stages of the oral proceedings, was focused on the third requirement, that of a subjective element on the part of the judge. The Spanish contention, based on arbitral awards, the replies of governments on the occasion of the 1930 Conference,

[28] Spanish Counter-Memorial, chap. IV, para. 121.
[29] Spanish Rejoinder, Part II, chap. IV, paras. 742–47.

and doctrinal opinion, was that the dividing line between a mere judicial error or misjudgment (*mal jugé*) and an injustice for which a state may be held to be internationally responsible consists of the presence of a subjective factor: bad faith and ill-will on the part of the judge, the animus to cause prejudice to the foreigner.[30] The practical consequence of this requirement is to lay upon the claimant state the onus of furnishing the evidence of that subjective element, since bad faith cannot be presumed.

It may have been due to the difficulties of evidence thus arising that Belgium strenuously opposed the view "that the subjective factor presented as indispensable by the Spanish Government must exist." [31]

The discussion between the parties as to the proper interpretation to be given to this subjective element in various arbitral awards reveals a reciprocal misunderstanding, a sort of *dialogue des sourds*. This was only cleared up when, in the oral proceedings, Professor Rolin invoked the "general principle of Roman law expressed in the concise formula *culpa lata dolo aequiparata*, . . . an unintentional fault but so serious, so excessive that it renders the debtor inexcusable." [32]

The Spanish side had not intended, when referring to a subjective element, to deny the equivalence of *dolus* and *culpa lata*, since it considered that both were equally manifestations of what was described as the subjective element. It was then realized that the divergences on the theoretical level were more apparent than real, even with regard to the question of evidence.

Professor P. Guggenheim, as Counsel on behalf of Spain,

[30] The United States reply to the questionnaire prepared for the 1930 Codification Conference was typical of the attitude of governments: "The State is not responsible for errors of national courts in the interpretation of municipal law, in the absence of fraud, corruption or wilful injustice" (cited in Annex 38 to Spanish Rejoinder). Counter-Memorial, chap. IV, paras. 106–20; Rejoinder, Part II, chap. I, paras. 26–43.

[31] Reply, para. 467.   [32] C.R. 69/2, 24.

was able to summarize the Spanish position with regard to the subjective element in the following three propositions:

Firstly, although the content of a municipal decision of last resort constituting a gross and inexcusable breach of municipal law may give rise to international responsibility, the subjective element of bad faith is always necessary.

Secondly, the onus of proving bad faith is on the applicant government.

Thirdly, only in cases where the breach of municipal law is exceptionally outrageous or monstrously grave does the presumption of the judge's bad faith or *culpa lata* arise. But they must be cases which, to use the expression of de Visscher borrowed by Freeman in this connection, "one can no longer explain the sentence rendered by any factual consideration or by any valid legal reason." [33]

Professor Rolin stated with reference to this admission by the Spanish side:

I can only express my satisfaction with the agreement which, for the moment at least, seems to have been established between us regarding the fact that both in international law and in civil law *culpa lata dolo aequiparata* and gross and patent error in the application of municipal law or in finding the facts upon the basis of which the law is to be applied gives rise to responsibility if palpable injustice results therefrom.[34]

THE REQUIREMENT OF GROSS INJUSTICE AND THE NATURE OF THE CONTROL BY AN INTERNATIONAL COURT OF MUNICIPAL JUDICIAL DECISIONS

It was common ground between the parties that, apart from cases of direct violation of international law or denial of justice properly so called, in order that a judicial decision should create international responsibility in international law it is indispensable—the more detailed requirements referred to

[33] C.R. 69/25, May 23, 1969, English translation, 23–24.
[34] C.R. 69/2, Apr. 16, 1969, 28–29.

above, aside—that the decision should have caused what arbitral tribunals and writers have described as a palpable injustice,[35] *une criante injustice,* which is something different from and far more serious than mere breaches or misapplications of municipal law.[36]

This has a bearing on the nature of the control which an international tribunal may exercise over municipal judicial decisions. It is not for an international tribunal to act like a court of appeal or of cassation and to verify in all its minute detail the correct application of municipal law in internal decisions. The essential business of the international tribunal is to see whether gross injustices have been committed against a foreigner and, if they have, whether the three requirements indicated above are present.[37] The angle of examination is different from that of an appeal judge: it is not the arguments or grounds invoked by the municipal tribunal which must be scrutinized, but rather the result of the decision which must be evaluated, taking into account factors of justice and equitable considerations.[38]

The International Court, in its judgment in the *North Sea Continental Shelf Cases,* made a pronouncement which may be considered relevant to the subject of state responsibility arising from the substance of municipal judicial decisions. It

[35] The British Government, defending a decision of its courts attacked in the Ambatielos arbitration case, stated: "Vattel uses the graphic term 'palpable.' The wrong must be so obtrusive that it can—metaphorically—be touched." (International Arbitration Tribunal, Ambatielos case, United Kingdom Counter case, p. 124 at 309.)

[36] Reply, paras. 449, 461, 462, and C.R. 69/37, hearing of June 11, 1969, 55–56.

[37] Spanish Rejoinder, Part II, chap. I, paras. 45–51.

[38] Sir Gerald Fitzmaurice, as Counsel for the United Kingdom in the Ambatielos arbitration, pointed out that an international tribunal must pronounce "not with reference to the original acts of complaint, but with reference to the character of the result arrived at before the Court." (Cited in Spanish Rejoinder, Annex 40.) He also added: "an international tribunal cannot review or reverse the decision . . . it cannot find it wrong in law—it can only find it wrongful according to international law, if the facts warrant this." (Spanish Rejoinder, Annex 39.)

said, "Whatever the legal reasoning of a court of justice, its decisions must by definition be just, and therefore, in that sense equitable." [39]

This is not appealing to equity and turning away from positive international law. The positive rules of customary international law on state responsibility for the contents of municipal judicial decisions require that, to create international responsibility, such decisions must be grossly unjust, notoriously unfair and manifestly inequitable.

The situation in this respect is the same as that accurately described by the International Court in the *North Sea* cases: ". . . in short, it is not a question of applying equity simply as a matter of abstract justice, but of applying a rule of law which itself requires the application of equitable principles." [40]

---

[39] North Sea Continental Shelf Cases, Judgment, [1969] *ICJ Reports* 48.
[40] North Sea Continental Shelf Cases, Judgment, [1969] *ICJ Reports* 47.

OLIVER J. LISSITZYN

Sovereign Immunity as a Norm of

International Law

THE SCOPE of the immunity of a sovereign state from the jurisdiction of the courts and other authorities of another state is one of the persistent uncertainties of international law. In much of the world, particularly in the older nations of the West, the trend is unmistakable. National courts in increasing numbers are asserting jurisdiction over foreign states and their instrumentalities in a variety of situations, rejecting the so-called "absolute theory" of sovereign immunity.[1] But the Soviet Union clings to the position that in practically all circumstances a state is absolutely immune from the jurisdiction of a foreign court unless it has expressly consented to submit to such jurisdiction. In this position it apparently has the support of the other states within the Soviet bloc.[2] The

OLIVER J. LISSITZYN is Professor of Public Law, Columbia University Law School.

[1] For extensive surveys of practice and doctrine, see H. Lauterpacht, "The Problem of Jurisdictional Immunities of Foreign States," 28 Brit. Y.B. Int'l L. 220 (1951); S. Sucharitkul, State Immunities and Trading Activities in International Law (1959); J. Sweeney, The International Law of Sovereign Immunity (1963); T. Giuttari, The American Law of Sovereign Immunity (1970).

[2] M. Boguslavskiy, Immunitet Gosudarstva (1962), also in German translation by Rathfelder, Staatliche Immunität (1965); see also, with special

views and practices of many new nations of the Third World have not been fully clarified.

Even among the states whose courts reject the absolute theory, there is no clear consensus on the limits of immunity. Despite, or perhaps because of, the continuing disagreement within the international community over this problem, international organs entrusted with the task of codification and progressive development of international law, including the United Nations General Assembly and the International Law Commission, have largely steered clear of it, although it has encountered a less inhospitable attitude in some regional organizations, notably the Asian African Legal Consultative Committee and the Council of Europe. Furthermore, no authoritative guidance has been provided by international tribunals, to which disputes over state immunity do not appear to have ever been referred.

Two extreme views are possible. One is that absolute immunity is a norm of general international law and, consequently, states which do not abide by it violate international law. This is the Soviet position. At the other extreme is the view that general international law contains no norm requiring the granting of immunity, leaving each state free to develop and apply such policies and rules of municipal law as it sees fit. Let us examine each of these extremes in turn.

The idea that absolute immunity is a norm of general international law rests in part on the fact that for some time in the past it was the rule predominantly applied by the courts of many states and asserted in diplomatic practice. Even some courts which in recent years have adopted the so-called "restrictive" theory have referred to absolute immunity as having been the general norm in the past. Hence, it may be argued, absolute immunity is still the norm on which states that have not consented to its modification can rely. On closer examina-

reference to public ships, V. Koretsky and G. Tunkin (eds.), *Ocherki Mezhdunarodnogo Morskogo Prava* 195–213 (1962).

tion, however, this argument loses weight. Absolute immunity never had the quality of a well-established and universally accepted rule. In the United States, it was not really established until 1926, when the Supreme Court in the *Pesaro* case upheld the immunity of a vessel owned and operated by the Italian state, despite the fact that it was engaged in the carriage of passengers and cargo for hire.[3] Prior to this decision, American case law was divided, while the Department of State rejected the absolute doctrine. In Great Britain, lower courts have generally followed the doctrine since 1880, at least with respect to arrest or attachment of foreign state-owned vessels;[4] the law officers of the Crown rejected it as late as 1872;[5] while the highest court—the House of Lords—has never had occasion to pass on it squarely. In the Netherlands, the doctrine of sovereign immunity does not appear to have been generally applied by the courts before World War I. In the meantime, the courts of certain other nations, notably Italy and Belgium, were developing and applying the restrictive theory, denying immunity to foreign states in suits growing out of acts done in a non-sovereign capacity (*acta jure gestionis*). The application of this theory by the Italian and Belgian courts and by the courts of an increasing number of other states did not give rise to effective protests by the states over which these courts assumed jurisdiction. This fact means that a number of states persistently and successfully challenged, over a period of many years, the claim that absolute immunity was a universally binding norm. By the time the U.S. Supreme Court espoused the absolute theory in the *Pesaro* case, several other states had thus rejected it. It may be concluded that at no time did international law require all states to adhere to the absolute theory.

Developments since World War II lend further support to

[3] Berizzi Bros. Co. v. S.S. Pesaro, 271 U.S. 562 (1926).
[4] The Parlement Belge, 5 P.D. 197 (C.A. 1880).
[5] McNair, 1 *International Law Opinions* 100–101 (1956).

this conclusion. As the practice of state trading has spread, the number of nations whose courts or governments reject the absolute theory has continued to grow. In the United States, the authority of the *Pesaro* case was short-lived. It was shaken by the Supreme Court's decisions in the *Republic of Peru* and *Hoffman* cases,[6] in which the Court took the position that the granting of sovereign immunity was a matter of national policy as determined by the executive branch of the government and that the courts should not allow immunity beyond the limits indicated by such policy. In the light of this judicial attitude, the announcement in 1952 by the Department of State in the so-called "Tate Letter"[7] that it was espousing the restrictive theory sounded the deathknell of whatever authority the decision in the *Pesaro* case had still retained. Since then, American lower courts have generally rejected claims of immunity not supported by the doctrine announced in the "Tate Letter" or by express recognition by the Department of State. The United States government, moreover, has adopted the policy of not claiming for itself diplomatically the benefits of the absolute theory when sued in the courts of foreign states.[8] In Germany, the absolute theory which prevailed before World War II was decisively rejected by the Constitutional Court of the Federal Republic in 1963.[9] Among the courts of the major Western nations, only those in the United Kingdom seem to continue to cling to the absolute theory, but the House of Lords still has not given its *imprimatur* to it. The views of some non-Western nations were reflected in the Asian African Legal Consultative Committee which in 1960 recommended

---

[6] Ex Parte Republic of Peru, 318 U.S. 578 (1943); Republic of Mexico v. Hoffman (The Baja California), 324 U.S. 30 (1945).

[7] Letter of Acting Legal Adviser, Jack B. Tate, to Department of Justice, May 19, 1952, 20 *Dep't State Bull.* 984 (1952); cf. Bishop, "New United States Policy Limiting Sovereign Immunity," 47 *Am. J. Int'l L.* 93 (1953).

[8] See Giuttari, *supra* note 1, at 317.

[9] Decision of April 30, 1963, 16 BVerfG 27, 16 N.J.W. 1732 (W. Ger.).

the rejection of the absolute theory by a majority of seven to one.[10] Perhaps even more significant is the fact that at the Geneva Conference on the Law of the Sea in 1958 a strenuous Soviet effort to provide for the immunity of foreign government-operated trading vessels mustered the support of only ten delegations (out of eighty-six) and was decisively defeated.[11] The attitude of many nations that have attained independence since 1960 remains unclear, but it is probable that not all of them are ready to subscribe to the absolute theory.

Again, as in the period before World War II, denials of immunity resulting from the rejection of the absolute theory either have not been protested or have been protested ineffectually. The significance of this fact is accentuated by the contrast with the insistence of states on the application of diplomatic immunities. For example, after some Italian courts had failed to extend certain immunities to foreign diplomats in accordance with the general practice of states, a formal protest by the diplomatic corps in Rome led to a reversal in 1940 of the Italian case law by the highest Italian tribunal, bringing Italian jurisprudence into line with the requirements of international law.[12] In the light of the practice of states both before and after World War II, it cannot be seriously maintained that the absolute theory of sovereign immunity is a norm of universally binding customary international law.

The Soviet insistence on absolute immunity, however, does not rest on the practice of states. Soviet writers, not surprisingly, reject custom as the source of this alleged norm. Like

[10] The majority was composed of the delegations from India, Burma, Ceylon, Japan, Iraq, the United Arab Republic, and Pakistan, while the Indonesian delegation, the sole dissenter, upheld absolute immunity. Asian-African Legal Consultative Committee, Report 66–69, 81 (3d. Sess., Colombo, 1960). It should be noted, however, that the delegations are not considered as acting in an official representative capacity.

[11] United Nations Conference on the Law of the Sea, 3 *Official Records*, 132, U.N. Doc. A/Conf. 13/39 (1st Cttee., 43d Mtg., April 11, 1958).

[12] De Meeus v. Forzano, 65 Foro Italiano, I, 336 (1940); also in H. Lauterpacht, *Annual Digest*, 1938–1940, Case No. 164.

some Western writers, they prefer to rely on the principle of sovereignty of states, of which, they contend, sovereign immunity is a corollary.[13] But the content of the principle of state sovereignty, like that of other general principles of international law, is defined by the consensus of states. As already shown, the practice of states does not indicate the existence of a general consensus in favor of absolute immunity. Such immunity, therefore, is not part of the generally accepted content of the principle of sovereignty.

The Soviet argument, furthermore, is inherently double-edged. A state can contend that by virtue of its sovereignty its courts may exercise jurisdiction pursuant to the law normally applied by them, regardless of the identity of the defendant, unless to do so would be to violate a treaty or a norm of customary international law. The invocation of the principle of sovereignty evidently does not and cannot resolve the issue. It can be resolved only by the consensus of states (that is, by international law) evidenced by practice or by treaty. The resolution or accommodation of conflicting claims of sovereignty and jurisdiction is, indeed, one of the primary functions of customary international law.

If the claim that absolute state immunity is a norm of general international law must be rejected, should we espouse the other extreme—the view that general international law leaves a state free to grant or deny immunity to other states as it sees fit?

This view may seem to have found support in the great variety of circumstances in which the courts of certain nations have denied immunity to foreign states and in the already noted lack of effective protests by the latter in most of these cases. In several decisions, moreover, the U.S. Supreme Court has disposed of the issue of immunity of foreign states without any reference to international law, apparently regarding the matter as one of national policy and law. Judge (then Profes-

[13] See works cited in note 2, supra.

sor) Sir Hersch Lauterpacht has also lent the weight of his authority to this position, though not without qualification.[14]

Nevertheless, there is evidently a very wide consensus in the world community that international law does contain a norm or norms limiting the freedom of states to deny immunity to other states. No state has ever officially claimed that no such norms exist. The courts of most states, in granting or denying immunity, refer to an international law standard, even though they may interpret it differently. This is emphatically true, for example, of the recent Austrian and German decisions espousing the restrictive theory, in which there are long discussions of the various relevant sources of international law.[15] The U.S. Department of State in recent years has referred to the requirements of international law in the matter of immunity.[16] Exceptionally, a denial of immunity has been effectively protested. In the Netherlands, denials of immunity by the courts led to intervention by the government and the passage of legislation designed to prevent such denials in violation of international law.[17] Judge Lauterpacht's authority is offset by that of Judge (formerly Professor) Philip C. Jessup, who has emphatically affirmed the position that sovereign immunity is governed by international law.[18] Judge Lauterpacht, moreover, seemed to recognize that the freedom of states to deny immunity to other states was subject to certain exceptions, such as that exempting warships from actions *in rem,* seizure, or arrest. The American Law Institute, in its *Restatement of the Foreign Relations Law of the United States,* published in 1965, indicates that the immunity of foreign states is a matter

[14] Lauterpacht, *supra* note 1.

[15] Dralle v. Republic of Czechoslovakia, Supreme Ct. of Austria, [1950] *Int'l L. Rep.* 155; decision of April 30, 1963, *supra* note 9.

[16] See, e.g., its statement in the case of Stephen v. Zivnostenska Banka, National Corp., 222 N.Y.S.2d, 128, 133–34, 15 A.D. 2d 111 (First Dep't 1961).

[17] See E. Allen, *The Position of Foreign States before National Courts, Chiefly in Continental Europe,* 103–38 (1933).

[18] Jessup, "Has the Supreme Court Abdicated One of Its Functions?" 40 *Am. J. Int'l L.* 168 (1946).

of international law.[19] On balance, it may be concluded that an assertion by a state that it is entirely free under general international law to deny immunity to a foreign state under all circumstances would encounter strong and probably effective resistance within the world community.

This conclusion, however, does not provide any real solution to the problem of the scope of a state's freedom to deny immunity to another state. The great variety of practice and opinion suggests that the limitations imposed by international law on this freedom may be minimal. Only in situations where all or almost all states would agree that there is an international duty to grant immunity could its denial be regarded as a breach of international law. The available information on the practice of many states, however, is too scanty to permit confident formulation of such a consensus in general terms. A survey of the opinions of many courts, governments, and jurists reveals the existence of widely divergent views. Among the adherents of the restrictive theory, there is no real consensus. Many believe that acts of states can be divided into two categories, *acta jure imperii* and *acta jure gestionis*, and that foreign states are entitled to immunity only with respect to the first category. As stated in these broad terms, this view seems to be widely shared. It is expressed in numerous judicial decisions, in governmental pronouncements such as the Tate Letter, and in the works of many jurists. But this distinction does not take us very far. It is conceded by many of its proponents that there is no single, generally accepted meaning of either of the two categories.

One possible meaning of the restrictive theory is that acts done by states for a "public purpose" are *acta jure imperii*. But this "purpose" test has been largely rejected in practice. It has been often pointed out that all acts performed by states must be assumed to have some public purpose. The "purpose" test could thus practically nullify the restrictive theory.

[19] See, e.g., Section 63 and Comment thereto.

Some courts and the U.S. Department of State [20] have taken
the position that the nature of the act, rather than its purpose,
is determinative of immunity. It is often said that if the act is
of such nature that a private person could perform it, the state
is not entitled to immunity. Consequently, some courts have
held that a foreign state which is sued for a breach of contract
need not be granted immunity, since private persons can enter
into contracts and the latter are usually governed by private
law. But this does not quite resolve the difficulty. Private persons, for example, do not maintain armed forces and therefore
do not undertake by contract to pay for supplies delivered to
such forces. In some countries, moreover, many other activities
are monopolized by the state. May a foreign state be sued for
an act, such as breach of contract, performed within the scope
of such activities? Courts and jurists have given different answers to this and similar questions.

Various limitations on the freedom to deny immunity, furthermore, have been applied or suggested within the general
framework of the restrictive theory. The U.S. Department of
State, for example, and many courts have held that the property of a foreign state is immune from execution even if the
judgment was rendered in a proceeding in which the foreign
state was properly denied immunity from suit; but the courts
of several nations deny immunity from execution in such cases,
at least with respect to property employed in connection with
activities *jure gestionis*.

The Harvard Research in International Law proposed in
1932 that immunity from suit be denied, inter alia, to a foreign
state when, in the territory of the forum state, it engages in a
business enterprise "in which private persons may there en-
gage, or does an act there in connection with such an enterprise wherever conducted, and the proceeding is based upon

---

[20] See, e.g., letter from the Department of State to the Argentine Embassy,
April 19, 1962, as quoted in W. Friedmann, O. Lissitzyn, and R. Pugh, *Cases
and Materials on International Law* 676 (1969).

the conduct of such enterprise or upon such act"; but it upheld immunity from a suit relating to the foreign state's public debt.[21] The *Restatement of the Foreign Relations Law of the United States* provides that a foreign state's immunity "does not apply to a proceeding arising out of commercial activity outside its territory." The Comment to this section of the *Restatement,* however, would permit the forum state to apply its own standard to determine what is "commercial activity," although "not in an unreasonable manner" such as treating "as commercial an activity generally considered governmental, such as the sailing of a warship in an organized navy." [22] The Harvard Research and the *Restatement* would thus condition the denial of immunity to a foreign state upon its activities being conducted or its acts done within the territory of the forum state (Harvard Research) or outside its own territory (the *Restatement*). But this "territorial limitation," as it may be called, finds no clear support in practice. For example, it is not mentioned in the Tate Letter.

The difficulties and uncertainties inherent in attempts to apply the distinction between *acta jure imperii* and *acta jure gestionis* have led to suggestions that immunity from suit be denied unless the acts out of which the action arises fall into certain defined categories. This solution was adopted by an American court in 1964 in the *Victory Transport* case. After rejecting both the nature-of-the-act and the "purpose" tests as unsatisfactory, the court declared:

Sovereign immunity is a derogation from the normal exercise of jurisdiction by the courts and should be accorded only in clear cases. Since the State Department's failure or refusal to suggest immunity

---

[21] Harvard Research in International Law, "Draft Convention on Competence of Courts in Regard to Foreign States," with Comment, Article 11, 26 *Am. J. Int'l L.* 597 (Sp. Supp. 1932).

[22] Section 69 and Comment thereto. The Institute of International Law in a 1954 resolution on sovereign immunity stated: "Whether an act is an 'act of State *or not is a question to be determined by the lex fori."* 45 *Annuaire de l'Institut de Droit International* 301–302 (1954-II).

is significant, we are disposed to deny a claim of sovereign immunity that has not been "recognized and allowed" by the State Department unless it is plain that the activity in question falls within one of the categories of strictly political or public acts about which sovereigns have traditionally been quite sensitive. Such acts are generally limited to the following categories:

(1) internal administrative acts, such as expulsion of an alien.

(2) legislative acts, such as nationalization.

(3) acts concerning the armed forces.

(4) acts concerning diplomatic activity.

(5) public loans.

We do not think that the restrictive theory adopted by the State Department requires sacrificing the interests of private litigants to international comity in other than these limited categories.

The court proceeded to deny immunity to a department of the Spanish government in an action by an American shipping company to compel arbitration of a dispute growing out of transportation of wheat purchased in the United States to Spanish ports pursuant to an agreement which contained an arbitration clause.[23]

Although the test set forth in this case appears to be intended to avoid the ambiguity of the nature-of-the-act test and to hold the scope of immunity within narrow bounds, it may be doubted that it effectively accomplishes either of these objectives. What is the meaning of the words "acts concerning" the armed forces or diplomatic activity? In 1963, for example, the highest Italian court denied immunity to the United States in a suit brought by an Italian company that had built sewers for a United States military command in Italy.[24] This decision was in accord with several previous holdings of Italian courts in similar situations. In the same year, the Constitutional Court of the Federal Republic of Germany denied immunity to Iran in a suit by a private firm which had en-

[23] Victory Transport, Inc. v. Comisaria General de Abastecimientos y Transportes, 336 F.2d. 354 (2d Cir. 1964).

[24] Governo degli Stati Uniti di America c. Soc. I.R.S.A., [1963] Foro Ital. 1405, 47 Revista de Diritto Internazionale 484.

gaged in repairing the heating system in the Iranian Embassy in Bonn.[25] Did the suits in these two cases arise out of "acts concerning" the armed forces and diplomatic activity respectively? The American court which laid down the test in the *Victory Transport* case apparently would have granted immunity in these situations, for the court, in criticizing the nature-of-the-act test, referred to its producing "rather astonishing results, such as the holdings of some European courts that purchases of bullets or shoes for the army, the erection of fortifications for defense, or the rental of a house for an embassy, are private acts." The test laid down in *Victory Transport* may thus have the result of expanding immunity without really clarifying the scope of the restrictive theory.[26]

The uncertainties of sovereign immunity, in addition to the divergencies and ambiguities involved in efforts to define the scope of the restrictive theory, also include several special problems. For example, a foreign state apparently is not immune from suit in proceedings concerning real property and decedents' estates in the territory of the forum state, but, as Lauterpacht has noted, this "is not altogether free of doubt" and should be further clarified. The immunities of corporations owned by a foreign state; the forms and effects of waivers of immunity; matters of security, costs, execution, and the like; questions of immunity from taxation and expropriation; and the role of reciprocity, all invite further inquiry.

The continuing uncertainty of the status and scope of the doctrine of sovereign immunity and its modalities in international law can hardly be resolved by further debates among jurists or by further private efforts to assemble fuller information on recent practice. Would its resolution be advanced, if not

[25] Decision of April 30, 1963, note 9 *supra*.

[26] This test appears to be borrowed almost *verbatim* from that suggested by Lalive, "L'Immunité de Juridiction des Etats et des Organisations Internationales," 84 Hague *Recueil des Cours* 205, 285–86 (1953-III); but Lalive, unlike the Court, indicated some uncertainty about the fifth category (public loans).

fully accomplished, by placing it on the active agenda of the international organs charged with the task of codification and development of international law, and in particular the International Law Commission? As far back as 1927, this topic was considered ripe for codification by the League of Nations Committee of Experts for the Progressive Codification of International Law, but it was not put on the agenda of the Hague Codification Conference of 1930. The International Law Commission placed it on its initial work program in 1949, but has not actually studied it.

What would be the advantages of having this topic studied by the Commission? Such a study may not lead to the adoption of a widely ratified convention. Indeed, the desirability of attempting to draft such a convention may be questioned. The issue of sovereign immunity continues to divide the international community but has not caused any major crises. It may be preferable to continue to develop the law through practice. Such development has already led to numerous modifications in the rules applied by the courts of a considerable number of states.

The drafting of a convention, however, need not be the result or even the major goal of a study of the topic by the International Law Commission. Such a study could serve to clarify the problem and its dimensions, both *de lege lata* and *de lege ferenda*. The facilities and resources of the Commission and the United Nations might make possible the collection and analysis of far more extensive data on the recent practice of states, including judicial decisions, than any yet available. Secretariat studies, questionnaires addressed to governments, and discussions within the Commission and in the General Assembly might also serve to elucidate possible solutions *de lege ferenda*. That such optimal results would be forthcoming is by no means certain. Much would depend on the willingness of governments to make full responses to questionnaires and on the resources made available to the Secretariat and the Commission. But even less than optimal results could be helpful in ascertaining the dimensions of consensus and of disagreement within the international community. If, as seems likely, considerable disagreement were manifested, this finding would serve to confirm the freedom of states to deny immunity in a large variety of circumstances, since the existence of a generally accepted norm limiting such freedom beyond minimal restrictions on which all or practically all states seem to agree would be impossible to demonstrate. The law could then continue to develop, perhaps more rapidly, through practice.

SHABTAI ROSENNE

Bilateralism and Community Interest
in the Codified Law of Treaties

AMONG THE insistent voices which, in the aftermath of World War II and following the initiation of the modern codification effort,[1] called for the reconstruction of the international law of treaties along new lines, one of the most significant and influential was that of Professor (as he then was) Philip, Jessup. His *A Modern Law of Nations* [2] was a sustained plea for the reconstitution of the international law to meet the new needs of the international community as it was then seen to be evolving after the climactic events of the present century. On the diplomatic level too, beside his doctrinal writings, he had been able to exert his considerable influence —both personal and political—on the elaboration of this facet of United Nations activities (enshrined in Article 13 of the Charter) through his official position as representative of the

SHABTAI ROSENNE is Permanent Representative of Israel to the United Nations, Geneva, and an Associate of the Institut de Droit International. The views expressed herein are personal to the writer.

[1] Professor Jessup was the United States member of the Committee on the Progressive Development of International Law and its Codification (the Committee of Seventeen), established by G.A. Res. 94, U.N. Doc. A/64/Add. 1 at 187 (December 11, 1946). For his report, see 17 *Dep't State Bull.* 121 (1947).

[2] (New York, 1948.)

United States and member of its delegations to various meetings devoted to the codification and the progressive development of international law during that early period.

A principal motive developed by Jessup as far as the reconstruction of the international law itself is concerned was his powerfully articulated call for the assertion of community interest in the law—in its substance and in its application. Thus we may read: "[T] here must be basic recognition of the interest which the whole international society has in the observance of the law." [3] And: "Sovereignty in its old connotation of ultimate freedom of national will unrestricted by law is not consistent with the principles of community interest. . . ." [4]

The essence of the application of this doctrine to the law of treaties is expressed in the following paragraph:

More broadly, the acceptance of the hypothesis of community interest should be considered to vest in all members of the international community a legal interest in respect for treaties. Despite the development of general international law, it is to be anticipated that much of the world's affairs will continue to be governed by agreements concluded by two or more states. Respect for the maxim *pacta sunt servanda* and the development of treaty law will be matters of concern to all states, and an infringement of the law will affect the interests of all.[5]

In this article, an attempt will be made to survey the codified law of treaties, now embodied in the Vienna Convention on the Law of Treaties of May 23, 1969,[6] and to evaluate it in terms of the balance struck between the interrelation *inter se* of the mutual interests of the parties to a treaty on the one hand, and the community interest in that treaty, its object and purpose, its application, and the resolution of differences arising out of it on the other hand.

[3] *Id.*, at 2, note 2. [4] *Id.*, at 41.
[5] *Id.*, at 154. Footnotes in original omitted.
[6] Not yet in force, done at Vienna on May 23, 1969, U.N. Doc. A/CONF.39/27 and Corr. 1 through 6. Also in 8 *Int'l Legal Materials* 679 (1969).

This problem is an involved and delicate one. It is not answered by mere invocation of the difficult concepts of the relativity of treaties or of the traditional rules governing the interrelationship of treaties *ratione personae*. This rule, embodied in the maxim, *Pacta tertiis nec nocent nec prosunt,* is dealt with in excessively formal terms in Articles 34 through 38 of the Vienna Convention. Those provisions formulate in detail the proposition that a treaty does not create either obligations or rights for a state which is not a party to the treaty —denominated a third state—without that state's consent. It might be thought, and indeed not without reason, that cast in that form and occupying literally the center of the Vienna Convention, these provisions constitute an emphatic reassertion of the individualized sovereignty of states vis-à-vis the law of treaties and negate any suggestion that the post–World War II codification of the law of treaties went any distance in acknowledging even the existence of community interest in the law. What is more, such a restricted view of the essential characteristic of the codification effort might receive some encouragement from a close study of the legislative history of those provisions in the 1964 and 1966 sessions of the International Law Commission and later in the Vienna Conference itself.[7] But it is believed that a more thorough look at the codification effort as a whole, with due attention to the limitations on its scope upon which the International Law Commission found it necessary to insist (and to insist deliberately), will erode away any superficial conclusions which a cursory reading of the Vienna Convention could engender.

In undertaking an investigation of this character, it is important not to read more than is warranted into the Vienna Convention—and it is equally important not to read less than

[7] Official Records of the United Nations Conference on the Law of Treaties, vol. 1(1968), vol. 2 (1969), vol. 3 (documents). U.N. Doc. A/CONF.39/11 and Add. 1 and 2. Hereafter cited as Official Records.

enough into it. The Vienna Convention is what it says it is—a codification of the law of treaties between states.[8] It is exclusively that, and no more. "Treaty," in this context, means "an international agreement concluded between States in written form and governed by international law, whether embodied in a single instrument or in two or more related instruments and whatever its particular designation."[9] These laboriously worded texts reflect early decisions of the Commission to the effect that the work of codification was to be focused upon the instrument embodying the international obligation, the treaty, and not upon the international obligation itself.[10] This is emphasized indeed by contrasting the provisions of Articles 6 through 10, on the preparation and adoption of the *treaty text*, with Articles 11 through 16, on the assumption of *treaty obligations*. The Vienna Convention does not contain a general statement of the law governing the international obligation of states: it is limited to a statement of the law as between states

[8] Vienna Convention, Art. 1. For a full account of the background and implications of this article, cf. The Question of Treaties concluded between States and International Organizations or between two or more International Organizations: Working Paper by the Secretary-General, U.N. Doc. A/CN.4/L.161 and addenda (1971).

[9] Vienna Convention, Art. 2 (1a). The position of international agreements not in written form is preserved by Art. 3.

[10] This decision is recorded in the Report of the Commission on the work of its second session, Yearbook of the International Law Commission (hereafter *Yearbook*), 1950, Vol. II, U.N. Doc. A/1316, Part VI, Chapter I, para. 161, as follows: "The Commission devoted some time to a consideration of the scope of the subject to be covered in its study. . . . A majority of the Commission favoured the explanation of the term 'treaty' as a 'formal instrument' rather than as 'an agreement recorded in writing.' Mention was frequently made by members of the Commission of the desirability of emphasizing the binding character of the obligations under international law established by a treaty."

See further the discussion at the 49th through 52nd meetings of the Commission. I *Yearbook* 64–84 (1950). Cf. also Art. 1(a) of the Draft Convention on the Law of Treaties of the Research in International Law of the Harvard Law School, 29 *Am. J. Int'l L.* 653 at 691 (Supp. 1935). "It is believed that . . . the instrument, rather than the intangible agreement which it records, should be considered as the treaty, because it is the instrument which can be seen and read and which must be interpreted and applied."

governing the instruments in which certain international obligations of those states are embodied. That is the law of treaties.

From that perspective, the classical severity with which the Vienna Convention retraces the traditional law, itself reposing securely on the fundamental doctrines of the sovereignty and the equality of states, is hardly surprising. That, indeed, was one of the main purposes of this codification effort. On that plane, but only on that plane, there is little scope for far-reaching innovations which in the long run would probably involve a restructuring of international law and a repatterning of the forms of present-day international relations, implicit in the assertion, as a doctrinal matter, that community interest is a factor to be accommodated in the modern law of treaties. It is thus consistent with this philosophy that the Vienna Convention avoids intellectually abstract classifications of treaties, of doubtful practical value, such as the theoretical distinction between the *traité-contrat* and the *traité-loi*, and limits itself to employing only a few pragmatic distinctions and differentiations which were found to be necessitated by the nature of things.[11] For example, in 1962 the Commission somewhat gingerly advanced the concept of "general multilateral treaty" (echoing the idea of the *traité-loi*), meaning a multilateral treaty which concerns general norms of international law or deals with matters of general interest to the states as a whole.[12] It came in for some scathing criticism from governments,[13] and it was dropped in the final version of the draft ar-

[11] Cf. J. Dehaussy, "Le problème de la classification des traités et le projet de convention établi par la Commission du Droit international des Nations Unies," *En hommage à Paul Guggenheim* 305 (1968).

[12] Int'l L. Comm'n, Report, II *Yearbook* Art. 1 (1c), U.N. Doc. A/5209 (1962).

[13] Waldock, "(Fourth) Report on the Law of Treaties," Art. 1, para. 1(c), Comments of Governments and Observations and Proposals of the Special Rapporteur, II *Yearbook* 13, U.N. Doc. A/CN.4/177 (1965).

ticles adopted in 1966.[14] This was partly because of its imprecision and ungainliness and partly because the Commission had no practical use for such a concept, especially after it had rejected the idea that there could be an absolute right for every state to participate in certain types of multilateral treaty regardless of the participation clause of the treaty itself.[15] It is equally consistent with this line of approach that in 1964 the Commission refused to accept a proposition to the effect that an "objective regime" could be established by treaty, that is, a regime possessed of an objective character *erga omnes* in obvious derogation from the basic principle *Pacta tertiis nec nocent nec prosunt.*[16]

These incidents have been deliberately mentioned at this stage because they relate to aspects of the law of treaties which had been singled out for special mention by Professor Jessup in his 1948 work already cited, and taken by themselves could reinforce the tendency to see in the Vienna Convention a reassertion of a conservative and regressive development of the law. Jessup had drawn attention to the growing tendency in international practice to acknowledge the existence of "law-making treaties." Without allowing himself to be misled by that expression, he saw in that trend in the use of the term a growing acknowledgment of a basic community interest con-

[14] Int'l L. Comm'n, Report, II *Yearbook* Part II, Ch. II, U.N. Doc. A/6309/Rev. 1 (1966).

[15] The proposal was later revived in the Vienna Conference and then dropped again. See U.N. Docs. A/CONF.39/C.1/L.19 and L.19/Rev. 1, and A/CONF.39/C.1/L.385 (all withdrawn). Particulars in Report of the Committee of the Whole on its work at the first session of the Conference, paragraph 35(ii)(b) and Report of the Committee of the Whole on its work at the second session of the Conference, para. 20(ii)(b). U.N. Docs. A/CONF.39/14 and A/CONF.39/15.

[16] Waldock, "(Third) Report on the Law of Treaties," Art. 63, II *Yearbook* 26, U.N. Doc. A/CN.4/167 (1964). And see the discussion at the 738th through 740th meetings of the Commission, I *Yearbook* 96–109 (1964). This notwithstanding, traces of the idea are contained, and deliberately so, in Art. 32 through 34 of the Vienna Convention.

trasting with what he called the "strict bilateralism of the law." [17] Further developing that line of thought, he considered that acceptance of the hypothesis of community interest would pave the way for the development of a system of international legislation under which an international body would have the legal authority to prescribe rules binding on the international community as a whole:

Presumably, the system would be created by an exercise of the will of States in becoming parties to some basic agreement; but if such a development takes place, it would not be long, as time is measured in the lives of nations, before the original basis of mutual consent would be submerged in the exercise of what was originally a delegated authority.[18]

It is in Part V of the Vienna Convention, entitled Invalidity, Termination and Suspension of the Operation of Treaties, that to all appearances, and at first sight possibly surprisingly, the "strict bilateralism of the law" is seen to be most firmly entrenched. In this respect, the Vienna Convention runs counter to many trends which had become visible, both in the writing of publicists—including Jessup—and in the work of earlier Special Rapporteurs that was presented to the International Law Commission before 1961 but not considered by it. While many of the substantive provisions of Part V are framed as abstract and generalized statements of principle, the deliberately for-

[17] Jessup, *supra* note 2, at 133.

[18] *Id.*, at 135. It is doubtful if in present-day practice the multilateral treaty as such performs this function, but there can be little doubt that the existence of multilateral treaties drawn up after careful preparation and adopted by widely representative international conferences are important indications of the direction of official thinking on the international level. The difficulty is that the drafting technique adopted to insure what United Nations jargon now calls "quasi-unanimity" frequently makes it difficult, if not impossible, to establish whether what is being laid down is a "principle," hardly given to implementation as it is, or a firm rule. The Vienna Convention itself furnishes many examples of this form of diplomatic compromise. Furthermore, there is considerable difference in intrinsic weight between a text adopted by a majority of two-thirds or more and one adopted by a "consensus" involving a procedure of non-vote.

mulated procedure for their application, as it appears in Articles 65 through 68 and the Annex, is strictly and exclusively bilateral (or more accurately unilateral) in its initiation, although not necessarily as to its subsequent evolution.[19] Even where the grounds upon which the consent of a state to be bound by a treaty may be struck down are novel, whether as concepts of international law or in formulation, and are intended to forestall abuses by Great Powers previously made possible by defects in the law of treaties (such as the provisions, to which we will return, regarding coercion, or regarding breach or fundamental change of circumstances as grounds for the termination of a treaty), the Vienna Convention develops its themes on the foundation that the procedure for their application is essentially bilateral, or at most limited to the parties to the treaty in question. In this respect, it can be anticipated that in the course of time polarities of tension will come into being between the requirements of traditionalist bilateralism thus set forth and requirements of community interest, which can be seen to exist beyond the reach of the Vienna Convention on the Law of Treaties.

Striking illustrations of this can be seen in Articles 51 and 52 of the Convention, relating to coercion in its two forms as vitiating the consent of a state to be bound by a treaty, and in Article 53 (and Article 64), where the illegality of the object (conflict with a rule of *jus cogens*) renders invalid (and irreparable) an initial consent to be bound by a treaty if the norm existed at that time or terminates the treaty in whole or in part if the invalidating norm is supervenient.

As to coercion, the Vienna Convention distinguishes between coercion against the person of the representatives of the

---

[19] For instance, insofar as "intervention" in one form or another by third parties is admissible in the judicial, arbitral, and conciliation procedures envisaged in Article 66 and the Annex of the Vienna Convention, a matter considered in an article on "The Settlement of Treaty Disputes under the Vienna Convention of 1969," to be published in the *Zeitschrift für ausländisches öffentliches Recht und Völkerrecht* (1971).

state and coercion against the state itself. Article 51, on the first type, provides that "The expression of a State's consent to be bound by a treaty which has been procured by the coercion of its representative through acts or threats directed against him shall be without any legal effect." Furthermore, by virtue of Article 45, the right to invoke this ground for invalidating the state's consent to be bound by the treaty may be lost by reason of that state's conduct (*allegans contraria non audiendus est,* sometimes denominated the principle of estoppel). On the other hand, for the second type of coercion, which is not open to the correctiveness of that rule, Article 52 is utter and absolute: "A treaty is void if its conclusion has been procured by the threat or use of force in violation of the principles of international law embodied in the Charter of the United Nations." In both cases, however, by Article 44, no separability of the tainted provisions is permissible. The treaty stands or falls *as a whole*.

As to illegality of object, the Vienna Convention distinguishes between illegality at the time of the conclusion of the treaty and illegality occasioned by a subsequent change in the law, and in neither case can the defect be cured by the subsequent conduct of the parties concerned (Article 45). According to Article 53,

A treaty is void, at the time of its conclusion, it conflicts with a peremptory norm of general international law. For the purposes of the present Convention, a peremptory norm of general international law is a norm accepted and recognized by the international community of States as a whole as a norm from which no derogation is permitted and which can be modified only by a subsequent norm of general international law having the same character.

And Article 64 adds,

If a new peremptory norm of general international law emerges, any existing treaty which is in conflict with that norm becomes void and terminates.

Furthermore, by virtue of Article 44, no separability of the tainted provisions is possible in respect of treaties within the

reach of Article 53 (it is otherwise as regards those caught by
Article 64). The distinction between the two aspects is crystallized in Article 71, on the consequences of the invalidity of a
treaty which conflicts with a peremptory norm of general international law. Paragraph 1 of that article deals with the initial illegality under Article 53, and paragraph 2, with the subsequent illegality under Article 64.

What, indeed, could be more reflective of community
interest than this very idea of *jus cogens?*

As stated, according to the Vienna Convention the validity of a treaty or of the consent of a state to be bound by
a treaty may be impeached (*contestée, impugnada, ospari-
vat'sya* in other language versions) only through the application of the Convention; and likewise the termination, etc., of a
treaty, including the suspension of its operation, may take
place only through the application of the provisions of the
treaty or of the Convention (Article 42). This, of course, refers
to "impeachment" of the treaty, or steps to terminate it, taken
at the initiative of the party desiring to invoke the particular
ground involved. Furthermore, that invocation has to be performed through the procedure laid down in Articles 65
through 68 and the Annex of the Convention. The term
"party," moreover, is strictly defined as meaning "a State
which has consented to be bound by the treaty and for which
the treaty is in force." [20]

Since it was primarily in connection with the hypotheses of
those two series of articles that the "community interest" issue
has been directly posed in the past, the history in the International Law Commission of the ideas which they express throws
much light on how the Vienna Convention can be read with
regard to the polarity of community interest versus the strict
bilateralism of the law. In the evolution of the topic in the International Law Commission, treatment of the illegality of object problem preceded that of the coercion problem. It is
therefore preferable here to treat them in that order and not in

[20] Vienna Convention, Art. 1 (1g).

the order in which they are set forth in the Vienna Convention.

The first member of the Commission to put the legality of object issue in the forefront and to formulate it in "community interest" terms was the late J. M. Yepes (Colombia). At the 78th meeting of the Commission in 1950, he proposed including in the articles adopted at that session (on the basis of Professor Brierly's first report) the following:

In order to be valid, a treaty, as understood in this Convention, must have a lawful purpose according to international law. In case of any dispute regarding the lawfulness of a treaty, the International Court of Justice shall state its opinion on the matter at the request of any State directly or indirectly interested, or of the United Nations.

A treaty with an unlawful object may not be registered with the Secretariat of the United Nations. Whenever the lawfulness of a treaty submitted for registration is in doubt, the Secretary-General of the United Nations shall ask the International Court of Justice for an advisory opinion.[21]

He later adumbrated those ideas in a memorandum which he submitted to the Commission in 1953,[22] embodying certain criticisms of the report submitted in the same year by the second Special Rapporteur on the law of treaties, the late Sir Hersch Lauterpacht, who seemingly had not incorporated those ideas.[23]

As I see it, the lawfulness of a treaty's purpose is not dependent on the mere fact that it is not contrary to the principles of public international law. . . . This view is directly derived from the idea that the will of the State is not the only source of law—far from it.

[21] I *Yearbook* 299–300 (1950). This proposal was advanced at a late stage of the session, when the Commission was engaged in approving its report on its work at its second session, and for that reason no reference to it appears in that report (*supra,* note 10). The Special Rapporteur intimated that the question would not be omitted.

[22] U.N. Doc. A/CN.4/L.46 (mimeographed only). French version printed in II *Yearbook* 163 (1953). Mr. Yepes ceased to be a member of the Commission in 1953, and his memorandum was not further discussed.

[23] Lauterpacht, "(First) Report on the Law of Treaties," II *Yearbook* 90, U.N. Doc. A/CN.4/63 (1953).

Apart from, and above, the will of the State there are other principles of nobler origin which the State must respect, because they
are anterior and superior to the State. It follows from this that
States have no right to include in a treaty every stipulation which
their preferences or interests may suggest. If they do so, however,
the treaty has an unlawful purpose and should be voidable.

It often happens that a weak State is obliged to sign an unlawful
treaty under pressure from a more powerful State. For this reason
it is necessary to provide for action by a kind of international common informer, so that any State, even if it has no direct interest in
the matter, can apply for the annulment of certain treaties. . . .
Without such action [by an international common informer] the
annulment of a treaty is often virtually impossible, especially in
the case of relations between a powerful State and a small country.[24]

Two features in that proposal and its justification are noteworthy and subsequently recur in one form or another. The
first is the desire to attribute a *locus standi in judicio* to any
state directly *or indirectly* interested, or to the United Nations,
in contentious proceedings in the International Court of Justice.[25] The second is the enlisting of the advisory jurisdiction
to prime the imposition of the formal sanction.[26]

[24] *Supra,* note 22, at section III. Without here embarking upon any prolonged discussion of the real value of the sanction of nonregistration of a treaty
in face of the mischief registration was designed to remedy, it may be pointed
out that for all practical purposes registration, or nonregistration, is rarely of
great political significance. In practice, states which knowingly conclude
tainted treaties are unlikely to be punctilious about registering them.

[25] We do not wish here to enter into the problematics of "interest" sufficient
to support *locus standi in judicio.* This is a highly controversial matter on
which the International Court itself has given contradictory and irreconcilable
opinions, for instance in the South West Africa Cases. Jessup dealt with this
issue in his separate opinion in 1962 and his dissenting opinion in 1966.
South West Africa Cases (Preliminary Objections) [1962] *ICJ Reports* 319, at
422 ff., and South West Africa Cases (Second Phase), [1966] *id.* 4 at 373 ff. In
procedural terms in an international tribunal, the question is closely intertwined with the definition of the term "dispute," on which the jurisdiction of
the court is based, and its practical application in the concrete case. One aspect of this problem was brought out in the 703rd meeting of the International Law Commission, I *Yearbook* 196 (1963).

[26] Again the procedural aspects, both as to the requirements for the request
for the advisory opinion and as regards the Court itself, are ignored. However,
it may be noted that in the advisory proceedings in the Reservations to the

In Article 15 of his first report on the law of treaties, to which Mr. Yepes had thus taken exception, Professor Lauterpacht had proposed: "A treaty, or any of its provisions, is void if its performance involves an act which is illegal under international law and if it is declared so to be by the International Court of Justice." If, on the aspect here being considered, there may be an element of ambiguity in that text, the Comment made it clear that the Special Rapporteur had in mind what would now be termed the voidability of that kind of treaty, or treaty provisions, "dependent upon the willingness of the party invoking it [the principle involved] to abide by the decision of an international tribunal upholding the allegation of invalidity or making, *proprio motu,* a finding to that effect." 27 In this respect, that proposal stands in marked contrast to Sir Hersch's proposal regarding the effect of coercion in Article 12, by which:

Treaties imposed by or as the result of the use of force or threats of force against a State in violation of the principles of the Charter of the United Nations are invalid if so declared by the International Court of Justice *at the request of any State* [emphasis added].

Commenting on that proposal, the Special Rapporteur wrote:

As the continued validity of a treaty imposed by force is a matter of concern for the entire international community, the present article gives to every Member of the United Nations—whether it has become a party to the Code of the Law of Treaties or not—the right to ask the Court to declare, in contentious proceedings, the

---

Genocide Convention case, the Court regarded every state entitled to become a party to the Convention as having sufficient "interest" in the Convention to be invited to take part in the advisory proceedings. This included not only the states entitled to become parties to the Convention at the time when the resolution requesting the opinion was adopted by the General Assembly and when the proceedings were instituted, but also states which subsequently attained that quality. Reservations to the Genocide Convention (Request for Adv. Op.), [1950] *ICJ Reports,* 406 at 407; [1951] *id.* 15 at 18. However, prudence is required before transferring to the contentious jurisdiction conceptions of "interest" evolved in the advisory cases, especially on the procedural aspects.

27 "(First) Report," *supra* note 23, Art. 15, Comment, Paragraph 7.

invalidity of a treaty imposed by force. The State directly affected may not always be in the position to do so.[28]

None of the reports and other documents submitted to the Commission in that phase were discussed by the Commission. However, it will easily be perceived that the major issues of the community interest versus strict bilateralism in the law of treaties had been clearly posed as a matter of principle, and that difficult questions of practice and procedure nevertheless remained to be solved. That having been done, and forcefully, the issue could not be avoided in the later stages of the work.

This notwithstanding, the reports submitted by the third Special Rapporteur, Sir Gerald Fitzmaurice, appear not to give any emphasis to the community interest aspect. The effort of the previous Special Rapporteur to bring about some progressive development of the law on the basis of a synthesis of the traditional contractual and essentially bilateral (or perhaps partisan) approach to the law was not repeated. This may be explained partly by the fact that what was now being proposed was an expository code and not a convention which would have to run the gauntlet of a diplomatic conference, there to be discussed in detail and each provision to be adopted by a majority of two-thirds. Nor did the spasmodic discussions on the law of treaties in the International Law Commission in 1956 [29] and 1959 [30] show any serious questioning of this approach by the members. For this reason, although those reports dealt in their own way with the issues of constraint and illegality of object as grounds for the invalidity of a treaty, they did so exclusively on the basis that only the injured state

---

[28] *Id.*, Art. 12, Comment, para. 11 *in fine*.

[29] See discussion at the 368th to 370th meetings. I *Yearbook* 216 ff. (1956).

[30] This discussion was devoted to a partial examination of Sir Gerald's First Report on the Law of Treaties, on the conclusion of treaties. See Int'l L. Comm'n, Report, *Yearbook*, U.N. Doc. A/4169 (1959). Sir Gerald's five reports on the law of treaties appear as U.N. Docs. A/CN.4/101, A/ CN.4/107, A/CN.4/115, A/CN.4/120 and A/CN.4/130 in Vol. II of the successive issues of the Commission's *Yearbook* between 1956 and 1960.

was entitled to invoke those grounds.[31] In that sense, they did not advance the investigation into the issues being discussed in this article.

Far-reaching changes were introduced when the Commission appointed Sir Humphrey Waldock as Special Rapporteur in 1961 and, after a brief but deep and sensitive discussion, gave him more precise terms of reference than had been vouchsafed any of his predecessors.[32] The central feature of the decision then reached was the determination that henceforth the aim was to prepare draft articles on the law of treaties to serve as the basis for a convention. From the outset, the Special Rapporteur seems to have appreciated, especially in reexamining the work of his predecessors in this field, that for this ambitious aim to have any chance of success, it must come to embrace not only the traditional bilateralistic elements of the law as it had developed in its historic period, but also the new trends which were coming into prominence, both in doctrine and, by 1961, in practice. Thus, he is on record as having said that treaty practice was developing in response to the needs of international life, as a reading of the *United Nations Treaty Series* would show. The drafts which he was submitting endeavored to reconcile considerations of the development of

---

[31] In his third report (*supra*, note 30) Art. 14, the concept of duress was limited to duress against the representatives or organs of the state concerned, on the ground that to extend it to duress against the state as such might open the door dangerously wide to the invalidity of treaties, possibly even leading to a threat to the peace, the maxim *Magna est pax: perstat si praestat* being cited. "(Third) Report on the Law of Treaties," para. 62. Illegality of object was also limited, since that Special Rapporteur thought that no international tribunal or other international organ existed which was in a position effectively to declare the invalidity of such a treaty, so that if the parties chose to apply it *inter se* and could do so without affecting the rights of any third state, they might be able to carry it out. The real point, according to him, was therefore that such a treaty was unenforceable. *Id.*, para. 76, footnote 61. Neither of these views are reflected in the Vienna Convention, as will be shown.

[32] See discussion at the 620th and 621st meetings. I *Yearbook* 247 ff (1961). For the Commission's formal decision then, see Int'l L. Comm'n, Report, I *Yearbook*, Ch. II, U.N. Doc A/4843 (1961). For an earlier discussion on the general directives to be given to the Special Rapporteur, see 32d meeting and 33d meeting, I *Yearbook* 235 ff (1949).

the law with the need for certainty in the law. He hoped that the text which the Commission ultimately adopted would maintain a judicious balance.[33] The Commission reacted favorably to this approach, and for the first time intimated in its report for 1962 that its general objective would be to initiate a process of codification designed to ensure "that the law of treaties may be placed upon the widest and the most secure foundations." [34]

It was in 1963, on the basis of the second report presented by Sir Humphrey,[35] that the major initiative was taken by the Commission in effecting that reconciliation. The conclusions reached by the Commission, and ultimately endorsed (with modifications) by the United Nations Conference on the Law of Treaties and thus embodied in the Vienna Convention, are based on a complex interlocking of a series of different elements. Those elements include the following: (1) exposition of the *law of treaties* on a bilateralist basis, in the sense that the law of treaties determines the rights and the duties of the parties to the treaties to which the Vienna Convention will apply; [36] (2) inherent in that exposition of the law of treaties is acknowledgment of a firm distinction between treaties which are void *ab initio* and treaties which are voidable; [37] (3) the

[33] 637th meeting. I *Yearbook*, at 46 (1962).

[34] Int'l L. Comm'n. Report, II *Yearbook* U.N. Doc. A/5209, Ch. II, para. 17. That phrase was subsequently taken up by the General Assembly in a series of resolutions adopted between 1962 and 1965, in which it encouraged the Commission to continue working along those lines. See G.A. Res. 1765, 17 U.N. GAOR Supp. 17, at 65, U.N. Doc. A/5217 (Nov. 20, 1962); G.A. Res. 1902, 18 U.N. GAOR Supp. 15, at 69, U.N. Doc. A/5515 (Nov. 18, 1963); G.A. Res. 2045, 20 U.N. GAOR Supp. 14, at 88, U.N. Doc. A/6014 (Dec. 8, 1965).

[35] U.N. Doc. A/CN.4/156 and Add. 1–3, II *Yearbook* 36 ff. (1963).

[36] See, above all, Part V, Invalidity, Termination and Suspension of the Operation of Treaties (Arts. 42–72) of the Vienna Convention.

[37] This distinction finds expression in subtle differentiations between the different formulas used in the substantive articles regarding the various grounds for what is collectively denominated in the Vienna Convention (Art. 69) the "invalidity of a treaty" or, more fully (in Art. 65), a "defect" in a state's consent to be bound by a treaty, or a "ground for impeaching the validity of a treaty," as well as in differences, at least as a matter of the *terminus a quo*, for the consequences of the invalidity to take effect.

codification of the law of treaties embraces complete and formal reservations of all other topics of international law which might have some bearing on the matter, and particularly the law of state responsibility in general [38] and the obligations in relation to a treaty that might arise for an aggressor state in consequence of measures taken in conformity with the United Nations Charter with reference to that state's aggression; [39] and (4) recognition in the Vienna Convention of the absolute supremacy of the Charter of the United Nations over the Vienna Convention itself and, by implication, over treaties which themselves would come under the regime established by the Vienna Convention.[40] Of these elements, it is believed that the reservation of state responsibility and other similar matters in combination with the distinction between void and voidable

[38] The reservation regarding state responsibility was first made in certain of the commentaries to the draft articles adopted in 1963, on the basis of Sir Humphrey's Second Report, *supra*, note 35. It was given a more pronounced status in the Commission's Report on its sixteenth session, where it was also formally included as para. 5 of what was then adopted as Art. 63, and which now appears as Art. 30 of the Vienna Convention. II *Yearbook* (1964), U.N. Doc. A/5809. In 1966 the reservation was completely generalized and is now embodied in Art. 73 of the Vienna Convention. See also para. 31 of the Commission's final report on the Law of Treaties, *supra*, note 14, at p. 177. Here, too, the reservation is repeated in the commentaries to several of the draft articles. The 1966 decision to insert this reservation in the form of an article and not to leave it to be implied from the introduction and the commentaries of the Commission's report emerged from the final discussion on the scope of the work, at the Commission's 888th and 889th meetings. I *Yearbook*, Part II, 295, 300 (1966). The Sixth Committee of the General Assembly of the United Nations in general accepted this limitation on the scope of the draft articles of 1966, while expressing the hope that the Commission would sson find it possible to deal with those aspects of the topic of state responsibility which were closely and directly related to treaty law. See, for example, Report of the Sixth Committee, 21 U.N. GAOR, Annexes, Agenda item 84, U.N. Doc. A/6516, *passim* (1966).

[39] See Art. 75 of the Vienna Convention. Nothing like this had appeared in the Commission's first draft. It was inserted in 1966 upon the insistence of a number of governments, including that of the United States. Waldock, "(Sixth) Report on the Law of Treaties, II *Yearbook* (1966), A/CN.4/186 and Add. 1–7, Art. 59, Observations and proposals of the Special Rapporteur, para. 4, at 69.

[40] This recognition follows from the preamble combined with Arts. 30, 52, 65, and 75 of the Vienna Convention.

treaties are probably the most significant aspects relevant to the matter here under discussion. At all events, one can find there a key to reconciliation of the strict bilateralism of the law with the requirements of community interest, which modern international experience has shown to be necessary.

The ideology and the general picture emerging from that conclusion can be observed in some of the statements made in the debate, especially by Sir Humphrey. During the initial discussion of what is now Article 52 of the Vienna Convention, he explained, in response to the debate, that international public order [41] was the principle on which that article rests.

Quite apart from the law of treaties as such, the act of any State seeking to procure the conclusion of a treaty by the use or threat of force could be challenged as a violation of the rules of international law concerning the maintenance of peace proclaimed in the United Nations Charter, and could be brought before the Security Council or the General Assembly by the injured party, whether a Member of the United Nations or not, or by any other State even if it had no direct interest in the object of the treaty.

He went on to indicate that the article had been framed in terms of the right of the victim to invoke nullity, but not in a manner that would in any way exclude the right of any other state to raise the matter in a United Nations organ.[42] This conception was carried through into the Commentary on Article

---

[41] This particular conception, of international public order, is highly controversial, and was in terms not adopted by the International Law Commission. See the discussions at the 720th and 828th meetings, with regard to the use of that expression in the Commentary on another article. I *Yearbook* 314 (1963); I *Yearbook* 38, Part I (1966).

[42] See his statement at the 683d meeting. I *Yearbook* 61 (1963). As early as para. 4 of the Commentary to what had been originally proposed as Art. 12 of his Second Report, Sir Humphrey had drawn attention to the existence of the United Nations, which provided the machinery through which the international community could have a voice in the way in which the right of the inured state to invoke the nullity of the treaty is exercised, so as to minimize the risks to international peace. This fact had deterred the previous Special Rapporteur from proposing the inclusion of such an article. For the Second Report, see note 35 *supra*.

49 of the final report on the law of treaties, adopted by the
Commission in 1966.[43] The Commission there expressed the
opinion that the existence, universal character, and effective
functioning of the United Nations in themselves provide the
necessary framework for the operation of the rule. To add emphasis to this and, in the words of its sponsor, "to provide
an organic link" for the declaration which the Conference
adopted on the prohibition of military, political, or economic
coercion in the conclusion of treaties, the Vienna Conference
later adopted a resolution requesting the Secretary-General of
the United Nations to bring that declaration to the attention of
all other states participating in the Conference and of all the
principal organs of the United Nations.[44]

The evolution of the provisions of the Vienna Convention
relating to the nullity of treaties which are void for illegality of
object is not dissimilar. Indeed, from some points of view the
two sets of provisions are seen to be closely connected. The
strong expression, "A treaty is void if . . ." with which Article
53 commences corresponds exactly with the initial phrase of
Article 52. It is self-evident that such language in each case
embodies the same reflection of community interest, along
with the assertion of bilateralism which it naturally embodies.
As Article 69 of the Convention proclaims: "A treaty the invalidity of which is established under the present Convention is
void. The provisions of a void treaty have no legal force."

However, in the case of the rules of *jus cogens* it was
strongly argued, especially at the Vienna Conference, that the

[43] *Supra,* note 14, at 247.

[44] The delegation of Afghanistan at the 20th plenary meeting of the Conference. 2 *Official Records,* at 100. The declaration and resolution are both
annexed to the Final Act of the Conference. U.N. Doc. A/CONF.39/26 and
Corr. 1 and 2. For the transmission of the declaration to the various principal
organs, see the letters of the Secretary-General in U.N. Docs. A/7697 of
S/9361, E/4723, T/1700 (at 5). The Secretary-General's letter to the President of the International Court of Justice of June 13, 1969 and the reply of
June 26, 1969, are apparently not reported in any of the publications or reports of the International Court of Justice.

community interest required a somewhat greater measure of protection than was granted it in Article 65 of the Vienna Convention (Article 62 of the draft articles submitted in 1966 by the International Law Commission). Thus, it was frankly stated by one delegate that questions of *jus cogens* involved the interests of the entire community of nations, and questions as to whether a provision of a treaty was in conflict with a rule of general international law, and whether that rule was to be regarded as a peremptory norm, could be settled authoritatively only by the International Court of Justice. That delegation could not agree that a dispute of that kind should be left to private settlement between the parties through procedures established on an *ad hoc* basis.[45] This aspect of the community interest, therefore, is not only reflected in the somewhat extensive revision of the definition of *jus cogens* which was introduced into the final text of Article 53 of the Convention (especially its new second sentence) as compared with Article 50 of the draft articles submitted by the International Law Commission. Perhaps of greater significance to the aspect here being discussed, it is also reflected in the explicit mention of the *jus cogens* articles in the new Article 66 of the Convention, they alone being subject to the compulsory jurisdiction of the International Court of Justice as the instance of last resort.[46]

At the same time, the Vienna Conference exhibited some curious reluctance toward granting full recognition to the community interest, even toward according complete acknowledgment to the proposition that states other than the parties

[45] The delegation of Japan at the 68th meeting of the Committee of the Whole. 1 *Official Records*, at 402.

[46] We have elsewhere indicated our strong reservations at this decision of the Vienna Conference. At the same time, it might be pointed out that the practical significance of that particular provision of Art. 66 may not be very great, since it is unlikely, as a matter of practical politics, that states will go about concluding treaties which conflict with the peremptory norms of international law. This has been forcefully pointed out by Sr. Eduardo Jiménez de Aréchaga in his note to the Institute of International Law. 52 *Annuaire de l'Institut de Droit international*, t. 1, at 378 (1967-Nice).

to a treaty themselves may have some "interest" in a dispute over the validity or the termination of a treaty. One instance in which this issue appeared was in connection with the place, and indeed the right, of such states to "intervene" in third-party compulsive proceedings then being discussed for the settlement of disputes relating to the application of Part V of the Convention. Little of this opposition appeared on the record of the Vienna Conference. However, a statement of one of the sponsoring delegations indicates that the issue of the rights of third parties had been raised in the consultations and had been the subject of a compromise,[47] which now, indeed, appears in Article 3 of the Annex to the Convention. According to that provision, a conciliation commission, which shall decide its own procedure, may, with the consent of the parties to the dispute, invite any party to the treaty to submit its views to the commission, orally or in writing. This is hardly any advance, especially considering that the International Law Commission had not had much difficulty in accepting the proposition that all parties to a multilateral treaty had an interest in the application and interpretation of that treaty, and even had rights as regards it: for instance in the case of breach.[48] Even more pointed, it is believed, is the insistence first of the International Law Commission and later of the Vienna Conference on drawing up the details of the law governing the rights and duties of the depositary of an international

[47] The delegate of the Netherlands at the 92d meeting of the Committee of the Whole, 2 *Official Records*, at 255.

[48] Note in particular the discussion at the 831st and 832d meetings of the Commission. I *Yearbook*, Part I, at 59, 64 (1966). In its commentary on Art. 57 (on breach of a treaty, now Art. 60 of the Vienna Convention) the Commission recognized that account had to be taken of the interests of all the other parties to the treaty. Document cited *supra*, note 14, Art. 57, Commentary, para. 7 at 255. It may be recalled that in his work cited in note 2, *supra*, at 154, Jessup had devoted a long and persuasive section to the topic of community interest and breaches of agreement. While the Vienna Convention may not go as far or always in the direction contemplated by Judge Jessup, there can be little doubt that the Convention does constitute an important step toward that goal.

treaty in terms which are exclusively procedural and administrative, and in excluding from them any element which might imply that the depositary is entitled to exert any control over the "life" of that treaty, including its very legality, or to pronounce itself on the conformity with the general law of notifications or communications made to it.[49]

Other provisions of the Vienna Convention may be briefly examined to see what acknowledgment they give to the concept that entities other than the states actually parties to a treaty may have some standing in relation to a given treaty.

The concept of the "object and purpose" of a treaty was formally introduced into the law of treaties by the International Court of Justice in the Reservations to the Genocide Convention case in 1951.[50] In that case, the Court described at some length the special characteristics, origins and character of that Convention, and its objects, by which was meant objects pursued by those states which joined together in order to adopt the treaty. Combining those elements, the Court employed the all-embracing formula "the object and purpose of the Convention," which it developed as a test for determining the admissibility of reservations to that Convention.[51] The Vienna Convention adopts the same criterion for the same purpose in

[49] Art. 76 through 80 of the Convention. In this respect the Convention places the seal on a course of development, which commenced in 1950, regarding the powers and duties of the Secretary-General of the United Nations, as depositary of multilateral treaties, in respect to reservations to multilateral treaties; and as a political matter the decision had already been made in the General Assembly. That development had made it plain that the majority would resent the exercise of substantive controls by the depositary. For a synopsis, see Resolutions of the General Assembly concerning the Law of Treaties: memorandum prepared by the Secretariat, II *Yearbook* (1963), U.D. Doc. A/CN.4/154, para. 106 through 124, 1 at 18. See in further detail our articles, "The Depositary of Multilateral Treaties," 61 *Am J. Int'l L.* 923 (1967) and 64 *id.* 838 (1970). It may be noted that no trace exists of the idea that the Secretary-General of the United Nations, as registrar of treaties under Art. 103 of the Charter and Art. 80 of the Vienna Convention, could sanction void treaties simply by refusing to register them. This idea is attractive in the abstract, but it is unlikely to mean much in practice.

[50] *Supra*, note 26.   [51] *Id.*, at 21, 22.

Articles 19 and following on reservations. However, it goes
further and employs the identical formula, presumably with
the same meaning, in connection with the interpretation of
treaties (Article 31), with the *inter se* amendment of a multilateral treaty by only some of its parties (Article 41), with the
inter se suspension of the operation of a treaty (Article 56),
and with breach (Article 60). If regard is had to the manner
in which the conception of the "object and purpose" of the treaty
was introduced into the law of treaties by the International
Court of Justice, with its close attention to the manner
through which, and the international organ in which, the
treaty in question was originally adopted by the states concerned, one may be tempted to reach a conclusion that in the
case of a multilateral treaty, especially one concluded under
the auspices of the United Nations and in a broadly representative conference or organ of the Organization, the Vienna
Convention does recognize the existence of a broad, although
ill-defined, community interest, with a standing in the law.
This could be reinforced by the appearance of broad and inde-
terminate expressions such as "the States entitled to become
parties" to the treaty in question in key procedural articles relating to the treaty as such, for example Article 77, already
mentioned in another context, regarding the functions of de-
positaries.

Two carefully drawn articles deal, albeit in a somewhat
roundabout manner, with some aspects of the relation between
the codified law of treaties embodied, *inter alia*, in the Vienna
Convention itself, and the customary law of treaties wherever
it may exist. They, too, accord formal acknowledgment to the
standing of community interest in relation to the law of treaties. By Article 38, in the section on treaties and third states, it
is provided that nothing in Articles 34 to 37 (i.e., the preceding
articles of that section) precludes a rule set forth in a treaty
from becoming binding upon a third state as a customary rule
of international law, recognized as such, This certainly takes

many of the rough edges off the severe enunciation of the third states rules. By Article 43, in the section on the invalidity, termination and suspension of the operation of treaties, it is laid down that:

The invalidity, termination or denunciation of a treaty, the withdrawal of a party from it, or the suspension of its operation, as a result of the application of the present Convention or of the provisions of the treaty, shall not in any way impair the duty of any State to fulfill any obligation embodied in the treaty to which it would be subject under international law independently of the treaty.[52]

This was deliberately intended to protect general international treaties against the deleterious effects of withdrawals from them. These provisions are themselves buttressed by a passage in the preamble by which it is affirmed "that the rules of customary international law will continue to govern questions not regulated by the provisions of the present Convention." There can be little doubt that provisions such as these, designed to strengthen the basic stability of the law, meet a general community interest which may override the strident verbal criticisms of the "traditional" international customary law as it was sometimes alleged to exist before the modern codification effort was consummated.

Equally significant is the general reservation which now appears in Article 5 of the Vienna Convention for treaties constituting international organizations and treaties adopted within an international organization. According to that article, "The present Convention applies to any treaty which is the

---

[52] It is possible that even in combination these two provisions do not cover all the eventualities. The resolution adopted by the Institute of International Law on September 14, 1967, worded the principle differently: "when an obligation embodied in a treaty is binding also by virtue of another rule of international law, the fact that a State has not become a party to that treaty, that the treaty has lawfully terminated or that a party has lawfully withdrawn from that treaty does not as such affect the existence of that obligation." *Annuaire*, *supra* note 46, t. 2 at 562.

constituent instrument of an international organization and to
any treaty adopted within an international organization without prejudice to any relevant rules of the organization." (The
expression "international organization" means an intergovernmental organization.) Vaguely worded and of variable scope
though this may be, it nevertheless acknowledges what international practice has already come to recognize, that certain
treaties closely linked to the activities of the major universal
international organizations may have to be applied and interpreted within the framework of a special regime of their own,
differing from the traditional legal regime commonplace in an
earlier era.

Incomplete though the foregoing description may be, it illustrates, it is believed, that first impressions notwithstanding,
the Vienna Convention on the Law of Treaties, when placed
in the context of the totality of public international law as it is
today, goes a long way toward reconstituting the law of treaties in such a manner that, alongside the bilateralism which
really is the essence of contractual law and jurisprudence, the
existence of broader interests is not only acknowledged but actually accorded a recognized place in the law. In this respect,
as in others, the Vienna Convention itself does not go into detail but limits itself to demarcating the points of contact of the
law of treaties with other relevant branches of international
law. Those other branches are widely spread and include not
only such "classic" topics as the law of state responsibility but
also newer topics such as the law of international organization
and its various incidences and manifestations. Some of these
other branches of the law are currently under investigation by
the International Law Commission itself, such as the law of
state responsibility, and no doubt in the course of time the apparent lacunae in the statement of the law of treaties as they
appear in the final report of the International Law Commission, as regards the impact of the principles and rules of the
law of state responsibility on the law of treaties, will be filled.

Other topics are or have been examined by other organs, such as the General Assembly and the Special Committee on Principles of International Law concerning Friendly Relations and Co-operation among States.[53] Eventually, it may be assumed, some of the more obvious gaps in the law, such as that deriving from Article 33 of the United Nations Charter (which is "embodied" in the law of treaties by virtue of Article 65, paragraph 3, of the Vienna Convention), will be narrowed.

It therefore seems to be justifiable to say that even if the law of treaties per se is, in essence, restated on a bilateralist basis, it would not be a proper construction of the Vienna Convention to assume that the law which it enunciates will be applied and developed on an exclusively bilateralist basis. Sufficient flexibility has been incorporated in the Convention to render possible, as the state of international organization and general developments in the international situation permit, the introduction into international treaty practice of a more broadly based international community interest designed to temper the severity and the rigidity of the strictly bilateral concepts which hitherto have held sway. If that is so, it may be postulated that the chief beneficiaries of this new formulation of the ground rules of international law and of international conduct embodied in the Vienna Convention will be the small and weak states, whose position, thanks to their own standing in the major relevant international organizations, will assist them in warding off the evil consequences which, to judge from the debates in the General Assembly and in the United Nations Conference on the Law of Treaties, flow from the illegal treaties indiscriminately imposed upon them.

[53] See the declaration on that topic adopted by the General Assembly in G.A. Res. 2625, 25 U.N. GAOR Supp. 28, at 122–24, U.N. Doc. A/8028 (Oct. 24, 1970).

J. E. S. FAWCETT

The Application of the European
Convention on Human Rights

IT IS fitting that essays in honor of Philip Jessup
should cover also the protection of human rights, for through
his work runs a deep sense not only that international law
reached individuals at many points, but that, informing international law itself, there is the "pertinent international community standard," of which he spoke in the *South West Africa
Cases.*

The European Convention for the Protection of Human
Rights and Fundamental Freedoms [1] illustrates both these features of international law. It makes it possible for the individual to complain to an international body of breaches of the
Convention by contracting states, including his own, a novel
and far-reaching step. Further, the substantive provisions of
the Convention set up common standards, which are the beginning of a public law of Europe. Since just over twenty years
have passed since it was signed, it is worth considering its application in certain broad aspects to see what lessons can be

J. E. S FAWCETT is Director of Studies, Royal Institute of International Affairs;
Member European Commission on Human Rights; and an Associate of the Institut de Droit International.
[1] 213 U.N.T.S. 221 (1950).

learned from it about the international protection of human rights and what changes might be made in the Convention. Let us examine, then, not the operation of the Convention in detail [2] but its political and moral base, its effects upon state sovereignty, and possible changes in its content and structure.

I.

In the preamble to the Convention the contracting states reaffirmed their

> profound belief in those Fundamental Freedoms which are the foundation of justice and peace in the world and are best maintained on the one hand by an effective political democracy (un régime politique véritablement démocratique) and on the other by a common understanding and observance of the Human Rights on which they depend (dont ils se réclament).[3]

This paragraph expresses very exactly the fallacy, which lies in supposing that there are certain values which are in human terms absolute.

If we use the notion of freedom to comprise the exercise of rights and enjoyment of freedoms guaranteed by the Convention, we can see that to describe them as fundamental may be to say that there are freedoms which must never in any circumstances be denied or restricted; or that certain freedoms are the foundation of the social order, which is a desired object; or that they are the condition for achievement by individuals in society of certain desired objects; or that they are themselves preeminently desired objects.

There can be few rights or freedoms which are fundamental

---

[2] For this see A. H. Robertson, *Human Rights in Europe* (1963); K. Vasak, *La Convention européenne des Droits de l'Homme* (1965); K. J. Partsch, *Die Rechte und Freiheiten der europäischen Menschenrechts Konvention* (1966); C. Morrisson, *The Developing European Law of Human Rights* (1967); H. Guradze, *Die europäische Menschenrechts Konvention* (1968); A. Khol, *Zwischen Staat und Weltstaat* (1969).

[3] "They" in the concluding phrase appears to be the contracting states.

in the sense that they can never be denied or restricted: indeed in the Convention it is only those covered by the prohibitions against torture and inhuman or degrading treatment in Article 3, against slavery and servitude in Article 4(1), and against retroactive penalties in Article 7(1), that could be so described. All other rights and freedoms are subject either to expressly permitted restrictions, to derogation under Article 15, or to both. But even though the prohibition against torture and ill-treatment can be described as fundamental, in the sense that under the Convention it is never to be disregarded or set aside, the protection it offers is still incomplete. For under certain conditions torture or ill-treatment comes to be inflicted almost as a matter of course, that is to say, where there is extreme social tension or open armed conflict, and political opponents of the government are seen as a threat to the nation; where the security forces, civil or military, are free, in law or in fact, from control by higher authority;[4] and where the security forces believe that political opponents whom they have detained can give vital information. Where these conditions have come about in combination, as in Greece, Brazil, or Vietnam, the infliction of torture or ill-treatment appears to be almost inevitable. The Convention should be strengthened to face this at least by dealing with the second condition, to assure higher responsibility for the acts of security forces.

As regards the other rights and freedoms guaranteed by the Convention we see that they are all subject in some degree to denials or restrictions, which are permitted by the Convention itself and therefore fundamental only in a metaphorical sense; in fact, it is around the character and extent of these permitted denials and restrictions that the application of the Convention in great part turns. For example, the Convention affirms the principles of personal liberty and respect for private and family life, and the freedoms of opinion, association, and assembly. But in its practical application, it has often to be determined

---

[4] So that Article 13 of the Convention is rendered, in effect, inoperative.

whether a given period of detention on remand is "a reasonable time" (Article 5(3)); or whether it is justifiable to make private homosexual behavior a criminal offense for the protection of morals, or to impose restrictions on immigration, so that families are divided, in the interests of the economic well-being of the country (Article 8(2)), or to deport an alien because his expression of political opinion [5] is regarded as threatening public order (Article 9(2)), or to limit the activities of political groups in the interests of public order.

II.

The criteria which the Convention provides for the acceptability of such restrictions [6] are that they shall be prescribed by law and shall be "necessary in a democratic society." The first of these criteria is not to be controverted, though the legal forms of prescription are not always satisfactory or suffiicient; it is the second which raises difficult questions and leads us back to the meanings of "fundamental." When it comes to their application, permitted restrictions are found to have a number of characteristics which together tend to weaken the Convention, and which may be described as subjectivity, rigidity, and the relativity of the values involved.

The judgment of what action is likely to be a threat, for example, to national security, public order, or public morals, is subjective in two senses: first, there is no clear standard, save in extreme cases, by which the threat can be measured; and second, the judgment is effectively made by a relatively very small number of people [7] to whom the responsibility for imposing restrictions is delegated, whether parliament or the gov-

[5] As distinct from his political *activities:* see Article 16.

[6] See Articles 2, 5(2), 6(1), 8(2), 9(2), 10(2), 11(2), 15(1), 16; First Protocol, Articles 1 and 2; Fourth Protocol.

[7] Walter Lippmann has remarked that, in the adoption of the Constitution, the expression "We, the people of the United States" covered, in fact, a bare 5 percent of the population.

ernment. This subjectivity is recognized in the notion of a "margin of appreciation" accorded to a government imposing or administering permitted restrictions. The notion received some attention in the *Lawless* case, but the European Court of Human Rights neither accepted nor rejected it, affirming simply that it could not displace its own competence to determine whether or not a permitted restriction is consistent with the Convention.[8]

Rigidity can show itself in the cover which permitted restrictions may give to the slowest runners among the Convention countries on the road to social reform. The taking of life by public authority is an example. Article 2 of the Convention allows this in certain prescribed cases, including capital punishment. But the movement away from capital punishment since 1950 in almost all the Convention countries renders Article 2 obsolescent in legitimizing the practice.[9] Article 60 recognizes that the state of particular rights or freedoms may be more favorable for individuals in some Convention countries than the provisions of the Convention itself require. But it goes no further than to state that the Convention shall not be so.applied as to limit or derogate from such rights and freedoms, and it does not oblige other countries to measure up to the same standard.

The subjectivity of the imposition of permitted restrictions, and their occasional rigidity, suggest that it is doubtful whether the Convention can be said to express "community values" or, even if it does, whether it necessarily expresses "community expectations" about them. To take capital punishment again as an example, and if "community" were to be identified with the majority of voters in a referendum on the abolition of capital punishment—and this would be at least a

[8] [1961] *Y.B. Eur. Conv. on Human Rights* 430.
[9] See G.A. Res. 2393, 23 U.N. GAOR Supp. 18, at 41, U.N. Doc. A/7218 (1968), which notes a "world-wide tendency" to reduce the number of capital offenses.

possible definition of community—it is probable that in more than one Convention country, the "community" would have different "values" and "expectations" from those who in fact make its laws.

This supposition is borne out by even a cursory look at the notion of value in the context of the Convention. Value is always relative, because it is a measure of what something is worth in terms of something else; and in saying that an object or activity has value, we mean that it is worth so much sacrifice, effort, or expenditure of resources, which we may or may not quantify. In saying that something is *a* value we can mean no more than that we think it is a good, a desired object, worth sacrifice or effort. The exercise of a Convention right of freedom can be described as a value only in one of these senses, and to call it an absolute or fundamental value would be a contradiction in terms. Even if value-language is not used, the permitted restrictions on the exercise of Convention rights and freedoms show that they are attainable in fact as desired objects only through a balancing of individual demands and the common interest.

It is here that the criterion of what is necessary in a democratic society comes in. Using Convention concepts, we may venture to define a democratic society as one in which the individual exercise of Convention rights and freedoms as they stand and as they may be extended is regarded as a common interest and indeed the principal social objective. Restrictions on this exercise are then permitted if they are necessary to secure this objective. But it is the characteristics of the permitted restrictions in the Convention, as we have described them, which obviously render most difficult the interpretation and application of Convention provisions which contain them, and in particular the determination of what is "necessary" in a democratic society. These difficulties have two practical consequences for the application of the Convention. First, there is a tendency to make the maintenance of the established social order itself a desired object, and, in a dispute as to whether a permitted restriction is necessary in terms of national security, public order, or health or morals, to give the benefit of the doubt to the restriction. Second, the record of applications to the Commission under the Convention since 1954 shows that those of its provisions which are subject to permitted restrictions, and particularly Articles 9–11, have been much less often invoked than, for example, Articles 5 and 6 concerned with detention and fair trial; but it can be observed that where they have been invoked, with the effect of being at least declared admissible by the Commission, they have raised major issues, as in the Belgian linguistic cases and the Greek case.

It is a fair inference, then, that the permitted restrictions not only discourage the invocation of and reliance on the Convention provisions to which they relate, but can also somewhat inhibit the effective application of these provisions by the Convention organs. This leads us to the extent of the impact of the Convention on state sovereignty, and how far its provisions encroach on the domestic jurisdiction of the Convention countries.

III.

Experience over fifteen years shows that the work of the Commission is not regarded as so gross an interference with the tasks of government, or as creating such difficulties in the application of the Convention, as to make it unacceptable. On the contrary, of the eleven Convention countries which have declared their recognition of the right of individual petition to the Commission, none has so far failed to renew these declarations; and a number of applications to the Commission have led to the friendly settlements envisaged in Article 28 of the Convention, to administrative changes, and even to legislative reforms. The results have not been sensational, but they have been by no means negligible.

Relations between the Commission and respondent governments in the handling of applications have owed much to the
skill and prudence of its Secretary. But the main reason why
the supposition or fear that the Convention would encroach
unduly on the domestic jurisdiction of states is shown to be
unfounded lies perhaps in the exaggerations which still surround state sovereignty. Notions of the sovereignty and equality of states in international law in their exaggerated form
have become a refuge for many countries whose domestic
power is at best precarious and whose external power is negligible.

Philip Jessup has done much with his concept of transnational law to clear away some attributions of sovereignty, and
the application of the Convention has followed a similar path.
Three features may be noticed: the national background of
certain applications to the Commission, the scope of possible
action by the Convention organs, and the points of contact between the Convention and the internal law and administrative
practice of Convention countries.

Applications to the Commission take a number of forms.
Complaints that the Convention has been breached may relate
to the individual applicant himself, who is alone the alleged
victim; or they may touch a particular legislative provision or
administrative practice which affects a number of people or
even the community at large, and in respect of which applications to the Commission by one or more individuals are in effect representative, a kind of *actio popularis*; or again applications may concern large issues of social policy, often the
subject of legislation and involving the whole community. In
the case of applications of the last two kinds, the complaints
made and the facts upon which they rest will almost certainly
be a matter of public concern and debate in the Convention
country from which they come; movement for reform of the
law or practice involved may already be afoot; and the national administration, if sympathetic to the reform, may even

find the invocation of the Convention an aid in achieving reform. Against this background, it would be a mistake to regard the handling of complaints by Convention organs about breaches of the Convention as an undue encroachment on domestic jurisdiction, or the introduction of Convention rules and standards as an alien element. On the contrary, the Convention countries have either incorporated these rules and standards as part of their internal law or have, by ratifying the Convention, affirmed the conformity of their law and practice with them. In finding in these circumstances breaches of the Convention, the Convention organs will almost certainly be supporting a body, and perhaps a large body, of existing opinion within the country.

The scope of action accorded to Convention organs is not such as to constitute direct intervention in the process of government or administration of justice. No order can be made by the Commission having effect in a Convention country, and no action can be taken by it reversing any decision or altering or annulling any measure in a country. Further, while the decisions of the Committee of Ministers and of the Court are binding on the Convention countries, they are not self-executing in internal law. They must be implemented by the procedure prescribed in Article 32 for the Committee of Ministers and in Articles 50 and 54 for the Court. These procedures do not exclude an arrangement with the government concerned as to the best means for repairing or compensating a breach of the Convention which has been found. A possible extension of the scope of action of the Convention organs by conferring upon them "a power to order interim measures in appropriate cases" is envisaged in a Recommendation by the Council of Europe Consultative Assembly [10] that a draft protocol to the Convention be prepared on these lines. The Assembly noted that "the practice of the European Commission of Human Rights and the Rules of the Court of Human Rights fill the gap partially

[10] Council Eur. Consult. Ass., *Texts Adopted*, Recommendation 623, 22 Sess. (Jan. 21, 1971).

but not completely." Here it may be added that, in a number of cases where an applicant to the Commission has said that his deportation or extradition to a particular country may expose him to persecution or worse, the government ordering the expulsion has voluntarily agreed with the Commission to suspend action until it has been able to consider the fears of the applicant in detail.

This instance of the practical working of the Convention leads us naturally to its points of contact with the internal law and administrative practice of Convention countries. Here it must be stressed that the application of the Convention by the Commission does not take the form of directives or recommendations addressed to individual governments or legislatures, but rather of a factual inquiry into the judicial or administrative action involved in an application before it and negotiation of a friendly settlement of the complaints of the applicant, if they are found to be justified. This process will comprise, for example, the examination of court files; the hearing of witnesses, including those exercising judicial or police functions; and the taking of evidence on the form and basis of various administrative practices. The process at the same time will be controlled by the Convention itself, in that the Commission will not, in handling applications, go outside the task which the Convention has set it. The application of the Convention is not then the administration of a treaty on an international plane between the Commission, as an international body, and the states parties to the treaty. Rather it is a case of a continuing interpenetration of the Convention and the internal law and practice of the Convention countries; the provisions of the Convention are a form of transnational law.

IV.

Some conclusions may now be drawn from this brief survey of the application of the Convention.

First, to describe the Convention rights and freedoms as

fundamental is erroneous or at least misleading. At most it is saying—and it may be saying less—that the social order and structure must be such as to secure certain rights and freedoms as generally desired objects. But it is also said that, for the maintenance of this social order and structure, some restrictions of those very rights and freedoms may be necessary. Both social order and structure and the rights and freedoms they serve are then variable. They can be expressed as functions of each other, but there is in human terms no constant, no absolute.

It follows that it would be desirable to review the substantive provisions of the Convention perhaps every ten years. While the extension of the Convention by new protocols can certainly be useful, the provisions of the Convention itself, now over twenty years old, need examination and amendment in light of the extensive experience of its application. Some suggestions may be offered.

Article 2(1) [11] is now out of date in many Convention countries. While it might be going too far, at present, to remove altogether the exception for capital punishment, the conditions on which it can be imposed should be restricted in the Convention to a small number of named offenses.

More difficult, but still needed, are closer definition and control of the permitted restrictions, particularly in Articles 8–11, since they should not be wider or vaguer than they have to be. First, it is not clear what is covered by "public safety" as distinct from "national security" on the one hand and "public order" or "prevention of disorder or crime" on the other hand. If the purpose is to permit measures designed to prevent or minimize physical accidents, it is difficult to see what restrictions on the rights and freedoms set out in these articles would

[11] "No one shall be deprived of his life intentionally, save in the execution of a sentence of a court following his conviction of a crime for which this penalty is provided by law (d'une sentence capitale prononcée par un tribunal au cas où le délit est puni de cette peine par la loi)."

be called for. Second, the area of the protection of morals should be more precisely defined. It would be consonant with the general character of the permitted restrictions, i.e., that they are to protect community interests, to qualify "morals" in Articles 8–11 as public and limit restrictions under this head to activities which can be seen to have a public or social moral impact.

The control of measures or orders imposing the permitted restrictions rests in part on the requirement that they must have the form of law, but it is desirable that this control be strengthened under the Convention, particularly where national security and public order are said to be involved. A closely related problem, noticed earlier in this paper, is that of controlling activities violating or likely to violate Article 3. Indeed, the Convention in general does not protect the individual against acts of the executive as clearly and firmly as it should. It is true that Article 13 [12] covers executive acts, but its interpretation is disputed, and it may be operative only when a breach of the Convention has been found by the Court or Committee of Ministers.

In any case, the operation of the Article may fail because the very generality of most of the permitted restrictions makes it difficult to demonstrate a breach of the Convention provisions to which they relate. It is suggested that Article 13 needs amendment on the following lines: first, it should be made clear that it applies to the case where an individual alleges a breach of the Convention and not merely to breaches of the Convention actually found to have occurred; second, it should declare that where a remedy is sought against an executive act, the proceeding should comply with the requirements of

[12] "Everyone whose rights and freedoms as set forth in this Convention are violated shall have an effective remedy before a national authority (un recours effectif devant une instance nationale) notwithstanding that the violation has been committed by persons acting in an official capacity (dans l'exercice de leurs fonctions officielles)."

Article 6(1), whether the "national authority" appointed to deal with the matter is judicial or administrative: that is to say, there should be a fair and public hearing by an independent and impartial body; third, "public" should be defined so as to allow exclusion of press and public in certain cases, as prescribed in Article 6(1), but to prevent the withholding of material evidence by public authority on the ground that its disclosure in the proceeding would not be in the public interest.

It should be noted that the whole problem of the protection of the individual against executive acts is now under active consideration in the Council of Europe.[13]

Finally, it must be stressed that there is room for study of what lessons can be learned, for the operation of other regional systems for the protection of human rights and even of the United Nations Covenants and Convention on Racial Discrimination, from the structure of the European Convention and what may be called the logistics of its enforcement.

Writing in 1947, Philip Jessup made some penetrating observations on the international protection of human rights, which are still highly relevant. He suggested, pursuing the analogy of practice in the United States federal system, that "in the early stages of the international development of the protection of human rights, enforcement [should be] left to the national state, subject to review by an international authority," but he went on to warn that "it is of primary importance that flexible administrative procedure be developed and that the system be not left entirely in the more rigid hands of strictly judicial tribunals." [14]

Both propositions are illustrated in the European system. Not only is the rule of exhaustion of domestic remedies a fundamental condition of application to the Commission, but the offices in some Convention countries of ombudsman, civil or military, show that the Commission has older national analo-

---

[13] See a draft questionnaire in U.N. Doc. D 42.472/05.11.
[14] P. Jessup, *A Modern Law of Nations*, p. 90 (1948).

gies. It may even be that the Commission is a transition to a general adoption of the ombudsman or Parliamentary Commissioner system. However, the experience of the Commission suggests that review by an international authority, of which Philip Jessup spoke, remains a useful and perhaps essential factor in the protection of human rights for at least one important reason. Proceedings before the Commission provide a unique opportunity for the actual practice, in law and administration, of the Convention countries to be compared by reference to a particular situation in one of them. From these comparisons not only may national administrations be led to change their methods, but the "international community standards" which Philip Jessup invoked can be gradually evolved.

His second proposition has been followed in principle by the establishment of both the Commission and the Court under the European Convention. This structure is not without its complications and disadvantages, but it at least serves the prime need in the protection of human rights—the finding of the facts.

KOTARO TANAKA

Some Observations on Peace, Law,

and Human Rights

IT IS regrettable that people who discuss world peace do not recognize the relevance of the rule of law to the maintenance of peace. They are either too idealistic, relying instead on religion and morality, or too realistic, putting their reliance solely on politics and economics. We must strive for a balanced recognition, without under- or overestimation, of the significance of law for the realization of peace.

The relation of law to peace in the world community is far stronger even than in national communities. The domestic community owes its peace and security not only to legal order but even more to other social norms to which individuals are subject, such as morality, custom, and religion. The role played by law is thus proportionately smaller than in the international sphere, where extra-juridical norms are few and cannot prevail on sovereign states, and order and security must depend upon law, agreed norms, and the general interest in maintaining them.

It is paradoxical and ironic that although the international

KOTARO TANAKA is a former Judge of the International Court of Justice and an Associate of the Institut de Droit International.

community has great need for the rule of law, and although we can trace considerable progress in international law in the last half-century, this community is in a primitive, almost anarchical state where the exercise of physical force still prevails, and the whole of humanity is threatened with nuclear annihilation. This paradox, of course, stems from the fact that the international community is composed of sovereign states that do not recognize authority higher than their own sovereignty, and that international law under traditional theory is subject to the will and consent of the individual state. International law, then, is "weak law," although a law to regulate relations between sovereign states has to be the strongest law.

A stronger international law is required to meet the needs of international peace. Peace requires the replacement of power politics with the rule of law. World peace obviously cannot be attained by law alone, but it cannot be attained without law.

There is an old saying, *Ubi societas, ibi jus* (where there is a community, there is law). The common need for peace and highly developed social and economic interdependence undeniably demonstrate the existence of a world community in which world law is not only a *Sollen* but a *Sein*. A world community requires an effective world law that imposes limitations upon the sovereignty of each state. Traditional international law, which was concerned only with relationships between nation states, has proved to be inadequate to cope with new requirements of the world community and the world economy. The legal structure of the world community has been made more complex and multidimensional by two developments—the creation of international organizations whose activities do not resemble the simpler traditional relationships between states, and the appearance of the individual and his human rights as a subject of international law.

It is natural and reasonable that such concepts as "transnational law" (Judge P. Jessup), "world law" (G. Clark and Professor L. Sohn), "universal law" (Dr. W. Jenks), and "global law" have been proposed to describe the different juridical spheres interwoven in increasingly complex relations. For my part, I have preferred the term "world law" (*droit mondial, Weltrecht*), which has been used for a long time by continental jurists such as Zitelmann, Ofner, Stammler, and Del Vecchio—forerunners of the idea of world law.[1]

In my view, world law comprises common national laws, private international law, and public international law; but world law is not a simple addition of these three. World law must be developed in step with the progress of the world community, uniting the three component legal spheres on the basis of the juridical common denominator, which is nothing other than natural law.

The essentially transnational, universal character of problems of peace and human rights and their natural law foundation lead inevitably to world law.

LAW AS PEACEMAKER

Every law has the objective of realizing some specific purpose, some common good, in its particular community. And although the purposes and content of laws are diverse—ethical, political, economic, or technical—and will vary with the character of the particular community, law also has the common purpose or function of realizing peace in the community. That is why Ihering calls law *Friedensordnung*. Every law, regardless of its content, is a peacemaker. This peacemaking quality, particularly emphasized by Professor Gustav Radbruch, is inherent in all norms of positive law, not only those (like procedural law) intended for the settlement of disputes.

Even an unjust and harmful law, one not in conformity with

[1] Kotaro Tanaka, "Esquisse d'une théorie de droit mondial," III *Annales de l'Institut de Droit comparé de l'Université de Paris* (1938), 303–15; "Du droit international au droit mondial," *Etudes Juridiques offertes à Léon Julliot de la Morandière*, 548–70 (1964).

ideas of justice and the common good, may nevertheless serve to establish peace in a community. A dictator may prescribe an unjust and oppressive law and proclaim, "Here is peace." But such a peace would not be just or in conformity with the common good, and would be neither desirable nor durable. An abstract peace without regard to its justice or stability is not worth striving for.

The relation between law and peace and justice applies as well in the world community. The rule of world law is the *conditio sine qua non* of the peace of the world community, which, because of its size, multiplicity, and ethnological, cultural, religious, sociological, and economic diversity, requires the regulation of law to establish the common basis necessary to make international life possible. We require, however, not only world peace through world law, but also that the content of the law be consonant with the common good and particularly with the ideals of justice of the world community. In short, we aspire to perpetual peace but without the sacrifice of justice.

HUMAN RIGHTS AND PEACE

The guarantee and protection of human rights and fundamental freedoms are an essential part of justice and the common good of a political community. Accordingly, the elimination of wars and the establishment of peace in the international community would have no value if human rights were not also protected. We do not seek peace of any kind, but peace whose content is worth seeking. If slavery exists in one state, peaceful relationships with other states would have little value. In an international community, where the weal and woe of all members are closely interconnected, one cannnot remain indifferent to the destiny of others.

History provides convincing evidence that human rights are worth protecting, even with blood. In our lives we may be confronted with two tragic alternatives—shedding tears or shedding blood. Sometimes we are obliged to pour out blood to avoid the shedding of tears. Peace would be temporarily sacrificed for the purpose of realizing a higher peace.

We desire peace and justice at the same time. In the reality of life we try to find a compromise between peace and justice, but we cannot deny the possibility that we may have to choose justice at the expense of peace (*Fiat justitia pereat mundus*).

If injustice prevails in the world community, even if there is no warfare or conflict between states, it is only a nominal and not a true peace that exists. I will not go into the causes of war, but surely violations of human rights, particularly the oppression of minority groups in certain countries, have been major causes of war. Human rights problems do not remain simply internal matters but develop into critical international disputes and worldwide wars. It was for this reason that clauses for the protection of minorities were inserted in the peace treaties after the First World War, and the execution of these clauses was placed under the guarantee of the League of Nations. These clauses, however, were concerned only with particular minorities: no general principle of protection of fundamental human rights was proclaimed. That had to wait for the Charter of the United Nations.

The development of the humanitarian principle and of the idea of universal brotherhood has intensified moral and political ties between nations and between individuals of the different nations. The protection of human rights has ceased to be the concern of municipal law only. But human rights must be seen in the light of the complex relationships in the hierarchy of legal spheres in the world community. Each of these spheres in the world community—families, local bodies, associations, corporations, universities, churches, nation states, the United Nations—has its specific mission, aim, and purpose, but they are all connected with and dependent on each other in various relations. Although each fulfills its role in the division of labor, there must exist a common denominator to establish harmony among them. There can exist no basic conflict of fundamental political ideals if the harmony of a world community is to be maintained. As Judge Levi Carneiro emphasized, homogeneity in fundamental political ideas is essential if there is to be integration of diverse political spheres in a community.

Agreement on the desirability and degree of protection of human rights and fundamental freedoms is certainly a *conditio sine qua non* of a pluralistic political community. A state that practices slavery or suppresses freedom of expression or other fundamental freedoms can hardly be said to be integrated into the world community. Democratic and totalitarian states cannot coexist, theoretically or practically, in a federal system. History provides evidence that for a state in which human rights are denied, as in Nazi Germany, peaceful coexistence with the other members of the international community is impossible. Whether liberal and communistic states can peacefully coexist will similarly depend upon the protection of human rights. If they are recognized and protected, the coexistence of diffferent political systems is not impossible, despite the adoption of a monarchical system by the one and a republican system in the other, or other political and administrative differences.

INTERNATIONAL NORMS ON HUMAN RIGHTS

Our discussion must also consider whether there are presently any international norms for the definition and protection of human rights, and to what extent they are legally binding on the world community.

The protection and guarantee of human rights and fundamental freedoms were first stipulated in the Bill of Rights of Virginia and of the United States Constitution and in the Declaration of Human Rights of the French Revolution. Similar protective clauses have been incorporated into most of the subsequent constitutions of the world. An effort to make an international law of human rights has been made under the auspices of the United Nations, and is still going on, as in the International Covenant on Economic, Social and Cultural Rights, and the International Covenant on Civil and Political Rights of 1966, now open for adherence. The earlier Universal Declaration of Human Rights, adopted by the General Assembly in 1948, although not binding on the member states, may be considered a general guide and a model code for national legislatures and constitutes evidence of the interpretation and application of the human rights provisions in the Charter.

It also is relevant to examine the binding force of the human rights provisions in the Charter of the United Nations. Do these provisions obligate each member state to guarantee and protect human rights, or only to promote and encourage human rights? The preamble to the Charter declares a determination "to reaffirm faith in fundamental human rights, in the dignity and worth of the human person, in the equal rights of men and women. . . ." Article 1 states that one of the purposes of the United Nations is to "achieve international cooperation . . . in promoting and encouraging respect for human rights and for fundamental freedoms for all without distinction as to race, sex, language or religion" (para. 3). Article 55(c) imposes upon the United Nations the obligation to promote "universal respect for, and observance of, human rights and fundamental freedoms for all without distinction as to race, sex, language, or religion." Under Article 56, "All Members pledge themselves to take joint and separate action in cooperation with the Organization for the achievement of the purposes set forth in Article 55."

The Charter also provides that "The General Assembly shall initiate and make recommendations for the purpose of . . . assisting in the realization of human rights and fundamental freedoms for all without distinction as to race, sex, language, or religion" (Art. 13 para. 1b). The Economic and Social Council "may make recommendations for the purpose of promoting respect for, and observance of, human rights and fundamental freedoms for all" (Art. 62(2)). Finally, Article 76(c) declares that one of the basic objectives of the trusteeship system is "to encourage respect for human rights and for fundamental freedoms for all without distinction as to race, sex, language, or religion. . . ."

This accumulation of references in the Charter to human rights and fundamental freedoms is one of its differences from the Covenant of the League of Nations. The Charter, however, gives no definitions of "human rights and fundamental freedoms," nor does it provide any machinery for implementing the protection and guarantee of these rights and freedoms. The Universal Declaration of Human Rights and Fundamental Freedoms of 1948 is no more than a declaration adopted by the General Assembly and is not a treaty binding on the member states. International codification of human rights has been achieved to only a very limited extent—in the European Convention for the Protection of Human Rights and Fundamental Freedoms of 1953, which has only regional validity, and in a few special conventions, such as those on genocide and the political rights of women, the application of which is limited to their respective subjects. The Human Rights Covenants of 1966 will bind only those who adhere to them.

It must be recognized that the international protection of human rights and fundamental freedoms is weak and imperfect. But there can also be little doubt that the Charter presupposes and recognizes the existence of human rights and fundamental freedoms: respect for that which does not exist would be logically impossible. Such rights and freedoms, moreover, could not exist without corresponding obligations upon others to honor them, without an underlying legal norm. There is no doubt that these obligations have not only a moral but a legal character, by the very nature of the subject matter and the interests involved.

Hence, the lack of definition of "human rights and fundamental freedoms" in the Charter and in later legislation and
the absence of juridical mechanisms for enforcing them do not
constitute a reason for denying their existence or the need for
their legal protection. That a norm is *lex imperfecta* does not
deprive it of its legal character.

HUMAN RIGHTS AS NATURAL LAW

The reason that these legal norms exist even though they have
not been enacted into positive law is that the juridical basis for
human rights and fundamental freedoms is natural law, not
national laws and constitutions or international agreements,
which merely reflect and recognize the existence and validity
of these rights and freedoms.

Human rights derive directly from the concept of "person."
As a "person," man, unlike other creatures, is endowed with
free will. By his own decision he can choose his destiny, his ca-
reer, his happiness. Man also possesses the faculty of ethical
valuation.

That man is endowed with free will does not mean that he
may do whatever he likes. The distinction between right and
wrong, between just and unjust, does not belong to the arbitrary and subjective decision of the individual; it is objectively
determined by the meaning of the creation of the world. Man
can participate in this process of creation by his own free will.
He may exercise his freedom of choice. But he may do only
what is good and just and must avoid what is bad and unjust.

If an individual had authority to determine what is good
and right, what is bad and unjust, he would be "the measure
of all things" (Protagoras) and the creator of truth, usurping
the position of God. On that hypothesis any abuse of freedoms
and rights could be justified.

The meaning of human life is found in the noble mission of
participating in the process of creation by realizing truth,

good, and justice in this world. In this mission all human beings are equal, notwithstanding individual physical, ethnological, religious, racial, linguistic, or other differences. All human beings are equal because they are brothers and sisters, under one and the same God. For that reason they, as "persons," are endowed with the same dignity and worth.

Human rights stem also from the indefinite and infinite possibilities that an individual has for contact with other individuals, intermediate groups and bodies, states. Professor Jacques Maritain has pointed out that a person is an "open whole" (*un tout ouvert*) with a window open in every direction. An individual can go everywhere he wants, can conclude contracts and enter into other legal relations, and becomes the subject of rights and duties vis-à-vis other individuals, groups, and states. That a person is the subject of rights and duties means that he is not simply the means for other persons to attain their particular ends; he is an end in himself. A person is master unto himself, unlike a slave or the individual under a totalitarian regime. The value of a person is a juridical concept of an absolute character. It is not deduced from other values; it is not only a technical term.

Furthermore, every human possesses human rights within all communities and groups in which he lives or has a part. Human rights must be protected against abuse by public authorities as well as by fellow citizens. In a pluralistic society of hierarchical structure, they should be protected in every group, association, or community to which an individual belongs.

Because the mission of protecting and guaranteeing human rights has been left to national states, most people tend to believe that human rights are derived from the respective legal systems. Inasmuch as the need for protection has indeed been most keenly felt when state authorities themselves violated these rights and freedoms, human rights law was first developed in national consititutional law. But human rights do not belong to any particular legal system or sphere; their proper *siège* is not the state to which an individual belongs.

In every legal sphere in which a person is involved he possesses human rights which do not derive from the constitution of a particular state. The state has effective means to protect and guarantee the human rights of its citizens, and protection of these rights by means of national law must be recognized as one of the most important methods. However, it has become insufficient. We cannot ignore the importance of the protection afforded by national constitutions, but such questions of human rights as equal treatment of members may arise in other groups as well and are not limited to political communities. Not only the state but also each local body, social and economic group, family, church, and university must respect, protect, and guarantee the human rights of its citizens and members. There must exist a concurrence of multiple protections concerning these rights under both municipal and international law. The world community should insure that a stateless person is also guaranteed his human rights at every place where he resides.

National laws protecting human rights have much in common, but that uniformity is not derived, as in the case of the law of contracts or commercial transactions, from considerations of expediency, recognized by different legislative organs, or from the creative power of custom in a community. These common laws already exist, notwithstanding their more or less vague form, in natural law.

There exists only one body of human rights for each individual, which is valid in every system of law and in every legal sphere in the hierarchical legal structure. This is different from, for instance, the laws of patents and copyrights, where registration under the specific national law is considered to be the source of the right and each right is alienable as a kind of property right.

In short, human rights have always existed with the human being. They existed independently of and before the state. Aliens and even stateless persons must not be deprived of them. Belonging to diverse kinds of communities and groups ranging from family to state and world community, the rights of man must be protected and guaranteed in every system in this social and political hierarchy. There must exist no legal vacuum in the protection of human rights. Who can believe, as a reasonable man, that the existence of human rights depends upon a legislative measure of a state or of an international organization and that, accordingly, they can be validly abolished or modified by the will of states or international organizations?

A law of human rights exists independently of the will of states and cannot be abolished even by their constitutions because it is deeply rooted in the conscience of mankind, and of any reasonable man, and is linked with human nature, which is in itself invariable. Constitutions of many countries characterize human rights and fundamental freedoms as "inalienable," "sacred," "eternal," "inviolate," recognizing that human rights and fundamental freedoms possess superconstitutional significance.

Such a concept would, of course, be categorically rejected from the viewpoint of positivism, which sees the law as an emanation of a sovereign will of a state and nothing else. From this viewpoint, a state's constitution presents itself as the highest law, and the legal character of international law should be denied, or at least its sources should be limited to those based on the will of the state. This viewpoint would exclude from international law, for example, "the general principles of law recognized by civilized nations" [2] which constitute a source of international law independent of the will of the state. It is extremely significant that Professor Brierly states of this provision: "its inclusion is important as a rejection of the positivistic

[2] ICJ Stat. Art. 38, para. 1(c).

doctrine, according to which international law consists solely of rules to which States have given their consent." [3]

The natural law character of human rights is clearly indicated in an advisory opinion rendered by the International Court of Justice in the case of "Reservations to the Convention on the Prevention and Punishment of the Crime of Genocide" on May 28, 1951:

The solution of these problems must be found in the special characteristics of the Genocide Convention . . . The origins of the Convention show that it was the intention of the United Nations to condemn and punish genocide as "a crime under international law" involving a denial of the right of existence of an entire human group, a denial which shocks the conscience of mankind and results in great losses to humanity, and which is contrary to moral law and to the spirit and aims of the United Nations (resolution 96 (1) of the General Assembly, December 11th, 1946). The first consequence arising from this conception is that the principles underlying the Convention are principles which are recognized by civilized nations as binding on States, *even without any conventional obligation.* A second consequence is the universal character both of the condemnation of genocide and of the cooperation required "in order to liberate mankind from such odious scourge" (Preamble to the Convention). [Emphasis added.] [4]

The spirit of this opinion of the International Court of Justice can be extended to human rights in general. The seat of human rights is not in any positive law, not in the public authorities, but in "the conscience of mankind" and "moral law," which are nothing else but natural law. In regard to such matters public authorities of any state play only a declaratory role.

INTERNATIONAL INTERVENTION TO
PROTECT HUMAN RIGHTS

We can now dispose also of the question whether human rights are "matters which are essentially within the domestic

[3] J. Brierly, *The Law of Nations*, p. 63 (6th ed. 1963).
[4] [1951] *ICJ Reports* 23.

jurisdiction of any State," and thus not a subject for intervention by the United Nations, or one that can engender disputes requiring submission to the U.N. for settlement under the United Nations Charter (Article 2, para. 7). The answer to this question depends on whether the sovereignty of a state gives it unlimited discretion in the treatment of its own nationals or whether humanitarian considerations limit this sovereignty, giving a right of international intervention when persecution by a state, even of its own nationals, is so egregious as to deny fundamental human rights and to shock the conscience of mankind.

I agree with the view that favors intervention in such cases. Promotion of respect for human rights and fundamental freedoms constitutes one of the principal purposes of the United Nations. The Charter of the United Nations recognizes the existence of human rights and therefore the concomitant duty to protect and guarantee these rights. Logically, then, the Charter should be interpreted as recognizing the principle of humanitarian intervention as basic to the international system. The denial of human rights, moreover, can create a serious threat to peace, and trouble which might be engendered by intervention would be less serious in general than that which might be caused by abstaining from intervention. Collective humanitarian intervention may also be justified as a manifestation of a homogeneity of principal political ideas among the members in a hierarchically constructed community and a manifestation of the roots of human rights in the common conscience of all mankind.

CONCLUSION

Human rights comprise many different rights that are still imperfectly developed. They include the right to life, liberty, and security of person; freedom from arbitrary arrest and detention; the right to a fair trial; freedom of thought, conscience, religion and expression; freedom of peaceful assembly and association; the right to equal protection of the law. These and other rights and freedoms are *conditiones sine qua non* of a democratic society, required for the purpose of attaining the end of life, which is the participation of the human being in the historical process of creation. They emanate from the status of man as "person." They are an indivisible, integral whole, one status and no more. The protection and guarantee of human rights are a minimum requirement and a common denominator of democratic communities, giving those communities a political homogeneity which is one of the essential conditions of world peace.

IV

LAW AND INTERNATIONAL

ORGANIZATION

LELAND M. GOODRICH

The Changing United Nations

WRITING IN 1956, Philip Jessup observed that "The establishment of the United Nations presents an opportunity for innovations. The development of the organization of the international community suggests the ultimate possibility of substituting some kind of joint sovereignty, the supremacy of the common will, for the old single state sovereignty." [1] This view regarding the possibility of the United Nations developing into an organization possessing powers and influence which would enable it more fully to give expression to generally accepted values and to achieve more fully the implementation of these values has been often expressed. Former Secretary-General Hammarskjöld, for example, in his lecture at the University of Chicago in May 1960, spoke of the possibility that the United Nations was in the course of development from an institutional framework of coexistence to a constitutional form of cooperation. [2] Others have also commented upon the possibilities of developing within the framework of the United Nations Charter the functions and powers of United

LELAND M. GOODRICH is James T. Shotwell Professor Emeritus of International Relations, Columbia University.
[1] P. Jessup, *The Modern Law of Nations* 13 (1956).
[2] *Dag Hammarskjöld: Servant of Peace* 251–60 (W. Foote, ed., 1962).

Nations organs more adequately to fulfill the purposes of the
Organization as set forth in Article 1.[3]

I.

The Charter, it is often stated, is not only a treaty but also a
constitution. The importance of this characterization lies in the
fact that, as a treaty to which two or more states are parties, it
might be thought of as an instrument defining the rights and
obligations of the parties and therefore subject to restrictive
interpretation. As a constitutional document, on the other
hand, the Charter not only defines the rights and duties of
members but also determines the functions, powers, and responsibilities of organs which are established for the purpose
of giving effect to the aims of the Organization. In this respect,
the Charter is similar to the constitution of a state, and particularly of a federal state such as the United States, which defines the functions and powers of organs and provides the legal
basis for the development of the powers of the central government to meet the demands which changing circumstances may
create. Its interpretation raises questions that do not arise in
the case of an ordinary treaty.

That the Charter would need interpretation and even
amendment was well recognized at the time the Charter was
drafted at San Francisco. The amendment procedure finally
agreed upon did not give assurance that change would be easy
and often, as it was of a highly complicated nature requiring
not only the approval of a proposed amendment by two-thirds
of the membership but also its acceptance by the permanent
members of the Security Council as well.[4] The question of interpretation also received extensive consideration at San Francisco. Two questions in particular received the attention of the

[3] See, for example, *The United Nations: The Next Twenty-five Years*. Twentieth Report of the Commission to Study the Organization of Peace.
[4] Arts. 108 and 109.

delegates: one, the procedure by which the Charter should be interpreted, and two, the extent to which an interpretation would be binding upon members of the Organization. One proposal was that any question of Charter interpretation should be referred to the International Court of Justice for an advisory opinion, with the serious expectation that the opinion given would be accepted by the members as an authentic interpretation of the Charter. This proposal, however, did not meet with the approval of some states, particularly some of the major powers, on the ground that it amounted to accepting the compulsory jurisdiction of the International Court of Justice, which these states were not prepared to do. In the end, no provision was made in the Charter for its interpretation; but in a statement adopted by the technical committee dealing with the matter, which was approved by the Conference, it was stated that

In the course of the operations from day to day of the various organs of the Organization, it is inevitable that each organ will interpret such parts of the Charter as are applicable to its particular functions. This process is inherent in the functioning of any body which operates under an instrument defining its functions and powers. It will be manifested in the functioning of such a body as the General Assembly, the Security Council, or the International Court of Justice. Accordingly, it is not necessary to include in the Charter a provision either authorizing or approving the normal operation of this principle.[5]

With regard to the binding character of such an interpretation, the statement concluded as follows:

It is to be understood, of course, that if an interpretation made by any organ of the Organization or by a committee of jurists is not generally acceptable it will be without binding force. In such circumstances, or in cases where it is desired to establish an authoritative interpretation as a precedent for the future, it may be neces-

[5] United Nations Conference on International Organization, XIII *Documents* 709–10 (Commission IV, Judicial Organization).

sary to embody the interpretation in an amendment to the Charter.
This may always be accomplished by recourse to the procedure
provided for amendment.[6]

Thus, it would appear that while each organ and the various
members have the responsibility for interpreting the Charter
insofar as they may be concerned, no such interpretation is to
be considered as authoritative unless it has the general acceptance of the membership of the Organization. Just how extensive this acceptance needs to be is a question with respect to
which many views have been expressed and on which full
agreement has never been reached. One view is that "unless
the expression 'generally acceptable' is given an unusual and
unwarranted meaning, with no basis in the Charter, it probably means, from a strictly technical point of view, acceptable
to the majority of the members of the organ in question, in accordance with the voting majority applicable to that organ
and to the nature of the matter being treated." [7] According to
this interpretation, the meaning of "expenses of the Organization" in Article 17 given by the International Court of Justice
in its 1962 opinion [8] and accepted by the General Assembly
through its resolution of December 19, 1962, adopted by a
vote of 75 to 17 with 14 abstentions, constituted an authoritative interpretation of the Charter, since the vote conformed to
the Charter provision governing General Assembly decisions
on important questions. This view would not only fail to take
account of a substantial number of negative votes but would
also give no weight to the importance of states casting negative votes, except when, as in the case of the Security Council,
the express consent of those states is required.[9]

On the other hand, there is the view that "an interpretation

[6] Id.

[7] J. Castañeda, Legal Effects of United Nations Resolutions 123 (1969).

[8] Advisory Opinion on Certain Expenses of the United Nations, [1962]
ICJ Reports 151, at 168.

[9] France and the USSR were among the 17 members voting against acceptance of the Court's opinion in the "Certain Expenses" case.

of the Charter adopted by all the Members (or even by the 'overwhelming majority' except for some abstentions) in the Assembly" would constitute an authoritative interpretation.[10] The same would be true of an interpretation based on a consensus made known through statements and actions expressed separately by governments either within or outside the Organization, even if no vote is taken. This view would seem to be more in accord with the statement approved at the San Francisco Conference than the first view. It still leaves open the question of what constitutes an overwhelming majority and how many abstentions are permitted.

II.

The full extent of the transformation that the United Nations has experienced in the course of the past quarter-century of its existence as the result of interpretation and adaptation to new circumstances and needs will be indicated only in broad outline. More detailed attention will be given to those changes having special relevance to the capacity of the Organization to deal with matters such as human rights, where the extent of the reserved domestic jurisdiction of the state is in question. In this area one can perceive certain tendencies toward a joining or fusion of sovereignties to give effect to a general will or "international public policy." [11]

When we look at the extent of the changes that the United Nations has experienced, we cannot but be impressed by the flexibility that the Charter has been shown to have. The record clearly demonstrates that it is in a real sense a living thing, capable of growth and adaptation. This has been clearly shown by the view widely held that any necessary and generally de-

[10] Schachter, "The Relation of Law, Politics and Action in the United Nations," 109 Hague *Recueil des Cours* 171, at 186 (1963-II).
[11] See R. Zacklin, "Challenge of Rhodesia," 575 *International Conciliation* 8 (November 1969).

sired changes in the United Nations system can be achieved under the provisions of the existing Charter without any need of formal amendment or even the holding of a review conference with that possibility in view. Any list of significant developments in the Charter system would include the following:

(1) The failure to implement the enforcement provision of the Charter and the consequent nonuse of the Security Council's enforcement power as a means of suppressing acts of aggression and other breaches of the peace.

(2) The use of military contingents for keeping the peace, under arrangements based on the consent of all parties concerned.

(3) The emphasis on disarmament or the regulation of armaments in the absence of effective measures for maintaining international peace and security.

(4) The assumption by the General Assembly, not without some significant dissent, of responsibilities specifically, if not exclusively, given to the Security Council by the terms of the Charter.

(5) The assumption by the Secretary-General of an executive role, more recently challenged and currently somewhat reduced.

(6) The concentration of the Organization's activity in the economic field on assistance to underdeveloped countries, leaving to the other agencies the primary responsibility for dealing with world problems of economic stability and underemployment.

(7) The assumption by the United Nations of power to seek compliance by individual member states with human rights standards through the use of such methods as condemnation and collective measures of coercion.

(8) The affirmation of the principle that colonial rule must be immediately terminated and that it is the responsibility of the Organization to bring this about by coercive means if necessary, in place of the earlier acceptance of

the principle of gradual evolution of non-self-governing territories to self-government or independence under United Nations supervision or prodding.

One of the major developments in the role of the United Nations has been in the field of human rights. In its provisions for the protection of human rights and fundamental freedoms the Charter broke new ground. Up until this time, except for provisions of the peace treaties and the minority treaties concluded at the end of the First World War for the protection of minority groups in certain of the defeated and succession states,[12] international law had provided little protection for the individual against the acts of his own government. The racial policies of the Hitler regime before and during the Second World War convinced President Roosevelt and others that an organization for the maintenance of peace must also provide for the protection of human rights.[13] Consequently, in Article 1 the Charter provides that one of the purposes of the United Nations is "[t]o achieve international cooperation . . . in promoting and encouraging respect for human rights and for fundamental freedoms for all without distinction as to race, sex, language, or religion."[14] The General Assembly is authorized to "initiate studies and make recommendations" for the accomplishment of this purpose.[15] Article 55 of the Charter states that "the United Nations shall promote . . . universal respect for, and observance of, human rights and fundamental freedoms for all without distinction as to race, sex, language, or religion." Responsibility for the discharge of this function is vested in the General Assembly, and, "under the authority of the General Assembly, in the Economic and Social Council."[16] By the terms of Article 56 members pledge themselves "to take

[12] See P. de Azcarate, *League of Nations and National Minorities* (Carnegie Endowment, 1945).

[13] See R. Russell and J. Muther, *A History of the United Nations Charter* 323–29 (1958).

[14] Art. 1, para. 3.   [15] Art. 13, para. 1.   [16] Art. 60.

joint and separate action in cooperation with the Organization" for the achievement of the purposes set forth in Article 55.

At the time these provisions of the Charter were under consideration at San Francisco some concern was expressed over the possibility that they would enable the Organization to intrude into areas hitherto reserved for action by national governments, and a statement was unanimously approved to the effect that nothing contained in Chapter IX dealing with economic and social cooperation could be construed "as giving authority to the Organization to intervene in the domestic affairs of member states." [17] This statement, taken together with the explicit provisions of Article 2, paragraph 7 safeguarding the domestic jurisdiction of members, created some ambiguity as to the extent of the competence of United Nations organs to adopt measures for the implementation of the human rights provisions of the Charter.

It was recognized from the beginning that it was clearly within the competence of the Organization to seek agreement by members on the definition of human rights, on the extent of their obligation to respect them, and on procedures for implementing this obligation. This clearly fell within the limits of promoting international cooperation and the responsibility which the Organization assumed under Article 55. Consequently, there was no serious objection to the proposal that a declaration of human rights in the form of a statement of standards to be achieved should be drafted, and when the completed text was voted upon by the General Assembly in December 1948 [18] there were no negative votes and a relatively small number of abstentions. In adopting the Universal Declaration the General Assembly clearly expressed its intent in the following words of the preamble:

[17] United Nations Conference on International Organization, X *Documents* 271–72 (Commission II, General Assembly).
[18] G.A. Res. 217 (III), Dec. 10, 1948. The vote was 48-0-8 (abstentions).

The General Assembly Proclaims this Universal Declaration of Human Rights as a common standard of achievement for all peoples and all nations, to the end that every individual and every organ of society, keeping this Declaration constantly in mind, shall strive by teaching and education to promote respect for these rights and freedoms and by progressive measures, national and international, to secure their universal and effective recognition and observance, both among the peoples of Member States themselves and among the peoples of territories under their jurisdiction.

Furthermore, the Commission on Human Rights, in its report submitting the text of the proposed declaration, pointed out that it was only the first step in the elaboration of a human rights program, that it was not a treaty, and that it did not impose legal obligations.[19] The Commission recommended that the next step be the preparation of a covenant or treaty which, when accepted by member states, would impose upon them legal obligations.

The preparation of the covenants was a work of greater difficulty, requiring a longer period of time due to recognition that the covenants, when operative, would impose definite legal commitments on the parties to them. Early in the process the decision was taken to prepare two covenants instead of one, one on civil and political rights and the other on economic, social, and cultural rights. The texts of the two covenants were finally approved in December 1966.[20] There was never any question that this represented a proper kind of United Nations activity, since the Charter expressly provides for the promotion of international cooperation by the drafting of treaty texts to enter into force when accepted by the requisite number of states in accordance with their constitutional procedures.[21] Similarly, the adoption by the General Assembly of the Declaration on the Elimination of all Forms of Racial Discrimination, followed by the preparation, approval, and

---

[19] 3 U.N. *ECOSOC*, U.N. Doc. E/800 (June 28, 1948).

[20] G.A. Res. 2200, 21 U.N. GAOR Supp. 16, at 49, U.N. Doc. A/6316 (Dec. 16, 1966).

[21] Art. 62, par. 2.

submission for ratification of the Convention on the Elimination of all Forms of Racial Discrimination,[22] presented no difficulties. What characterized the approach of the Covenants
and the Convention was that the General Assembly, and the
Economic and Social Council acting under its authority, prepared drafts of international agreements which were then
opened for signature and did not enter into force and become
binding for the parties until ratified in accordance with constitutional procedures.[23]

While the preparation of declarations and draft conventions
defining the human rights to be respected has proceeded with
a considerable degree of success, the same cannot be said of
efforts to provide for the implementation of agreements once
entered into. The importance of established machinery and
agreed implementation is clear. As one commentator has observed, "[w]ithout such machinery, implementation would always remain piecemeal, hesitant, and inevitably political, and
would be dependent on the availability of a solid, if not overwhelming, majority." [24] Of the two covenants on human rights,
only the Covenant on Civil and Political Rights and its Optional Clause make provision for a special procedure of implementation, and this only in the form of a conciliation
procedure to be used on a voluntary basis, with the possibility
of allowing individual petitions under the Optional Clause. A
proposal for the use of judicial procedures met with little support. A proposal to establish a United Nations High Commissioner for Human Rights, with limited reporting and advisory
functions, has met with opposition on the part of many governments.

---

[22] G.A. Res. 2106, 20 U.N. GAOR Supp. 14, at 47, U.N. Doc. A/6014. The
Convention entered into force in January 1969 on receiving the requisite number
of ratifications.

[23] See Goodrich, Hambro, and Simons, *Charter of the United Nations: Commentary and Documents* 416–18 (3d ed. rev. 1969).

[24] W. Korey, "The Key to Human Rights—Implementation," 570 *International Conciliation* (1968).

Members have been prepared to go somewhat further in providing for the implementation of the Convention on the Elimination of all Forms of Racial Discrimination, in that provision is made for a committee to supervise implementation on a continuing basis. The committee receives biennial reports from governments on the measures they have taken to implement the Convention and reports each year to the General Assembly. It may act as a conciliator in disputes between governments and in an advisory capacity to United Nations organs dealing with non-self-governing territories. Furthermore, under an optional clause, not yet adhered to by any states that have ratified the Convention, individual petitions may be submitted to the committee.

No one has seriously questioned the competence of the United Nations to prepare declarations, draft treaty texts, and propose methods of implementation for consideration by governments, but there has been considerable difference of opinion as to the extent of the competence of the Organization to deal with specific cases where individual rights are alleged to have been violated. The problems presented and the general development of attitudes within the Organization can best be illustrated by reference to the handling of the question of racial discrimination in the Republic of South Africa.

The question first came before the General Assembly in 1946 in a complaint by India that persons of Indian origin were being illegally discriminated against. The competence of the General Assembly to consider the question was challenged on the ground that it was a matter falling within the domestic jurisdiction of South Africa. The first resolution that the General Assembly adopted [25] reflected the division of opinion that prevailed with regard to the basis of United Nations competence and the propriety of General Assembly action. The resolution was ambiguous as to whether the obligations, if any, of

[25] G.A. Res. 44, U.N. Doc. A/64/Add. 1 (Dec. 8, 1946).

South Africa arose under the Charter or under terms of the Cape Town agreement between India and the Union of South Africa. The Assembly limited itself to calling upon the interested parties to negotiate with a view to finding a satisfactory solution consistent with South Africa's obligations. This was the approach which the General Assembly continued to take down to 1952. It is noteworthy that during this time a significant number of members consistently questioned the competence of the General Assembly to take even this limited remedial action in the case of an alleged violation of human rights by a member state.[26]

In 1952 the General Assembly adopted a new approach. While continuing to deal with the original Indian (now Indian and Pakistani) complaint by urging negotiations between the parties, it adopted a separate resolution, in its first part calling upon governments to put an end to racial and religious persecution in conformity with the letter and spirit of the Charter, and in the second part, declaring that in multiracial societies harmony and respect for human rights and freedoms are best assured by legislation and policies based on racial equality, and that policies not so based are "inconsistent with pledges under Article 56." [27] The first part of the resolution was adopted by a vote of 35-1-23, Australia, Belgium, Canada, France, Sweden, and the United Kingdom being among the abstainers. The vote on the second part was even more indecisive, being 24-1-34, with the Communist bloc joining the group of abstainers. While the Assembly continued to consider at its subsequent sessions the Indian and Pakistani complaint,

[26] G.A. Res. 511, 6 U.N. GAOR Supp. 20, at 11, U.N. Doc. A/2119 reiterating the provisions of earlier resolutions in somewhat more urgent terms as the result of the South African enactment of the Group Areas Act of March 30, 1951, was adopted by a vote of 40-0, with 14 abstainers, including Australia, Canada, France and the United Kingdom, who were not satisfied on the question of competence.

[27] G.A. Res. 616 A and B, 7 U.N. GAOR Supp. 20, at 8, U.N. Doc. A/2361 (Dec. 5, 1952).

racial discrimination in South Africa in its larger aspects was henceforth the Assembly's principal concern.

In 1953, the Assembly reiterated its position of the previous year, adopted the view of its Committee on the Racial Situation in South Africa that policies of racial discrimination "are contrary to the Charter and the Universal Declaration of Human Rights," and asserted that genuine and lasting peace depends on the observance of the purposes and principles of the Charter and the implementation of United Nations resolutions.[28] The vote was 38-11-11, France and the United Kingdom casting negative votes, while the United States abstained. The negative votes and abstentions were indicative of serious doubts still entertained by members as to the competence of the General Assembly in the light of Article 2, paragraph 7, or to put the matter in another way, the extent to which South Africa was legally obligated under the Charter and General Assembly resolutions to abstain from the practice of racial discrimination.

By 1958 we see a weakening of opposition to General Assembly action on the ground of lack of competence and a greater willingness on the part of members to support strong measures. The expansion of General Assembly membership as the result of the breaking of the membership deadlock in 1955, the obduracy of the South African government, and the adoption by that government of more extreme measures were undoubtedly factors in producing this result. The Assembly's 1957 resolution,[29] reaffirming its previous positions and renewing its appeal to South Africa, was adopted by a vote of 59-6-14, with countries such as Australia, France, and the United Kingdom denying competence on the ground that the Organization was specifically precluded from adopting a resolution

---

[28] G.A. Res. 721, 8 U.N. GAOR Supp. 17, at 6, U.N. Doc. A/2630 (Dec. 8, 1953).

[29] G.A. Res. 1178, 12 U.N. GAOR Supp. 18, at 7, U.N. Doc. A/3805 (Oct. 30, 1958).

reflecting on domestic policies. Argentina, Canada, Italy, and the United States, among the abstaining members, agreed with this position and also questioned the propriety or desirability of adopting further resolutions. At the thirteenth session in 1958, however, a somewhat stronger resolution [30] expressly declaring South Africa's policies to be inconsistent with pledges under Article 56 was adopted by a vote of 70-5-4, with Argentina, Canada, Italy, and the United States casting affirmative votes. Italy still questioned competence but saw a possible contradiction in Charter provisons. Argentina thought that competence had been confirmed by repeated Assembly votes. Canada and the United States were willing to consider General Assembly action more sympathetically, but stressed the limitations of Article 2(7) and emphasized the need for balance between the rights of the state and the individual.

The Sharpesville incident of March 21, 1960 resulted in a new approach to apartheid, though this had been suggested in earlier discussions. As the result of inflamed feelings and a new sense of urgency, the General Assembly not being in session, the matter was brought to the attention of the Security Council, which adopted a resolution [31] recognizing that the situation had led to international friction and "if continued might endanger international peace and security." The Council called upon South Africa to take measures to achieve racial harmony. When the General Assembly met in its fifteenth session later that year it reaffirmed its previous resolutions and repeated the Security Council call by a vote of 96 to 1 (Portugal), with no abstentions.[32] While this near unanimity was probably in large measure the result of the Sharpesville incident, it is important to note that the change in member atti-

[30] G.A. Res. 1248, 13 U.N. GAOR Supp. 18, at 7, U.N. Doc. A/4090 (Oct. 30, 1958).

[31] S.C. Res. S/4300, 15 SCOR, 856th meeting (April 1, 1960). The vote was 9-0, with France and the United Kingdom abstaining.

[32] G.A. Res. 1598, 15 U.N. GAOR Supp. 16A, at 5, U.N. Doc. A/4684/Add. 1 (April 13, 1961).

tudes on General Assembly action had begun before the incident occurred.

The next significant development was the use of collective measures to bring South Africa to terms, when methods of persuasion had failed. The initial step was taken by the General Assembly in 1961 when, after repeating its earlier requests, it urged all states to take separate and collective action to secure South African compliance and called the attention of the Security Council to Article 11, paragraph 3 of the Charter, under which the Assembly may call the attention of the Security Council to situations that are likely to endanger international peace and security.[33] This was followed the next year by a resolution of far-reaching scope [34] in which the General Assembly, reiterating its earlier positions and reaffirming that "continuance of these policies seriously endangers international peace and security," requested that members take specific diplomatic and economic measures, separately or collectively, in conformity with the Charter. It also established a Special Committee to keep South Africa's racial policies under review. The resolution was adopted by a vote of 67-17-23. Negative votes were cast by Australia, Canada, France, the United Kingdom, and the United States. Latin American and Scandinavian states were prominent among the abstentions. Opposition to the resolution was clearly based more on grounds of expediency and doubts as to the likely effectiveness of the proposed measures than on reservations regarding the competence of the General Assembly. Subsequent resolutions of the General Assembly and the Security Council repeated and strengthened efforts to achieve the termination of South Africa's racial policies by collective measures, though the Security Council has not been willing up to now to use its powers

[33] G.A. Res. 1663, 16 U.N. GAOR Supp. 17, at 10, U.N. Doc. A/5100 (Nov. 28, 1961).
[34] G.A. Res. 1761, 17 U.N. GAOR Supp. 17, at 9, U.N. Doc. A/5217 (Nov. 6, 1962).

under Chapter VII of the Charter to order collective measures.[35] On October 11, 1963, by a vote of 106 to 1 (South Africa), the General Assembly requested the termination of "arbitrary" trials in progress and the granting of unconditional release to all political prisoners and persons imprisoned or interned for opposing apartheid.[36]

The significance of these and subsequent resolutions of the General Assembly and the Security Council lay in the fact that over the years members of the United Nations have generally come to accept the view that the practice of racial discrimination is in violation of the Charter and the Universal Declaration and that, notwithstanding the provisions of Article 2, paragraph 7 protecting the domestic jurisdiction of the state, the organs of the United Nations have the competence to bring strong pressure to bear upon the government of South Africa to modify policies, legislation, and administrative acts which that government has insisted are "essentially within [its] domestic jurisdiction." Such opposition as was expressed during the period of the sixties to proposals adopted by the Assembly, except for the consistent position taken by the Republic of South Africa itself, was mainly based on doubts regarding the likely effectiveness of the proposed measures rather than doubts as to United Nations competence. It is important to recognize that changes in national attitudes that took place during this period were to a considerable extent the result of political pressures and the desire of Western states to avoid being placed in the position of resisting proposals which were recognized to have moral and ethical justification, even though

---

[35] On August 7, 1963, the Security Council called upon states to cease the sale and shipment of arms and ammunition to South Africa (S.C. Res. S/5386, 18 SCOR, 1056th meeting 1 (1963), and on December 4 it called upon all states to cease the sale and shipment of equipment and materials for the manufacture and maintenance of arms and ammunition (S.C. Res. S/5471, 18 SCOR, 1078th meeting 1 (1963).

[36] G.A. Res. 1881, 18 U.N. GAOR Supp. 15, at 19, U.N. Doc. A/5515 (Oct. 11, 1963).

some reservations may have existed on other grounds. Nevertheless, whatever the motives for changes in member attitudes, the fact remains that members have come to accept General Assembly competence generally and to recognize the importance of General Assembly resolutions dealing with questions which earlier were widely regarded as "essentially" within a member's domestic jurisdiction.[37]

Another and closely related area in which the United Nations has developed over the years a responsibility and capacity for action exceeding what the framers of the Charter had in mind when the Charter was drafted, has been that of political development of non-self-governing peoples. The Charter system initially adopted two major approaches to the problem of the political development of colonial peoples. One approach was that of the trusteeship system, which was a modification of the League mandate system. The other, broader approach was contained in Chapter XI of the Charter, which placed upon all members administering non-self-governing territories the obligation to assist in their economic and political development and to make factual reports on economic, educational, and social conditions to the Secretary-General.[38] Following in the tradition of the League mandate system, the United Nations approach in both cases was premised on the assumption that the development toward self-government or independence would be a gradual one, with the United Nations performing a supervisory function and if necessary exercising some influence to prevent the administering state from prolonging unduly the period of tutelage. In fact, however, there was no general agreement at San Francisco that the performance of obligations under Chapter IX was subject to any kind of United Nations supervision or control, and the Charter makes no explicit provision for such supervision or control.

[37] See R. Higgins, *The Development of International Law through the Political Organs of the United Nations* 120–23 (1963).
[38] Art. 73.

In actual practice, during the first decade and a half, in spite of resistance from certain of the administering states, the process of development in the case of trust territories was speeded up considerably; and in the case of territories not under trusteeship the General Assembly assumed a role comparable to that which it and the Trusteeship Council explicitly held under the Charter in the case of trust territories.[39] With few exceptions, members came to recognize that the General Assembly was competent to discuss economic, social, and educational conditions in non-self-governing territories as reported by the administering states, and to express its views regarding the adequacy of economic, social, and educational development. While the General Assembly did not claim the right to supervise political development, as in the case of trust territories, it did nevertheless welcome the submission of information on a voluntary basis and asserted the right to decide whether a particular territory was or had ceased to be non-self-governing.

The year 1960 was of special significance in the development of the United Nations role. In its fifteenth session, the General Assembly adopted by a unanimous vote the Declaration on the Granting of Independence to Colonial Countries and Peoples.[40] In doing so, it invoked the principle of self-determination [41] as the basis for competence to consider and take action on questions involving the right of colonial peoples to self-government or independence. By this Declaration, the General Assembly declared that all peoples had the right to self-determination by virtue of which they might freely determine their political status and pursue their economic, social, and cultural development; that inadequate political, economic,

[39] Goodrich, Hambro, and Simons, *supra* note 23, at 448–62.

[40] G.A. Res. 1514, 15 U.N. GAOR Supp. 16, at 66, U.N. Doc. A/4684 (Dec. 14, 1960).

[41] Art. 1, par. 2.

social, or educational preparedness should never serve as a pretext for delaying independence; and that immediate steps should be taken in all non-self-governing territories which had not yet obtained independence to transfer powers to the people of those territories without conditions or reservations. What is particularly significant is that the Declaration was adopted with no opposing votes and that the number of abstentions was very low. It must consequently be accepted as representing the will of the membership of the United Nations [42] and certainly represents a radical change from earlier attitudes which insisted upon a more limited role for the United Nations and more extensive discretion by the administering states in determining whether or not conditions justified independence. While in the case of many General Assembly resolutions setting forth highly idealistic propositions in general terms, it may be said that states may accept them for political reasons without committing themselves to any specific course of action, it is difficult in the case of the Declaration to explain the affirmative votes in this way. Many governments which had previously refused to accept self-determination as a right to be exercised nevertheless in this instance voted in favor of a resolution which was very specific in certain of its provisions. Some governments may have regretted giving their support to the Declaration, as evidenced by their refusal to cooperate with the committee established by the General Assembly to supervise its implementation. Their position would have been strengthened if they had made clear their reservations at the time the Declaration was being voted upon. Not only has the right of self-determination been generally accepted, but the competence of the General Assembly to adopt certain specific measures for the implementation of that right, Article 2, paragraph 7 notwithstanding, has been established.[43]

[42] See Higgins, *supra* note 37, at 99–101.   [43] *Id.*, at 102–103.

III.

In the course of twenty-five years the United Nations has shown a capacity to evolve and adapt to new circumstances and needs within the limits of the original Charter. In no area has it shown this capacity for growth to a greater extent than in the promotion of respect for human rights. In responding to demands made upon it, the Organization has been sensitive to the widely prevalent opinion that respect for human rights and self-determination cannot be adequately achieved by independent actions of national governments responding to pressures from within their own territories. The Organization has remained, however, an organization of states. States are its members, states are represented in its organs, and states are responsible for the decisions that are taken. Thus, in the last analysis, the advances that are made in expanding the responsibilities and effectiveness of the Organization are conditioned by the extent to which member governments give their consent to proposals, are influenced by United Nations purposes, principles, and resolutions, and are prepared to assist in their implementation.

The composition of United Nations membership and the particular interests and objectives of member states have contributed to a somewhat uneven concern with the problems of human rights. The approach has often been a political one and decisions and programs are often determined by considerations of political expediency. In the case of apartheid in South Africa, it is significant that many members who for a time supported the South African position on the question of the General Assembly's competence were members of the Commonwealth who, while regretting and being unwilling to justify the policies of racial discrimination being followed, were nevertheless reluctant to be too severe upon a member of the family. When a member of the North Atlantic Treaty Organization, Portugal for example, was being criticized for failure to

recognize the human rights and political aspirations of its colonial peoples, the other members of NATO appeared to be balancing their Charter commitment to human rights and the
principle of self-determination for peoples against their strategic interest in doing nothing to weaken or displease a fellow
member of a collective self-defense organization considered
important to their security. While the Soviet Union refused to
admit the competence of the General Assembly to deal with
the complaint that freedom of association was being denied in
its territory, it nevertheless was quite willing to join in the
condemnation of South Africa for its policies of racial discrimination and to support the competence of the General Assembly to take quite drastic measures to put an end to these policies and practices.

The continued evolution of the United Nations as an
organization of sovereign states must depend to a large extent
on the restraint shown by member governments and on their
willingness to accommodate their attitudes and policies. An organization constituted as the United Nations is cannot assume
the powers of a world government and cannot by majority
votes adopt rules and enforce standards of conduct which do
not represent a broad consensus among its members. In fact,
its capacity for enforcement is very limited in any case, as is
evidenced by its limited success to date in persuading the Republic of South Africa, Southern Rhodesia, and Portugal to
comply with the standards contained in the Charter and in
resolutions adopted by United Nations organs relating to racial discrimination and self-determination. Experience of the
last quarter-century suggests, however, that the United Nations, through its principal organs, and more particularly the
General Assembly, has come to be recognized as having a considerable competence and capacity for developing international standards in the broad area of human rights which individual governments can disregard only at considerable risk to
themselves.

EDVARD HAMBRO

Some Notes on Parliamentary Diplomacy

THE TERM parliamentary diplomacy was given
its first wide publicity by Judge Philip C. Jessup in his lectures
at the Academy of International Law at The Hague in 1956.[1]
His great experience as a diplomat, jurist, and statesman gave
added weight to his legal acumen and the elegance of his presentation.

"Parliamentary diplomacy" has been given wide currency
but is not very exact or precise. The term conjures up at least
two different pictures in the mind of the reader who sees it for
the first time. It could mean the application of parliamentary
techniques in diplomatic gatherings; and, on the face of it,
large meetings of diplomats might benefit from the experience
of national parliaments. It could also mean the application of
diplomatic skill and tact to parliamentary proceedings; and
many parliamentarians would welcome the decorum of old-
world diplomacy. The term might also be used for the new international meetings of parliamentarians in l'Union interparle-
mentaire, the Council of Europe, and similar gatherings, but it

EDVARD HAMBRO is Ambassador of Norway to the United Nations; President of
the General Assembly (1970–71); and Member of the Institut de Droit International.
[1] Jessup, "Parliamentary Diplomacy," 89 Hague *Recueil des Cours* 185
(1956-I).

is probably accepted today as a description of the particular kind of negotiations which take place in assemblies within permanent international organizations, and, of course, most particularly, in the General Assembly of the United Nations.

The difference between conventional diplomacy and parliamentary diplomacy is to some extent a difference in degree. Conferences of an international character are nearly as old as modern diplomacy itself. And it is clear that some of the techniques used in the United Nations derive from diplomacy by conference in the eighteenth and nineteenth centuries. But a new dimension was added when this kind of diplomacy started to become universal and permanent. The existence of a nearly universal organization such as the United Nations is fairly recent. It is also a modern development that nearly every state is represented by a permanent delegation or mission. It is probably also significant that meetings at headquarters take place nearly all year round.

All these trends were present in the League of Nations. Much could or should have been foreseen, but the speed of development has been revolutionary.

Rules of procedure are adopted by all the main organs of the United Nations, and they are applied from year to year. This body of precedents should be easily available, but the Organization has not published a digest of the application of Rules of Procedure in analogy with the practice of the General Assembly and the Security Council in application of the Charter. It is not excluded that meetings of the General Assembly would benefit considerably from such a publication, which would certainly make the tasks of the presiding officers and their advisors considerably simpler.

The rules of procedure play an important role in the day-to-day work of the organs of the United Nations. They are necessary for the orderly conduct of business and to ensure fair play in the Organization. But on the whole they do not play a preponderant part. There are certain delegates who love the sport of raising technical points of order. And a nervous chairman or president trembles when a number of delegates simultaneously stand up in different corners of the room and shout "point of order"! One sees happy smiles on the faces of some of the adepts at this sport once the going is good, particularly in the legal committee, where it has been developed into a fine art. But the wise chairman tries to avoid this sport, which is time-consuming and, on the whole, rather uninteresting and profitless. A presiding officer who knows his rules and applies them impartially is generally spared.

There are, however, certain other aspects of life in the Glass House at Turtle Bay which can more profitably be studied for a greater understanding of this aspect of world politics.

First of all, it must be understood that the United Nations is not, or at any rate not yet, the center of the world. In contradistinction to members of national legislatures, the delegates to the United Nations act on instructions.[2] They are not—in principle—free agents. There is constant interplay between the delegations in New York and the national headquarters.

Another important difference between national parliaments and international conferences and organizations consists in the composition and selection of delegations; another phenomenon of great importance is the emergence of political and geographical groups in the United Nations.

It is the purpose of the present paper to investigate some of these problems as they look from the point of view of a delegate to the General Assembly.

I.

The delegates represent their states, which means that they represent a government and not a political party or other

[2] It is, of course, admitted that certain parliamentarians in certain countries consider themselves more as spokesmen for their electors than as independent legislators. They may feel the "mandate" of the constituency as binding as any "instruction."

group.[3] They are all bound by instructions, which, as will be seen later in this paper, may vary in character. Instructions all have something, in common, however, in that they are only of importance to the delegates and their governments. If the delegates violate their instructions, it may have serious consequences for them in their own countries, but it does not affect the international character and importance of their speeches in the current debate in the United Nations. The only document which has any effect on the validity of the vote cast in this connection is their credentials, which are public and official and which are examined by the credentials committee and passed on by the General Assembly. This may be of the greatest political importance, as was seen in the League of Nations in the Ethiopian crisis and in the United Nations in the cases of China and the Congo. The question concerning the credentials of South Africa very nearly precipitated a crisis during the twenty-fifth session. But once the credentials are accepted, the instructions given by the government to the delegations are outside the purview of the United Nations.

In the daily life of the Organization, the permanent representative with the rank of ambassador heads the delegation and represents his country in all the organs of the United Nations. At times, he is not an ambassador but has cabinet rank, and thereby greater authority and possibly greater freedom in relation to his government. During the meetings of the General Assembly, most delegations are—for a certain time, at least—headed by the prime minister, the foreign minister, or another cabinet minister. The delegations, which vary in size and importance, consist of politicians, diplomats, and technicians.

Certain governments appoint parliamentarians to their delegations, which, of course, makes the term parliamentary diplomacy even more apposite. In some cases, only parlia-

---

[3] It is admitted that certain governments consider themselves as more representative of a party than of a nation and that the difference between state and party may be nonexistent in one-party states.

mentarians from the government party and, in other cases, some members of parliament from the opposition are included. The government of Norway is of particular interest in this connection, because members of all the important political parties—also the opposition parties—have, since the days of the League, been members of the delegation. This has been done to manifest that Norwegian foreign policy, or rather that important part of it which is enacted in New York and Geneva, is not the privilege of one party but is a national and largely nonpartisan concern. But even in this case it is the policy of the government which is pursued. The members from the opposition are still under government instructions and cannot pursue any particular party interest or personal aim, if there should be disagreement with the government on any point.

II.

The group structure of the United Nations tends to become ever more important. For many purposes the whole Organization is divided into groups which at times are geographical and at times political. The main groups are the African, the Asian (at times combined to form an Afro-Asian group), the Latin-American, the Eastern European, and the group called Western European and Others. The "Others" refer to Canada, Australia and New Zealand. Certain states belong to no group, namely Israel, South Africa, and the U.S.A., whereas Cyprus and Turkey belong to both the Western European and the Asian group.

Within these groups there are subgroups like the Arab group, which cuts across other groups and has both African and Asian members. The same is the case with the group of the (British) Commonwealth. And there are groups within groups like the Nordic states and the Benelux states. Certain other special groupings come into existence for specific purposes during the sessions of the General Assembly. One example is the Western European group working during the meetings of the Second Committee. The U.S., the Federal Republic of Germany, and Japan also work in this group, which to all intents and purposes works like a group of the OECD. And the most powerful group of them all, when it meets, is the group of seventy-seven, which really is the equivalent of the group of the developing nations in the United Nations Conference on Trade and Development (UNCTAD) but which also meets from time to time during the General Assembly and can command the majority of the membership. At present it consists of 96 members.

These groups are not all of the same character, and the Western European group is in a way the weakest of the lot, since it only meets formally to consider elections for U.N. bodies and never takes a vote.

Little is known about procedures within these groups. It is certain that they meet for consultations fairly often, and it is clear that a nucleus, which may change from time to time, meets very frequently during the whole session of the General Assembly. Groups within groups meet with very great regularity. The ambassadors of the Nordic states meet at least once a week during sessions and at times much more often. Similar meetings take place among the deputy representatives and among the secretaries and experts on what—in an odious comparison with the ambassadors—is called the working level.

During meetings of the Economic and Social Council (ECOSOC), to take an example, this collaboration goes so far that the Nordic states meet as one delegation. One of them is at all times a member, and the four Nordic states which are not members have one of their representatives meet as a special adviser in the delegation of the state which is a member. They participate in all the delegation meetings.

The collaboration among these states continues all through the year. Twice a year the foreign ministers meet at Nordic meetings, in which the permanent representatives to the U.N. generally participate. A communiqué in English is issued after each meeting. These meetings are preceded by a Nordic meeting of the officers in the foreign ministry who are chiefs of the United Nations office and are succeeded by meetings of the directors general of the political sections of the ministry. These personal contacts are continued all through the year either by meetings or by telephone. Occasionally, one of the ambassadors in New York asks his foreign ministry to try to settle for a common Nordic policy by telephonic conversation among all the capitals.

The collaboration between this group of states may be stronger and more intimate than in most other groups, but there is no reason to think that other groups do not also to some extent follow the same pattern.

III.

It is suggested that the most important single issue which should be studied in depth in order to understand the essence of parliamentary diplomacy is the question of instructions.

If a representative is bound by strict and unchangeable instructions, he is in fact acting as a diplomat and has no serious political role to play. (Needless to say, even ambassadors on the bilateral level may at times have flexible instructions.) If, on the other hand, he has no instructions at all, he is hardly an ambassador and becomes really a politician or statesman, as the case may be; but his word may not always have sufficient weight if it is believed that he does not bind anybody but himself.

It is difficult to know how the instructions are formulated since they are not published and, in any event, would probably be considered confidential and not available to scholars until much later.

The rigidity or flexibility of instructions is perhaps the most important element in judging, first of all the character of the permanent mission, but also the role to be played by the delegation in every session of any organ of the Organization.

Rumor has it that a permanent representative from a country which shall remain unnamed, cabled home for instructions during one important crisis and was told in no uncertain terms that he was sent to New York to take care of that part of the policy of his country and that his asking for instructions was quite uncalled for.

Another delegate, it is told, not only gets detailed instructions about every vote but has all his speeches sent verbatim from his capital with instructions of when to speak with sincerity and when to inject an ironic inflection.

There are great variations between these two extremes according to national traditions, the standing of the permanent representative, the character of the foreign minister, or the atmosphere in the ministry. In most cases, it is believed, there is a certain element of flexibility. All contingencies cannot be foreseen. And this uncertainty must be reflected in the instructions. They must be fairly general in character and outline the policy the government wishes to pursue. On the most important items of the agenda, which is distributed well in advance of the session, it is possible to give instructions on how the delegation shall vote.

This, however, is not the end of the story. New items may be included, and the items which have been presented can in the course of the debate be changed out of recognition. A well-known item may still result in unforeseen proposals. In order to meet such contingencies, it is wise to have flexible instructions and also to have constant communications between the delegation and the foreign office.

A really effective delegation probably collaborates with the government in the formulation of the instructions.

The delegation will during the whole session be in permanent touch with the foreign office. There will be a constant

flow of information and an uninterrupted series of consultations. It may be difficult for the delegation to know at which
point it will be most convenient to ask for instructions; the
exact point in the development of an item which is the best for
this purpose must be chosen by the leader of the delegation
according to his discretion and in the light of his relations with
the home government.

Certain items at every session are purely formal and others
are noncontroversial, but as a general rule it may be stated
that each and every proposal travels a long way. After a general debate on the item in question, certain exploratory meetings take place. Delegates begin to discuss informally what a
draft resolution should contain. During this period, no "paper"
is presented at all. This, however, does not mean that delegates have not put their thoughts in writing. Several of the
more active among them move around with all their pockets
full of the most tentative and informal suggestions, which are
too exploratory in character even to be shown let alone delivered to friendly delegations. Some ambassadors move around
like disturbed porcupines, bristling with secret non-papers instead of quills. In some mysterious way these papers become
known and serve as a basis for other papers which will circu-
late freely. Secrets—unlike speeches—last a very short time
during sessions.

The task of these informal negotiations is a double one. The
first is to explore what kind of text has a chance of being
adopted and the second is to find out which state or states
should be chosen to present the proposal with the greatest possibility of positive result.

At this time, most delegates would probably still deem it
premature to ask for instructions. This is the stage of the negotiations when the new kind of multilateral diplomacy has its
greatest scope. During these days small groups are formed to
discuss informally whether, how, and when a proposal shall be
made. An active and forward-looking representative will often

participate in such groups on a pre-negotiation basis. He will not and cannot ask for formal instructions each time he is asked to participate in this way. If all representatives asked for instructions every time they took any step, however informal, the work of the Assembly would be paralyzed.

At times the ambassador will participate himself, thereby showing his strong personal interest in the matter; at other times he will ask the representative in the relevant committee to participate. In either case, he will make it clear that he participates only in his personal capacity. He will underline the fact that he has not yet received instructions. He may say so, as a safeguard, even if he has received instructions.

The idea that the ambassador acts in his personal capacity is, of course, a device to ensure greater freedom of action and does not correspond to reality; and this ploy is accepted by everybody for what it is worth. Tom, Dick, and Harry do not act in the United Nations. The actor is always the official representative of Ruritania, Mixolydia, or Utopia. That is why he is in New York. That is his whole *raison d'être*. By saying that he acts in his personal capacity he simply indicates that he reserves the entire freedom of action of his government and that he can withdraw at any moment without losing face. On the other hand, it is reasonably clear that an ambassador's credibility will to some extent be diminished if he gets the reputation of indulging in this game too often and withdrawing at the last moment. The ever-present risk is that a diplomat in this way is drawn in step by step and is at last so involved in the negotiations that he may finally feel the risks of participating in this particular form of parliamentary diplomacy.

These groups may in the very beginning be very informal indeed and very small. At times, two or three delegates get together who belong to the same geographic group—for instance, two Scandinavian representatives, two Benelux representatives, or two diplomats from Latin America. Later they may consult more people from the same geographical group, but a proposal should, if possible, not be a Western European proposal, or Latin American or Eastern European. Consultations therefore start with diplomats from other groups so that there will be no danger of confrontation. The informal debates will very often consist of a search for cosponsors.

The idea of cosponsorship is a peculiar innovation in the life of the United Nations. The fate of a proposal may depend on the group of sponsors. Efforts should ideally be aimed at obtaining a balanced group of sponsors. The best group is small, compact, and responsible. One or two Latin Americans, one or two Western Europeans, one Eastern European, one from Asia, and, if possible, one from the anglophone and one from the francophone African states.

But a resolution of a somewhat nonpolitical nature may need fewer sponsors and still obtain very large support. The Resolution on Marine Science and Technology [4] is a case in point. The sponsors were Belgium, Iceland, Norway, Uruguay, and the U.S.A. It was unanimously adopted. The Resolution establishing the International Year of Human Rights [5] was sponsored by Ecuador, India, Indonesia, and Cyprus. It was adopted 110-0-4.

A resolution of a noncontroversial character may get a very large number of cosponsors because certain governments wish at the last moment to share the honor of having introduced it. Often the number will grow tremendously and without any control.

The unanimous Resolution on the Human Environment [6] was sponsored by 55 states.

The "original" sponsors, and not the great number who jump on the bandwagon, form the important group which pre-

[4] G.A. Res. 2560, 24 U.N. GAOR Supp. 28, at 35, U.N. Doc. A/7630 (Dec. 13, 1969).
[5] G.A. Res. 2588, 24 U.N. GAOR Supp. 28, at 60–61, U.N. Doc. A/7630 (Dec. 15, 1969).
[6] G.A. Res. 2581, 24 U.N. GAOR Supp. 28, at 44–45, U.N. Doc. A/7630 (Dec. 15, 1969).

pares the text circulated among many delegations with a request for support. And a crucial moment comes when last-minute sponsors may still have some chance of influencing the wording before the proposal is officially filed. This is the point at which many prudent delegations cable or telephone for instructions. Now the proposal is fairly near its official birth and it is reasonably clear what it will look like. On the other hand, it is still not quite impossible to have it changed. A government may then instruct its representative to promise support with or without amendment or may promise to sponsor it. Certain governments may request minor changes as a condition for support. This explains why it is fairly important not to have too large a sponsor group. In principle, every single one of the sponsors must consent to every change in the text. Often, the representative may feel under the obligation to ask for permission to accept changes and this may make it well nigh impossible to effect the last-minute changes which will insure the largest possible adherence.

After all these negotiations, a proposal is tabled as an official U.N. Document. It is nearly certain in advance how the document will fare, which changes will be proposed and which will be accepted. The debate on the official proposal will be reasonably short in committee and will rarely be repeated in the General Assembly in plenary meetings.

This "democratic" procedure will take place in most instances. The only dramatic exception is a proposal of particular interest to the developing nations. In such a case the "group of 77" (96 at present) will debate the matter themselves and will all act as cosponsors. This means that they have the majority in advance and that there is little give and take. However, in most cases, they prefer not to use this kind of "railroading," but to have a resolution adopted unanimously or at least by a great and representative majority.

One particular characteristic of United Nations diplomacy —but not necessary of parliamentary diplomacy elsewhere—is that the debates, both in committee and in plenary, take place in public. Nearly all the debates in plenary and some important committee debates are sent out over radio and the more spectacular of them on television. This adds a sense of drama and urgency to the proceedings which certainly changes the character of the debates and gives a chance for demagogy and even emotional appeals which had no place in old-fashioned diplomacy. It may happen that one or two important speeches may change the atmosphere of the Assembly to such an extent that delegates hurry off to inform their governments and eventually ask for new instructions.

IV.

A complete study of parliamentary diplomacy should also examine the practice of delegation meetings—how often these meetings take place, who participates, and whether votes are taken.

It is believed that most delegations have frequent meetings where all matters of importance are discussed; but since the policy pursued by the delegation is the official policy of the government, most delegations probably do not take formal votes.

The Norwegian delegation, for one, has a meeting every single day except weekends during the session, and all members of the delegation, the permanent staff as well as *ad hoc* members, participate: parliamentarians, diplomats, and technicians. No distinction is made between delegates, substitute delegates, advisers, experts, and secretaries.

These notes of a purely factual and explanatory character may throw some light on the workings of the machinery of the United Nations and may be useful if the General Assembly in historical perspective should be proved to have been a forerunner of a world legislature.

But in such an eventuality a very critical evaluation of the decision-making procedure is called for.

The delegates themselves feel that the machinery could and should be improved upon. From time to time efforts are made to change the rules of procedure.

This is reflected in the debates during the twenty-fifth session of the General Assembly.

In paragraph 11 of the Declaration on the Occasion of the Twenty-fifth Anniversary of the United Nations it is stated:

It is furthermore desirable to find ways and means to strengthen the Organization's effectiveness in dealing with the growing volume and complexity of its work in all areas of its activities, and notably those relating to the strengthening of international peace and security, including a more rational division and co-ordination of work among the various agencies and organizations of the United Nations system.[7]

And in Resolution A/2632(XXV) the Assembly decided to appoint a committee of thirty-one member states:

to study ways and means of improving the procedures and organization of the Assembly in accordance with the provisions of the Charter of the United Nations, including the allocation of agenda items, the organization of work, documentation, rules of procedure and related questions, methods and practices, and to submit a report to the Assembly at its twenty-sixth session. . . .[8]

One very great weakness of the system is that decisions are taken by a vote where every nation, irrespective of its contribution to world government, to world welfare, to world security, and to the budget of the Organization, has the same vote. This may lead to decisions being taken by a majority of states representing little in the actual world except numbers.

Parliamentary diplomacy could counteract this danger with-

[7] U.N. Doc. A/L.600.
[8] G.A. Res. 2632, 25 U.N. GAOR Supp. 28, at 5, U.N. Doc. A/8028 (Nov. 9, 1970).

out the necessity for a formal change in the Charter, by using this power with wisdom and prudence. Procedures may be easily evolved whereby no serious decision is taken without due regard being paid to the responsibility for carrying out the decisions.

A system of conciliation is already used in international assemblies. A gentlemen's agreement may be reached whereby a resolution is not pressed to a formal vote in plenary if it has not been adopted by a qualified majority in committee. Imagination and goodwill could undoubtedly devise still other formulas.

Once this is achieved, it might perhaps be proposed that the World Assembly not adopt decisions which would remain a dead letter because they would not be carried out. The temptation to vote for a resolution because it has no binding force would disappear, and all delegations and all states would realize that it is a violation of the tenet of good faith to vote in favor of a resolution with the mental reservation that it does not matter anyhow since it need not be carried out. It must also be understood that no resolution in itself solves a problem. The following up of a resolution is much more important than the resolution itself.

If this were clearly understood, perhaps delegates would attach slightly less importance to each word in the text, and one could eliminate all the votes and sterile debates on subclauses in preambular paragraphs without any real meaning. It would be much more reasonable to have a legislative office in the Secretariat to ensure good, clear drafting and a certain consistency in the vocabulary of resolutions. Too little use is made of the very competent officers in the department of legal affairs in the Secretariat.

Another weakness in the system of decision-making in the United Nations is that resolutions can be adopted with a very small number of votes. It is theoretically possible to adopt a resolution with two votes in favor, one against, and 123 abstentions. Although such a vote is still in the realm of nightmares, it happens frequently that the number of votes in favor of a resolution is smaller than the combined number of abstentions and negative votes.

The habit has insinuated itself into the practice of the United Nations of registering disagreement with a proposal only by abstaining. The casting of a negative vote is today interpreted as such a strong demonstration that it might very nearly be considered an offense against good manners.

The majority required is only a majority of the delegations present and voting. Delegations which are absent, which do not participate in the vote, or which abstain are not counted, although all delegations present, voting or not voting, are counted for the quorum. This means that those delegations who do not vote against a proposal automatically diminish the number of votes necessary for adoption. They consequently carry a certain responsibility for the adoption of the relevant resolution.

A better voting practice might also reduce the "explanations of vote." This is a very peculiar habit in parliamentary diplomacy. It takes place after the debate has been closed and is in its form a part of the voting procedure. The "explanation" can take place either before or after the vote. It is often used to explain for home consumption why a certain vote was taken. At other times, it is used to mollify other delegations that might resent the policy pursued. Often it may look like a result of bad conscience, either to hide or to underline the difference between the vote cast and the real desire of the delegation. It is often difficult to see the difference between a speech in the debate and an "explanation of vote" if the explanation is given before the vote. But as a general rule the chairman will feel very reluctant to stop such a speaker. According to the rules of procedure, a sponsor cannot explain his vote; but even on this point most chairmen show a great indulgence.

V.

There are also other aspects of the resolution-making which are of a doubtful character, namely, repetitive resolutions on the same matter. The Assembly has during its first twenty-five years adopted 15 resolutions concerning apartheid. It may seem peculiar to repeat the same debate year after year and to adopt a series of similar resolutions over the years. But it has a certain sense. If the Assembly one year refused to debate apartheid or failed to vote a resolution, it might be interpreted by the government of South Africa as a moral victory showing that the Organization had given up the fight and had realized that the whole matter was within the domestic jurisdiction of that government. There are certain items which must be treated again and again, and certain principles which must be restated with short intervals.

It should be remembered that the General Assembly is not only, not even chiefly, a legislative assembly. It is also a sounding board for the world. It must act as the public conscience of mankind. Declarations of a general character have also a long-range effect in educating world public opinion and influencing governments. In this way, the Organization helps to create a climate and to develop standards of international behavior which will eventually become general principles of international law and, to put it on the lowest level, be one of the elements that helps to create customary international law.

Certain resolutions of the Assembly are intended to create law, namely declarations giving expression to legal principles. If these were adopted unanimously or with an overwhelming majority, it would be difficult to ignore them, even though the Assembly is not in a formal way a legislative organ.

It may as yet be difficult to state with legal accuracy what is the effect of a general declaration of the General Assembly. Such declarations are often used as a substitute for international legislation by states who deem that the ordinary procedure of law-making in the international community is too slow. And it is a paradox that often the states who act in this way are in other ways the staunchest defenders of the absolute sovereignty of states.

Such contradictions will persist as long as statesmen, politicians, diplomats, and even serious scholars uphold sovereignty as the basis of our society instead of stressing international solidarity, mutual interdependence, and the absolute obligation to respect the principles of the Charter and to live together in peace with one another as good neighbors. Parliamentary diplomacy is in a stage of development, just as international community is in a stage of transition between the fragmentary international society of yesterday and the organized and integrated international community of tomorrow. Techniques and procedures could and should be improved, but the all-important need is to imbue the statesmen of the world with a strong conviction that the strengthening of our feeling of solidarity is a necessity for our survival.

SUZANNE BASTID

Have the U. N. Administrative Tribunals Contributed to the Development of International Law?

1. In his famous lectures of 1956, Judge Philip C. Jessup drew attention to law as applied by international administrative tribunals. He saw in it one of the aspects of transnational law, the law applicable to acts and facts which go beyond national considerations and concern physical and moral persons other than states.

At that time Judge Jessup referred to the jurisprudence of the Administrative Tribunal of the United Nations, of the Administrative Tribunal of the International Labour Organisation (ILO), and of the Administrative Tribunal of the League of Nations, with which the former tribunals are closely linked.

Since that time virtually all international organizations have made use of jurisdictions of this type, either by having accepted the competence of one or the other tribunal of the fam-

SUZANNE BASTID is professor at the Université de droit, d'économie, et de sciences sociales de Paris; Member of the Académie des Sciences Morales et Politiques; First Vice-President of the Institut de Droit International.

ily of the United Nations,[1] by having established an institution of their own, or by having entrusted disputes concerning their staff members to a jurisdiction possessing other and wider competence, as is the case for the Court of European Communities.

The North Atlantic Treaty Organization has been faced with rather complex problems by reason of the existence of numerous civil or military organs whose respective heads make individual decisions concerning the agents placed under their orders. At one point, with the agreement of the officials in question, the disputes were submitted to the arbitration of the Secretary General, who rendered his judgments with the advice of committees specially constituted for that purpose. But it became apparent that a standard procedure should be instituted. Therefore, on October 20, 1965, the Council of NATO adopted "regulations for claims and appeals procedures," creating a Complaints Commission[2] of a jurisdictional nature, competent to rule on individual litigation which might arise from any decision by the head of a civil or military organ of NATO with regard to an agent with an international status. The Commission was constituted in 1966 and since then has had to rule on a fairly large number of cases. Complaints commissions of this kind exist for five other international organizations whose dealings are not worldwide: the Council of Europe, the OECD, the Western European Union (WEU), the European Organization for Space Research and the European Organisation for the Development and Construction of Space Vehicle Launchers. These commissions are separate, but they emanate from organizations which have established a system of coordination for questions of the salaries of staff members

[1] IMCO and ICAO for the Tribunal of the United Nations; UNESCO, ITU, WMO, FAO, CERN, GATT, IAEA, BIRPI, Euro-Control, UPU for the Tribunal of the ILO.

[2] Guillaume, "La Commission de Recours de l'OTAN et sa jurisprudence," 14 *Ann. Fran. Droit Int'l* 322 (1968).

and various statutory questions, and they are similar in many ways.

The Franco-German Youth Office, provided for by the Franco-German Treaty of January 22, 1963, also possesses a Complaints Commission. The Paris Court of Appeals stated in a judgment of June 18, 1968 that the agents of the Office "have a special juridical status of an international nature" and "are to be regarded as international officials," and upheld the decision of incompetence rendered by the lower court in a suit brought by an agent dismissed for serious misconduct, who had brought the case before French tribunals. The case finally had to be submitted to and decided by the Complaints Commission.[3]

Except in the case of the European Economic Community and of Euratom,[4] these jurisdictions are established by resolutions of the deliberative organs, based on their competences as recognized in the Constitution of the organization dealing with staff members, and thus by a unilateral international act.

2. The widespread adoption of this system is a rather remarkable fact. In the advisory opinion of July 13, 1954, on the *Effect of Awards of Compensation Made by the United Nations,* the International Court of Justice said that "It would, in the opinion of the Court, hardly be consistent with the expressed aims of the Charter to promote freedom and justice for individuals . . . that [the United Nations] should afford no judicial or arbitral remedy to its own staff for the settlement of any disputes which might arise between it and them." It also pointed out that "the power to establish a tribunal, to do justice as between the Organisation and the staff members, was

[3] Larger, "L'affaire Klarsfeld devant les tribunaux français," 14 *Ann. Fran. Droit Int'l* 369 (1968); D. Ruzié, "De l'obligation du réserve des fonctionnaires internationaux et des conditions de leur licenciement—A propos de l'affaire Klarsfeld," 16 *id.* 417 (1970).

[4] E.E.C. Treaty, 298 U.N.T.S. 11, Art. 179; Euratom Treaty, 298 U.N.T.S. 167, Art. 152. For the C.E.C.A., competence was based on Art. 78 and on an arbitration clause contained in the contract of staff members. The staff members' statute today provides for the competence of the Court.

essential to ensure the efficient working of the secretariat, and to give effect to the paramount consideration of securing the highest standards of efficiency, competence and integrity. Capacity to do this arises by necessary intendment of the Charter." [5]

In 1957, the Institute of International Law considered the question in general terms at its session at Amsterdam. The resolution entitled *Judicial Redress against Decisions of International Organs* affirms the duty of every international organ and of every international organization to respect the law, poses the principle of judicial control of decisions of international organs, and, "as a minimum, expresses the wish that, for every particular decision of an international organ or organization which involves private rights or interests, there be provided appropriate procedures for settling by judicial or arbitral methods juridical differences which might arise from such a decision."

It must be noted that the Institute deemed it desirable that —with the exception of special jurisdictional regimes—the International Court of Justice be called upon to decide as to "grievances based upon the lack of competence or grave irregularities of procedure of judicial or arbitral organs" charged with deciding these differences.

These texts are the remainder of much more ambitious proposals which tended to generalize the system of jurisdictional control provided for in the European Coal and Steel Community Treaty, but their practical importance in the current state of development of international organizations has been emphasized by C. W. Jenks.[6]

The Institute undoubtedly did not in 1957 intend to express the *lex lata*. The formulas it uses leave no doubt in this respect, but the practice which has taken hold since then makes one wonder whether international organizations do not today

[5] [1954] *ICJ Reports* 47, at 57.
[6] 47 *Annuaire de l'Inst. Droit Int'l* 30 (1957-I).

consider themselves obliged to assure for their personnel a judicial remedy, in the absence of possible access to national tribunals. The fact that certain organizations with headquarters in Washington have remained apart from this movement cannot be ignored; however, it does seem that the reasons for instituting this recourse are ever more evident, no doubt in the interest of the staff, but also in the interest of the smooth functioning of each organization. There is thus an orientation toward the recognition of demands implied by the characteristics peculiar to that unique social structure, the international organization.

3. In most cases the right of access to the Tribunal or to the Complaints Commission results from the contract concluded by each staff member with the organization. This contract refers to the statute established by the deliberating organ, in which are remedies, and in particular juridical remedies, are laid down. Thus, the contractual link with the organization is, as a rule,[7] the basis of the competence of the judge. But the judge is called upon to consider disputes against the organization by persons other than those linked to the organization by a contractual tie. In general, the statutes provide for the tribunals or commissions to be open not only to present or former staff members but equally to those who have succeeded *mortis causa* to their rights, and also to those who can establish rights resulting from a contract of employment or from texts applicable to personnel; thus, the widow of an official is capable of bringing an appeal concerning her pension rights.[8]

4. Two problems have arisen with respect to the competence *ratione personae* of these jurisdictions. One concerns the staff of offices placed in special jurisdictional situations and for which the competence of the international administrative ju-

---

[7] The juridical regime of staff members has sometimes changed; see Decision of the Commission of the OECD No. 37, Jan. 9, 1964 on the substitution of the statutory regime for the contractual regime.

[8] Adm. Trib. of the ILO, April 10, 1965, No. 81, Metzler vs. I.T.U.

risdiction is not expressly provided. Case law is favorable to
the extension of this competence except when resort to a national jurisdiction is possible; the organization also must agree
to be subject to that jurisdiction and to implement its decision.
The Complaints Commission of NATO has stated this point
precisely in the case of a local statutory agent of the Atlantic
Supreme Command's Research Center on Anti-submarine
Warfare, whose contract made reference to Italian law and
collective bargaining agreements.[9] The absence of recourse to
a national tribunal was pointed out by the Tribunal of the ILO
in the famous *Desgranges* case,[10] asserting its competence to
rule on a case concerning an agent of the branch office of the
ILO in Paris. In order to affirm its own competence, the U.N.
Administrative Tribunal specifically invoked the fact that the
Secretary-General had formally requested jurisdictional immunity for the Agency before the Egyptian tribunals in which
an agent of the UNRWA brought a suit.[11] In this matter the
Tribunal brought out the fact that its competence is not limited to the "staff members of the United Nations Secretariat,"
and it admitted that the right of appeal may be extended by
virtue of special agreements applicable to the personnel of a
specialized agency (*organe subsidiaire*).

Concerning a petition brought by a former finance clerk of
the U.N. Emergency Force, the Tribunal recently declared
that referral to an advisory organ such as the Joint Appeals
Board did not ensure the judicial or arbitral remedy to which
an official is entitled, and that recognition by the administration of this reference of the dispute necessarily implied the
right of recourse to a complete appeal procedure, including access to the Tribunal following such reference.[12]

In these cases the competence of the Tribunal was based on
provisions opening certain procedures to the staff member

[9] Case No. 5.   [10] Judgment No. 11, August 12, 1953.
[11] Judgment No. 57, Hilpern.
[12] Judgment No. 144, Samaan.

concerned but without express provision for juridical remedy. As for the Tribunal of the ILO, it emphasized the question of principle: earlier, in the *Desgranges* case, it had stated, "The absence of positive legal provisions concerning the employees of the Branch Offices would make their situation extremely precarious. . . . It is unthinkable that the ILO, which was established to ensure the security of all wage-earners, does not desire to assure that of all of its own officials. . . . The Administrative Tribunal . . . should be considered as governed by general legal principles with the necessary powers to guarantee the security of employment of all officials attached to the ILO."

It is thus with a noticeable reticence that the Tribunal of the ILO declared itself incompetent to rule on the claim of a temporary agent of UNESCO whose contract provided that she would not be regarded as a staff member of the organization.[13] It defined this condition as that of a "purely casual" employee, and, based on its nature as a court of "limited jurisdiction," it yielded, noting, however, the "regrettable" deprivation of any means of judicial redress.

Certain commentaries seem to suggest that this decision was rendered with great hesitation.[14]

In line with the *Desgranges* judgment, the Tribunal in 1968 declared itself competent to decide a petition brought by a member of the English-language translation service, an autonomous service within the framework of the Universal Postal Union (UPU). This service is directed and financed by the member states of the "English-Language Group," and the staff rules and regulations of the UPU are not applicable to these staff members.

One of them, having presented a petition to the tribunal of the ILO, whose competence had been accepted by the UPU,

[13] Judgment No. 67, Darricades (October 26, 1962).
[14] Lemoine, "Jurisprudence du tribunal administratif de l'O.I.T.," 9 *Ann. Fran. Droit Int'l* 501 (1963).

faced the objection that the terms of his contract had not included the benefit of the appeals procedure laid down in the Staff Regulations of the UPU. The judgment vigorously opposed this contention:

While the Staff Regulations of any organisation are, as a whole, applicable only to those categories of persons expressly specified therein, some of their provisions are merely the translation into written form of general principles of international civil service law; these principles correspond at the present time to such evident needs and are recognised so generally that they must be considered applicable to any employees having any link other than a purely casual one with a given organisation, and consequently may not lawfully be ignored in individual contracts. This applies in particular to the principle that any employee is entitled in the event of a dispute with his employer to the safeguard of some appeals procedure.[15]

This judgment, rendered October 15, 1968, constitutes a very important precedent, and one may consider that in the Samaan case the Administrative Tribunal of the United Nations confirmed, in 1971, the principle of contentious recourse as a rule incumbent upon the international organization with respect to all its personnel.

5. However, it is still necessary for the organization in question to have accepted the competence of an Administrative Tribunal: the Tribunal of the ILO, regretfully it seems, declared itself incompetent to hear an appeal against the dismissal of an officer of the Pan-American Sanitary Bureau, which is an administrative secretariat of the Pan-American Health Organization reorganized in 1958 and serving as a regional office of the World Health Organization (WHO) in Washington, while still maintaining its principal activity within the Pan-American framework. The officers of the WHO and those of the Bureau work side by side, and a functional and administrative integration has been achieved. However,

[15] No. 122, Chadsey.

although the rules and regulations of the personnel of the Organization have been assimilated into those of the WHO, some minor differences remain, and the only recourse provided for the benefit of the staff members of the Bureau is a proceeding before a Board of Inquiry and Appeal; the Bureau has no administrative tribunal.

As a staff member of a regional bureau, the complainant had thought that he could lodge an appeal against the WHO in the capacity of a regular WHO staff member.

The Tribunal found that he was an employee of the Pan-American Sanitary Bureau, and that that organization, despite its ties with the WHO, constituted "an independent body with its own staff under its sole authority." In the absence of any agreement with the WHO, the staff members of the Organization could not enjoy the jurisdictional guarantees benefiting the staff members of the WHO.

The Tribunal recognises that as a result of holding that it lacks jurisdiction complainant is thereby regrettably deprived of any means of judicial redress against the injury sustained as a result of the alleged breach of his contract. However, the Tribunal, being a court of limited jurisdiction, is bound to apply the mandatory provisions governing its competence, and it is for the Organization concerned itself to determine whether it is desirable to provide its employees with a safeguard which is enjoyed by the great majority of international officials at the present time.

The judgment was not confined to the pronouncement of these considerations. Although it dismissed the complaint, the Tribunal deemed it "equitable" to award costs to the complainant in the amount of 3,000 Swiss francs, "in view of the reasonable doubts that the complainant may have had on the question of jurisdiction." [16]

These expenses were chargeable to the WHO, even though the situation could certainly not be imputed to it. One may wonder whether, through this unexpected action, the Tribunal

[16] Judgment No. 137, Mr. Brache, November 3, 1969.

was not attempting to furnish an argument for WHO in its relations with the Pan-American Health Organization, to overcome the previous obstacles to the establishment of a means of redress for the officers of the Bureau.

In this regard, it must be pointed out that in 1971 a plan to establish an administrative tribunal was brought before the first regular session of the General Assembly of the Organization of American States.[17] This tribunal could have its competence extended, by agreement, to specialized inter-American organizations connected with the OAS and to any American intergovernmental organization. If the statute of the Tribunal comes into force, the Pan-American Sanitary Bureau could perhaps participate in such an agreement and overcome the resistance which up to now has prevented the acceptance of the jurisdiction of one of the Administrative Tribunals of the United Nations family.

It thus appears that even if one cannot speak of a real obligation imposed upon organizations to institute legal remedies, they are at least bound, when they have accepted this principle, to extend its benefit to the entire body of their personnel. In the social pressure being exerted in favor of the institution and expansion of this recourse, the jurisprudence of administrative tribunals has undoubtedly played an appreciable role.[18]

6. From another point of view, jurisdictional protection has been understood in a rather broad manner; here it is a question of candidates for international posts who are not hired and who eventually do not obtain the status of staff members. In the opinion of October 23, 1956, relating to judgments of the Administrative Tribunal of the ILO on complaints against

[17] OAS/Ser.P (?) A6/Doc. 116 rev. 1, March 16, 1971.

[18] It may be noted that, subsequent to the Hilpern judgment, a special regulation was established for the staff members of the UNRWA, July 1, 1957, providing an arbitration procedure. Judgment No. 70, Radicopoulos, declares that this procedure could be judged by competent authorities as answering the needs mentioned in the advisory opinion of 1954. The Tribunal of the ILO may rule as an arbitral body in a dispute concerning a person employed by the WHO not having the status of staff member. Judgment No. 77, Rebeck.

UNESCO, the Court said: "Clearly, an applicant for a new appointment who fails to obtain it cannot properly invoke the jurisdiction of the Administrative Tribunal." [19] The Court contrasted this situation with that of a staff member with a fixed-term contract who did not obtain the renewal of the contract.

This is the view expressed by the United Nations Tribunal in declaring its incompetence to rule on a complaint brought by a candidate who had taken a translator's examination and had been informed that the Board of Examiners had recommended him for a probationary appointment. The judgment states that the communications addressed to the complainant constituted neither an offer of employment nor notice of a future nomination and therefore could not create any rights, for neither the statutes nor the personnel regulations governed operations preliminary to recruitment. [20]

On the other hand, the law of the European Communities allows candidates to bring before the Court possible violations of the rules governing recruitment competition. The right of appeal is, in effect, open to persons covered by the personal statute; and an appendix to this statute generally refers to "candidates" for the recruitment competition, without specifying whether or not they are already staff members of the Communities. [21]

The Administrative Tribunal of the United Nations has been brought to recognize its competence in two cases (Judgments No. 96 Camargo and No. 106 Vasseur) where the parties concerned had received offers of employment coming from competent authority and where, subsequently, the nomination procedure had not been carried out. The Tribunal deemed that the question at issue "must be resolved essentially on the basis of

[19] [1956] *ICJ Reports*, 77, at 92.

[20] Judgment No. 115, Kimpton; Adm. Trib. of the ILO, Sept. 11, 1964, Silenzi de Stagni vs. FAO.

[21] Court of Justice, March 31, 1963, case 23, 64 Melle Vandenyvère vs. European Parliamentary Assembly (Parlement). (Rep. vol. XI, p. 214.)

the rules of law which it is the responsibility of the United Nations Administrative Tribunal to apply," and declared itself competent on the basis of the nature of the questions being litigated, not on the legal status of the petitioner.

In the *Vasseur* case it considered that "a real contract by which the Respondent undertook to employ the Applicant" had been established, a contract connected with the nomination procedure provided for in the statute and the personnel regulations; and it rendered its opinion on the dispute with respect to the amount of indemnity due by reason of the rescission of the offer of employment. This was a particularly bold solution, since it involved making good damages caused by an action of the administration to a person who never had the status of staff member.[22] This solution was reasonable, however, since the defendant had invoked immunity of jurisdiction when the complainant brought the case before a national tribunal.

One always returns to the fundamental problem of assuring a guarantee in the application of the law while maintaining the immunity of jurisdiction of the international organization. This last principle obviously depends on the international juridical order, as does also the obligation of the organizations to ensure respect for the law established by their organs in accordance with their constitutions. The availability of a legal remedy—as a guarantee of respect for the law—may now be considered a general principle of law in the sense of Article 38 of the Statute of the International Court. This is so by virtue of a customary international rule that is tending to assert itself more and more, that international organizations today appear bound to establish legal remedies for the good of all their personnel and of those who may invoke statutory rules. The formation of this

----

[22] In Judgment No. 68, Bulsara, Aug. 22, 1957, the Tribunal of the United Nations considered that there was a "contract *for* employment," but there was no appointment; however, since the matter dealt with a former official, the defendant did not raise the issue of incompetence.

rule is undoubtedly still meeting certain resistance, but the plan of the OAS in this regard is an indication of a major step in an evolution to which the jurisprudence of administrative tribunals has greatly contributed.

7. This jurisprudence has also affirmed certain principles applicable to staff members that complete, or rather include, the provisions of the Statutes and regulations and appear to partake of the international juridical order as much as the texts established by international organs by virtue of the constitutions of the organizations.

We shall limit ourselves to two examples. We may mention first of all the rule *audi alteram partem*. Presented by the Court of Justice of the Communities as "responding to the demands of sound justice and good administration" and as a "general principle universally recognized," according to the Administrative Tribunal of the United Nations [23] the principle has been asserted in various circumstances: integration procedure within the framework of the Communities; [24] annulment of a contract of employment of an official in a trial period; [25] appeal procedure against a decision giving grounds for appeal; [26] procedure before the Admission Board on Compensation Claims; [27] decision to terminate the secondment of an official; [28] disciplinary procedure; [29] dismissal of an expert.[30]

The requirement of a regular procedure may furthermore involve other aspects than the right of the interested party to be informed of the grievance and to be called upon to explain himself. Thus consideration has been given to the identity of the person who makes the final decision, [31] the nature of a

[23] Judgment No. 103, Azzu.
[24] July 4, 1962, Case 32–62, Alvis vs. Council of the E.E.C.
[25] Adm. Trib. of the ILO, Judgment No. 69, Kissaun.
[26] *Id.*, Judgment No. 92, Varla-costa Patrono.
[27] Tribunal of the United Nations, Judgment No. 103, Azzu.
[28] Tribunal of the United Nations, Judgment No. 92, Higgins.
[29] Tribunal of the United Nations, Judgment No. 74, Bang Jensen; No. 123, Ray; No. 130, Zang Atangana.
[30] Tribunal of the United Nations, Judgment No. 113, Coll.
[31] Complaints Commission of NATO, April 19, 1967, Decision No. 4.

medical procedure followed, [32] the accuracy of information considered, [33] etc.

8. On the other hand, it may be noted that the international administrative judge has asserted a right to control the discretionary competence of the administration in certain cases which are more or less well defined: manifest error, [34] unlawful purposes (*fins illicites*), [35] verification of the materiality of facts,[36] competence of the author of a measure, regularity of the procedure followed, error of law, omission of consideration of essential facts, manifestly erroneous conclusions drawn from the documents of the dossier,[37] bias,[38] etc.

Thus, the jurisprudence of administrative tribunals has established a body of rules governing the conduct of heads of international administrations whose status results from the treaty establishing the international organizations. These rules are undoubtedly inspired by the internal law of certain states, but it does not appear that they are being applied as general principles of law. Here again, one may consider that a custom is being established which has not been contested, notably by the organs which could have recourse to the International Court of Justice against the judgments which apply the custom.

Undoubtedly, the conditions in which international administrative tribunals operate engender appreciable nuances in the expression of these principles, even certain divergences. However, the cases mentioned above, and still others, are rather significant and correspond to the requirements imposed by the very system of international organizations in the absence of any written rule. Considered as recognized and necessary con-

[32] Tribunal of the United Nations, Judgment No. 83, Miss Y.

[33] *Id.*, Judgment No. 98, Gillman.

[34] Grievances Commission of the OECD, Decision No. 35, Doronzo.

[35] Tribunal of the United Nations, Judgment No. 90, Chiachia; No. 93, Cooperman.

[36] Court of Justice of the Communities, cases 35–62, Leroy vs. High Authority of the ECAC.

[37] Adm. Trib. of the ILO, Judgment No. 84, Gale.

[38] Administrative Tribunal of the United Nations, Judgment No. 93, Cooperman.

sequences of this system of concerted action among states, they may be seen as a new aspect of the law of international society, an aspect deriving from the modifications occurring in the very structure of that society in the contemporary era.

ANDRÉ GROS

Concerning the Advisory Role of the
International Court of Justice

IN THE course of a lecture given on July 22, 1970
at the Academy of International Law in The Hague, [1] Philip
Jessup put forward various suggestions with a view to more
effective use of the International Court of Justice. Since then,
the General Assembly of the United Nations has placed the review of the Court's role on its agenda. The time has therefore
come for a closer look at some of the reforms proposed by
Philip Jessup at The Hague, reforms typical of a trend of
thought of which he has long been one of the principal advocates.

In order to keep this study within bounds, it will be confined to the Court's advisory function—the more so because
the tendency today is to consider that any rise in the number
of contentious cases brought before the Court is bound to be
slow and difficult, whereas advisory opinions might more frequently be requested of it if only certain procedural reforms

ANDRÉ GROS is a Judge on the International Court of Justice and a Member of
the Institut de Droit International.
[1] "To Form a More Perfect United Nations," 129 Hague *Recueil des Cours* 5
(1970-I).

could be introduced (for example, by delegating power to request an opinion to a standing committee of the General Assembly, or by conferring a right to request opinions on the Secretary-General of the United Nations). Without going into the details of such possibilities, it would be interesting to try and determine whether, in this field, the obstacles in the way of the development of the advisory function would in fact be removed by improvements of a technical and procedural nature; or whether the difficulties encountered in the contentious field would not to a large extent remain, thus seriously restricting any significant development of the advisory function, whatever procedural reforms might be introduced.

It seems to be generally admitted that the distinction between the Court's judgments and its advisory opinions cannot be taken too far. When the Court replies to a request for an advisory opinion, it does not transform itself into a committee of fifteen legal consultants; it continues to be the principal judicial organ of the United Nations and to act as such. On this point the procedure, the rules governing deliberation and voting (the Resolution of July 5, 1968 concerning the Court's internal judicial practice applies to advisory proceedings), separate opinions, the delivery of an opinion at a public sitting, and every detail from the reception of a request down to the placing of an original copy in the archives of the Court (Rules, Article 85) leave no room for doubt. Moreover, this was pointed out by the Court in its *Advisory Opinion on the Constitution of the Maritime Safety Committee of the Inter-Governmental Maritime Consultative Organization:* "The Court as a judicial body is . . . bound, in the exercise of its advisory function, to remain faithful to the requirements of its judicial character." [2] Similarly, in the *Case Concerning the Northern Cameroons* the Court stated that "the Court's authority to give advisory opinions must be exercised as a judicial function." [3]

[2] [1960] *ICJ Reports* 150, at 153.   [3] [1963] *ICJ Reports* 15, at 30.

Article 38, paragraph 1(d), of the Statute refers to "judicial decisions" as constituting a subsidiary means for the determination of rules of law, and this includes advisory opinions as well as judgments. It is known that in giving their decisions the tradition of the two Courts (the present one and its predecessor) has been to cite only their own pronouncements, whether made in advisory opinions or in judgments, both ranking as statements of international law. The distinction habitually drawn between advisory opinions and judgments, whereby the former do not have the binding character of the latter, is not an absolute one. In the first place, it is only the operative part of a judgment that is distinct from an advisory opinion as to its obligatory force. As regards the reasoning, this, in both cases, represents the Court's legal conclusions concerning the situation which is being dealt with, and its weight is the same in both cases: there are no two ways of declaring the law. Second, even advisory proceedings may involve acts that operate with finality both for the Court itself and for the participating states or organizations.

The case concerning the *Legal Consequences for States of the Continued Presence of South Africa in Namibia* (*South West Africa*) *notwithstanding Security Council Resolution 276* (1970) furnishes several examples of this. Thus, the Court decided on its composition by Orders Nos. 1, 2, and 3 of January 26, 1971; then by an order of January 29, 1971 it decided to dismiss the South African Government's application to nominate a judge *ad hoc;* finally, without making any order, but by a unanimous finding, read out by the president at the start of the public sitting of February 8, 1971 (Verbatim Record, 71/1, p. 4), which was, in consequence, a judicial act, the Court decided not to entertain an objection relating to the possible disqualification of the Court as such from giving an advisory opinion. The terms of that unanimous decision serve to underline the judicial character of the Court's advisory proceedings:

The Court has decided to examine first of all the observations which the Government of the Republic of South Africa has made in its written statement and in its letter of 14 January 1971 concerning the supposed disability of the Court to give the advisory opinion requested by the Security Council, because of political pressure to which the Court, according to the Government of the Republic of South Africa, had been or might be subjected.

After having deliberated upon the matter, the Court has unanimously decided that it was not proper for it to entertain these observations, bearing as they do on the very nature of the Court as the principal judicial organ of the United Nations, an organ which, in that capacity, acts only on the basis of the law, independently of all outside influence or interventions whatsoever, in the exercise of the judicial function entrusted to it alone by the Charter and its Statute. A court functioning as a court of law can act in no other way.

These decisions, dealing with preliminary questions, were binding in character, and the Court reminded the states and organizations participating in the oral proceedings that the respect accorded to a *res judicata* was due to them. Thus, in the course of the same hearing the president intimated that it would no longer be in order for any oral comment to be made on the questions raised by the Government of South Africa that had been the subject of adverse decisions of the Court already made public. (Verbatim Record 71/1 (corrigendum), p. 45.)

The general characteristics of the Court's judicial role in answering a request for an advisory opinion flow from those provisions of the Statute and the Rules which deal with advisory procedure. These contemplate the application of a principle of convergence in the contentious and the advisory fields, as laid down by Article 68 of the Statute and Articles 82–85 of the Court's Rules.

A first problem arises out of the notion of "a legal question actually pending" mentioned in Article 82 of the Rules. The distinction thus drawn between the two categories of advisory opinion must always be a matter for appreciation in each particular case; but the reason for it must not be lost sight of, since it involves the very foundations of international justice in the world of today. Professor Charles de Visscher has vividly called attention to this in a recent work:

The whole evolution of advisory opinions and, more particularly, the gradual assimilation of advisory to contentious procedure shows a concern to eliminate any possibility of introducing compulsory jurisdiction surreptitiously, so to speak, by the back-door of an advisory opinion, and to avoid a dispute between States being in practice decided by the answer given to a question about it that "may constitute a key question in the dispute." [4]

The fact that a political organ of the United Nations concerns itself with a situation cannot, as a legal effect, produce the automatic disappearance of a dispute between two or more states interested in the maintenance or modification of that situation. (The word "dispute" is used for the sake of brevity, instead of the formula, "Legal question actually pending between two or more States," used in the Court's Rules.) In such a case there are two different and parallel levels: at the one, there is a manifestation of the United Nations' political interest in facilitating the regulation of a situation of general concern for the community of states; at the other, there is a recognition of the existence as between certain states of opposed legal interests giving them a special place within a situation of general concern. The mere evocation of a "situation" by the political organs of the United Nations cannot automatically and always bring about the disappearance of the element of dispute between states if there exists such an element underlying the general situation. It is therefore necessary every time an advisory opinion is requested to ascertain whether or not the Court is confronted with a dispute between certain states, the evocation of the matter by political organs being insufficient to

[4] de Visscher, *Aspects récents du droit procédural de la Cour internationale de justice*, 196–97 (1966). See also the dissenting opinions of Judges Winiarski, Basdevant, and Koretsky, appended to the advisory opinion on "Certain Expenses of the United Nations," [1962] *ICJ Reports* 151, 227 ff.

nullify the dispute element to which the provisions of the Court's Statute and Rules refer.[5]

It is necessary to beware lest any contrary interpretation, pushed to its limit, should render all acceptances of the Court's compulsory jurisdiction nugatory, since this would mean that the mere fact of raising a problem before the General Assembly or the Security Council and dealing with it by means of a recommendation could lead to a preexisting legal dispute being disposed of on a basis not necessarily one of law, or at least to a disregard of any intention by the parties to have their dispute settled by judicial means. No doubt such a process might appear to provide a method of handling certain situations by means of peaceful negotiation; but in cases where it was used as a substitute for a settlement on a basis of law accepted in principle by the states concerned, no very obvious progress would ensue.

Quite apart from the difficulties always liable to arise over the distinction made by Article 82 of the Rules between the two categories of advisory opinion, other problems of a general character are involved in the suggested expansion of the Court's advisory function.

If the question really is one of enhancing the Court's judicial activity through the agency of its advisory function, what means are there of overcoming these obstacles to the development of the Court's role, whose existence as regards the contentious procedure cannot well be denied? It is very possible that the obstacles would persist, at least for the most part. If so, these would be the real problems requiring investigation, for in that case no improvements in the advisory machinery, however good in themselves, would make any effective contri-

[5] See Advisory Opinion on Legal Consequences for States, June 21, 1971, paras. 30–41; see also Judge Sir Gerald Fitzmaurice's dissenting opinion, Annex, paras. 26–32; Judge Onyeama's separate opinion, pp. 2–5; and my dissenting opinion, paras. 5–17.

bution to the transformation of the Court's role in present-day international relations.

With regard to such obstacles to the development of international justice, it seems to me that, while different opinions may give weight to this or to that factor, there ought to be general agreement in favor of the analysis made by Charles de Visscher in the fourth edition of his excellent *Théories et Réalités en droit international public* (Paris 1970), in particular on pages 382–401, to which I whole-heartedly subscribe.[6] In close reliance on this analysis, the obstacles in the way of the development of international judicial settlement may be summarized under two heads:

1. In the first place, what is in question is the general structure of international relations, from which it is not possible to isolate the problem of judicial settlement, so that this first category of obstacles arises out of the fact that, on the one hand, international law does not correspond to any hierarchically organized order and, on the other, the sphere in which states have freedom of action is constantly being extended to fresh matters through the progress of science and technology.

2. The second general obstacle to judicial settlement lies in the fact that the applicable system of rules is incomplete or contested. These are classic problems. The rules of international law are as much the subject of controversy today as are the relations between the citizen and the state in certain municipal systems. The increased number of states belonging to the international community and the tendency to transform economic considerations into legal claims or pretensions have resulted in a calling into question of established rules. Together with these factors, there has arisen a certain mistrust of the adjudicator, not, generally, as a person but as representing either a "traditional" legal outlook or an attitude of "chal-

[6] See the observations on the same subject which I addressed to the International Law Commission on June 11, 1970. U.N. Doc. A/CN.4/SR. 1068.

lenge" to established law. States which accept judicial settlement do so only on the basis that accepted law is applied for
the solution of disputes, so that the prospect of being adjudged
according to new theories which they do not accept as being
part of international law is likely to turn them lastingly against
adjudication as a means of settlement.

Add to that a pronounced tendency to regionalize the law
applicable in international relations, and the main outlines of
the obstacles to judicial treatment of international legal problems will become sufficiently apparent.[7]

What view, then, should be taken of the proposals for expansion of the Court's advisory function, having regard to the
general difficulty of any judicial inquiry into legal questions
dividing states and international organizations? The problems
raised by the reserved domain of the state are not any less because the case is advisory; in the oral proceedings on the
*Legal Consequences for States of the Continued Presence of
South Africa in Namibia (South West Africa) notwithstanding
Security Council Resolution 276 (1970)*, the representative of
the United Nations Secretary-General made the following remark:

Turning to certain specific limitations set out in the Charter on the
powers of the General Assembly and the Security Council, the Secretary-General would refer by way of example to paragraph 7 of
Article 2. . . . [Verbatim Record 71/18, page 42].

It is not hard to imagine advisory opinions being requested on
recommendations or resolutions of United Nations organs invoking the purposes and principles of the Charter but involving a state's national sphere of jurisdiction. Is the Court therefore to be asked, on the basis of a request for an advisory
opinion, to choose between two criteria—that of Article 2, paragraph 7, and that of the purposes of the Charter as inter-

[7] On the idea of a socialist international law with its own rules and principles, see Khlestov, "New Soviet-Czechoslovak Treaty," *International Affairs*
(USSR, July 1970), especially page 13.

preted by a United Nations organ? If so, the Court would come up against the same obstacle of an incomplete and contested system mentioned above. To seek obliquely, through advisory jurisdiction, the settlement of what is not yet regulated would probably be more likely to sow the seeds of new conflicts than would attempting to deal with existing ones out of court. The precedent of *Certain Expenses of the United Nations* indicates the limits within which states will accept conclusions whose legality they contest.[8] It is not good enough, even with the best of intentions, to set up a "forward-looking" interpretation of the Charter against a "strict" one, for this would amount to solving the problem by begging the question of whether states are ready to accept the development of the Organization's powers and functions through a process of majority decision. It cannot be recalled too often that the difficulties of the Organization are in reality those of the states composing it. It must not be forgotten that it is the states themselves—and not only the larger ones—which (Chapter VII of the Charter apart) do not admit that matters directly concerning them can be disposed of by majority resolutions. And, here again, it is necessary to look beyond specific problems in order to find the reason for this cautious attitude on the part of states toward international settlement. For, of course, everything would be simpler if the "forward-looking" conception of international relations, to which the Court subscribed in principle in its Advisory Opinions of April 11, 1949 [9] and July 13, 1954 [10] had the backing of an unbroken international solidarity in support of its precepts. In this respect, the parallel often drawn with the development of the federal state in America appears devoid of

[8] See on this point the declaration of the United States on the subject of Art. 19 of the Charter in "Two Neglected Problems in Drafting Regimes for Deep Ocean Resources," 64 *Am. J. Int'l L* 905, at 920, note 2 (1970).

[9] Advisory Opinion on Reparation for Injuries Suffered in the Service of the United Nations, [1949] *ICJ Reports* 174.

[10] Advisory Opinion on the Effect of Awards of Compensation Made by the Administrative Tribunal of the United Nations, [1954] *ICJ Reports* 47.

relevance, because in any federal constitution the hierarchical relationship between the federal and component states is accepted as a principle by the whole body of citizens; whereas the United Nations is still at the stage indicated by the representative of the Soviet Union in his oral statement made before the Court in the case of *Certain Expenses of the United Nations:*

The opposing of the effectiveness of the United Nations Organization to the observance of the principles of the United Nations Charter is legally groundless and dangerous. It is clear to everyone that the observance of the principles of the United Nations Charter is the necessary condition of the effectiveness of the United Nations. The experience of the United Nations clearly shows that only on the basis of the strict observance of the principles of the United Nations Charter can the Organization become an effective instrument for the maintenance of international peace and security and the development of friendly relations among States.[11]

Procedural machinery is no substitute for the solidarity of a community which has decided to set up a certain form of international organization. The measure of that solidarity is to be found in the balance established in the constitution of the organization between its purposes and its powers. The characterization of the organization, which is the sole basis of agreement, cannot be modified by an extension of implied powers to accommodate such broad, open-ended purposes as "international co-operation" without producing the unexpected result that an organization constituted as an association of states for the purpose of cooperation would prove to be endowed in practice with the same powers as if its constitution had been

[11] *ICJ Pleadings* 411 ff. On the limited nature of the General Assembly's budgetary powers, see the written statement of France, *id.* at 134, and, in general, the closely reasoned refutation of the implied powers theory in Tunkin, "The Legal Nature of the United Nations," 119 Hague *Recueil des Cours* 1 (1966-III); see also the statement made in Parliament on behalf of the Government of the United Kingdom concerning the legal nature of the obligation arising out of Security Council recommendations, 812 *Hansard* 1763 ff. (No. 96, March 3, 1971).

that of a "federated" or "integrated" community. A scrutiny of the detailed clauses of the founding instruments of multistate organizations actually endowed with a "federal" or "integrated" constitution shows that the *raison d'être* of such precise rules would disappear if the same compulsory powers could, by virtue of the implied powers theory, be ascribed to *any* organization with economic and social purposes.[12] The effort of continuous creativeness required for any international organization has to be directed along the line of thought which originally determined its constitution.[13]

The present crystallization of ideas around particular objectives, such as decolonization or the protection (within limits here) of human rights, is distracting attention from the fact that the purposes of the Charter also include the solution of international problems of an economic and social character, and that since this, at bottom, means nothing other than a securing of the general common weal, the forward-looking development of international rules to that end presupposes the parallel disappearance of the exclusive national competence of states in those fields. This, again, is allowing a great deal.

I therefore fear that, as regards the development of the Court's role, the quest for devices directed to enlarging its advisory function may only lead to an impasse. As a great European jurist said in the interwar period, "International law may, to be sure, progress, but only by the occasional nudge." And that is also the sense of the following generalization by Professor Charles de Visscher:

When certain theoreticians assign absolute primacy to the judicial function in the international order and in the maintenance of peace they are artificially inverting the terms of the problem. So

[12] See the 208 articles of the Treaty of March 25, 1957 defining the principles, basis, and policy of the European Economic Community, its institutions, and the mode of exercise of the powers involved, 298 U.N.T.S. 11.

[13] See Advisory Opinion on Legal Consequences for States, June 21, 1971, paras. 110–16; Judge Sir Gerald Fitzmaurice's dissenting opinion, paras. 35–36.

long as the individualistic distribution of power among sovereign
States endures, peace will better serve the cause of justice than justice that of peace.[14]

The facts of international life operate as limitations on all reform. Over twenty years ago the Court clearly intimated that
it considered itself under an obligation, in principle, to reply
to requests for advisory opinions, inasmuch as they represented
"its participation in the activities of the Organization." [15] But
when the Organization was created, that participation was restricted from the outset by a refusal to institute any judicial
supervision over the decisions of the Organization; [16] and the
work of the Institute of International Law has plainly shown
that this point must be the focus for any possible reform of the
relations between the Organization and the member states.[17]

Yet there has been no progress so far. Is it really conceivable
that the development of the Court's advisory function might
provide an indirect path to a judicial supervision of the decisions of organs of the United Nations and other international
organizations, without the fear that an advisory opinion ven-
turing to declare such a decision incompatible with the applicable law would close that path up again? Here of course, we
get back to the hard kernel of our problem: the role of the
judge in contemporary international relations.

[14] *Théories et Réalités en droit international public* 383 ff. (1970).

[15] Advisory Opinion on the Interpretation of Peace Treaties with Bulgaria,
Hungary, and Romania, [1950] *ICJ Reports* 65, at 71.

[16] Cf. Advisory Opinion on Legal Consequences for States, June 21, 1971,
paras. 87–89; Judge Sir Gerald Fitzmaurice's dissenting opinion, Annex, paras.
9–12; and my dissenting opinion, paras. 18–23.

[17] Resolution on Judicial Redress against the Decisions of International Organs, 47 *Annuaire de l'Institut de Droit Int'l* 276 ff. and 488–91 (1957-II).